Detour on The Path

Brad Jones

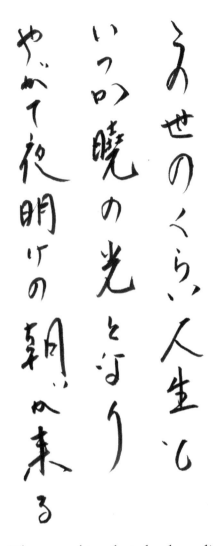

The grey skies that cloud our lives
Are sure to clear
As dawn breaks the endless night.

Detour on The Path

A martial artist's brief foray as a smuggler

— A true story —

by Brad Jones with Gene Shanon

White Knight Books

Copyright © 2008 Brad Jones

All rights reserved. The use of any part of this publication reproduced, transmitted in any form of by any means, electronic, mechanical, photocopying, recording or otherwise or stored in a retrieval system, without the prior consent of the publisher, is an infringement of the copyright law.

National Library of Canada Cataloguing in Publication Data

Jones, Brad, 1955-
    Detour on the path / Brad Jones.

ISBN 978-1-897456-04-0

1. Jones, Brad, 1951-. 2. Martial artists—Canada--Biography. 3. Ex-convicts—Rehabilitation—Canada. 4. Ex-convicts—Canada—Biography. I. Title.

GV1113.J65A3 2008   796.815092   C2008-902716-7

1 2 3 4 5 – 12 11 10 09 08

Design: Fortunato Design Inc.
Chapter head calligraphy: Noriko Maeda
www.norikomaeda.com

Printed and bound in Canada

To those who dedicate their lives to training and teaching the martial arts. In our modern world, it is much needed.

To my teachers and mentors, Tsuruoka Sensei in Toronto, Yamaguchi Sensei in Gotemba, Japan, and all the instructors of the Japan Karate Association in Tokyo, Japan.

Most of all, I would like to dedicate this book to my mother, who never questioned my life decisions and forgave me for my mistakes.

Even though this event happened a long time ago, I have never forgotten the help and support I was given by my family, friends and colleagues. Thank you to all of you who kept the Dojo running during my absence: George Taylor, Jon Juffs, John Walker, Leo Cossetto, Les Smith, my administrator Joan White and all the other instructors and assistants training at the Dojo at the time.

To Susanne, for all her help in gathering information to help in my case.

To Gene Shannon, my writer, it would have been impossible to do this book without him. Thanks to Fortunato Aglialoro for the cover design and layout of the book, and for his insights on how to get the book published. And Japanese calligrapher Noriko Maeda for the chapter head calligraphy.

Sensei
Teacher

Prologue

June 1984

"ONE MORE TIME!"

Again, I thrust my body forward. My front foot smacks down in unison with fifteen others onto bare hardwood, rattling it like an approaching army, while my fist, the knuckles on my first two fingers swollen into gnarled stumps, snaps forward. My legs, on the brink of mutiny, scream for stillness, but there is no time for that; I am already moving, back foot shooting out to my right like a pendulum, then swinging beneath me and settling into another *zenkutsu-dachi* stance, my lean 200-pound frame shuddering ever so slightly as I hold my balance. There is ragged breathing all around me, and the blood pounds at my temples like a mob at the door of a walled city, but my body is singing. Block. Pivot. Reverse punch. Step. Kick. Block. I keep moving, gliding across the floor, thinking only of the next movement, all available reserves of energy emptying into each kick and thrust. My *gi* hangs loose and open at the waist, while the sweat pours off me like a river, the heavy fabric clinging to my arms like wet sandbags.

"Again!"

Next to me, a voice curses softly, from a lanky, wheezing brown belt who has made the mistake of taking two weeks off class. The sequence begins again, mercilessly, each motion of the kata *bassai-dai* passing under the microscope buried in the eyes of Tsuruoka Sensei. He is pacing slowly at the front of the dojo, terse, belting out instructions, his head turning to follow each of us, his *karate-ka*, struggling to perform with our usual grace. His moon-shaped face is impassive behind a full, close-cropped beard of inky blackness and matching glasses—to a stranger he would look every bit the stern, serious college professor. He is not; rather, in our minds, he is a man just arrived from the Japanese feudal countryside, an exiled warrior who has stepped out of our imaginations and into life to bring us his gifts, doling out his knowledge in exchange for our sweat. Behind him a long bank of mirrors reflects back on us, exposing our labour to execute motions we have done thousands of times before. I am no different, stealing a glance at the clock as I pivot into the next movement: it's been more than ninety minutes of this agony.

"*Yame!* Partners. *Jiyu kumite.*"

I pause for breath, head down, as people hurry into pairs. The sun has dropped into view through the leaded windows that rise behind me to the ceiling, a tangle of naked joists and exposed wires. I can see the evening traffic below us lumbering along Davenport Road, the sound coming through the windows that are open to the stifling air saturated with June's humidity.

Warren a slight but lightning-quick Chinese second-dan, steps in front of me. We face each other, and bow.

"*Hajime!*"

I have barely moved into a fighting stance before a sidekick snaps at my ribs and then a back-fist at my head. I dance aside, landing a blow to his exposed kidney, just slapping him enough to sting. My *gi*, laden with moisture, cracks like a whip when I strike. Undeterred, he throws two punches at my head, but my guard is back up and I block, our forearms colliding as I shift my weight to throw a kick of my own. He is trying to keep me moving, assuming that because I am bigger I am slower, but I just hold myself in good position and use my reach to keep him at bay. I let him land one solid kick, spanking me in the small of the back, to encourage him.

Sensei signals for a partner change and in comes Rico, an

aggressive, newly minted black belt with a fearsome punch—it is packed with steel, courtesy of a prosthetic hook that hangs in place of his missing left arm. His body is hard in the same way, lean, wiry and well-defined, and he starts playfully, leading with his hook, wrapped in a towel for sparring. I slide left and come inside, bringing the front two knuckles of my reverse punch up under his chin to graze his Adam's apple. He laughs, his olive-skinned head falling back in appreciation, and we start again. I am having fun now, holding in a smile, marshalling energy for a quick strike. As we circle I go for his head, but the punch ends up hitting steel, the shock vibrating through the thin towel and up my arm. He grunts a half-apology, looking for his opening. He is quick and becoming skillful, but not enough to put me in any danger; we play cat-and-mouse for a minute before Tsuruoka calls out again and we bow to each other and move on.

Then Ted, a very seasoned fourth-dan about ten years my senior, steps in. Sparse patches of grey at his temples slide into a chiselled jaw, carved from the same rock as the rest of his physique. Now retired from competition, he was Canada's first national champion of karate, a title he carried easily for four years. My shoulders go tense—even though I am now the one on the national team, this is a man who can dominate me. We bow and begin.

I am nervous, making me slow on the counter-attack, and he pulls me out of position with a lunge punch to my head and then punishes me down low, landing a hard kick to the abdomen that throws me back a step. He holds little back—pain radiates out from the impact, but I keep my face still. I am breathing hard, but my mind is empty and clear, attuned to every flicker of movement. I decide to come at him with everything I have. When he begins to change stances I attack, launching forward with a front kick to make him scurry to my right, then throwing a combination of punches that force him into blocking low with both arms, leaving me an opening for a roundhouse kick to his head.

He dodges, but I have seized the initiative. I keep throwing combinations, trying to overwhelm him with speed, and within the space of five seconds we throw at least ten attacks and counters, but he swats my advances aside with alarming ease. Finally we disengage and I step away to catch my breath, happy to have stood my ground.

At last Tsuruoka Sensei calls for the sparring to stop. We fall into line in front of the mirrors and kneel, every chest heaving, Ted and the Sensei at the front, the rest of the students to my right in a straight line.

"*Hansei.*"

Sensei's voice reverberates through the quieting room. My heart still pounds, but the river of sweat has eased to a trickle, with drops rolling gently down my back. My spirit purrs; my body tiptoes the fine line between exhaustion and elation. I close my eyes and my breathing becomes more even: inhale through the nose and slowly exhale through the lips. I feel good.

"*Hansei yame. Shomen ni lei.*" Stop meditation. Bow to the front.

"*Sensei ni lei.*" Bow to Tsuruoka sensei.

"*Sempai ni lei.*" Bow to Ted.

"*Yudansha ni lei.*" Bow to the black belts.

We rise and walk off the floor in single file, stopping to bow to Tsuruoka a final time. In the shower I take an extra minute to enjoy the hot water enveloping me. I'm bone-tired, and all I want to do is go home, eat a simple meal and sleep, but I know I have to get to my own dojo in Newmarket first. Everyone else is charged up from the work-out, and the voices bounce around the cinder-block walls like kids waiting for recess, the possibilities of the summer night taking over the conversation.

"Who wants to hit Queen Street?"

"Are you hanging out with those punks again?"

"Better than you punks."

"Forget Queen, I'm going to a party on campus."

"I thought you had to be of age to get into those."
"I'm twenty-three!"
"Yeah, sure…"

Every body radiates health, ripples with muscle. No one cares about the spartan surroundings, the bare pipes jutting out from the walls, the single rough-hewn bench where everyone's clothes are stacked. It's a confident group, men who believe that there is nothing the world can throw at them that they can't handle.

"Hey Brad, let's go for a beer," shouts Rico, towelling off.

"Nah, I can't, I got to go to Newmarket and teach an advanced class."

"Ah, your class isn't for a couple of hours, you don't have time for one beer?"

"No, not tonight, I need to get up there now so I can take care of some things."

I step out of the showers and start dressing quickly. Rico comes over and sits down on the bench next to me, snapping his towel at one of the lower-ranked belts walking by.

"C'mon man, let's get just one drink."

"Nope, can't do it."

I'm putting away my *gi*, wringing it out and folding it carefully in the prescribed way before placing it inside the gym bag at my feet. I've known Rico for years, training beside him, but now I'm rushing, not looking at him, just trying to pack my bag and get out.

"Brad." Rico leans towards me as he speaks. "Did you think about what I had to say earlier?"

"No, I haven't had time."

"Ok, well think about it, alright?"

"Ok."

"Let's get a beer next class."

"Ok."

— ★ ★ ★ —

I think about "it" as I inch up the 400 highway with the evening commuters heading north out of the city. I've been thinking about it for days, ever since Rico made the proposal—accompany him to Pakistan to do "a run." I still shake my head every time I think about it. Drop everything and take a job as a dope runner.

It's crazy, of course, but the way Rico explains it there is a certain logic that keeps tugging at me. He had asked me once before, months ago, and I dismissed it out of hand, but this time it keeps slinking back into my mind, popping in at all hours of the day. I review the reasons in my head one more time as I follow the brake lights ahead of me:

This is how he earns his money. He's done these runs before, many times.

He has a proven system, so the chances of getting caught are small.

He'll be there to show me how it's done.

It is just hashish oil, it won't hurt anybody.

I'll get to travel to parts of the world that few Westerners have ever seen.

I'll make a lot of money.

The money. That's what it comes down to in the end. There are a lot of things I could use that money for. A lot of things. But smuggling dope? It isn't the best answer to my problems, but it is an answer. And part of me has to admit it does sound like a very interesting trip—tribal areas, warlords, ancient civilizations. I've heard his stories many times. It would certainly be *an adventure*.

I shift down and pull into the off-ramp for Newmarket. *Still, smuggling, I don't know…*

"Hi Brad."

"Hi Angie. Any messages?"

"Phone's been ringing off the hook. The modelling agency called to say you have a casting call on Wednesday and they expect to see you at the party at The Bamboo tomorrow night. Dress nice."

"Great."

"The landlord called to remind you that the rent is overdue again and that he would have kicked you out by now if he wasn't such a nice guy."

"Alright. Any messages from DeHavilland about being called back to work?"

"Nope. But Mia called and said to phone her right away, it's something important."

"Ok. Thanks for minding the store, Ang. How are classes going tonight?"

"Good. The kids are excited about their grading next week. George and I worked with them on some of their katas, I think they're really coming along."

"That's great."

I step into the main dojo area and watch George put a class of higher belts through its paces. It's near the end of the session and many of the faces are flushed. They are such good students. No one complains about the nondescript little room, the cheap pine flooring, the lack of air conditioning or the lack of equipment. They all come and forget about their busy lives for this hour or two and give themselves over to karate. Some of them fumble with the movements, but they are all intent. I stand and watch them for a minute as they struggle with a new combination. I can't help looking at their progress with all the pride of a den mother watching her young fight towards the day when they can hunt for themselves.

I look over at the clock on the wall, beside the faded photograph of Master Funakoshi that furnishes every Shotokan karate dojo I've ever entered; it's almost 8 p.m. I quickly change into a new *gi* in my office and return just as George calls an end to his class.

"*Oss!*" He bows and the students all turn towards me and do the same. "*Oss!*"

"*Oss.*" I bow in return and take the floor with three of our black belts. Now it is my turn to lead.

I get back to my apartment close to 11 p.m. and heat up a simple meal of rice, beef and vegetables. I'm cooking the meal on a hot plate with my old camping pots; that's all the kitchen equipment I have left since Suzanne moved out. It doesn't bother me, I like keeping things simple, but I have to admit that most people would laugh if they walked in—there are just a few pieces of furniture in the room: a beat-up old dresser, an unmade queen-sized bed against the far wall and an antique barber's chair by the window. Everything else had been Suzanne's.

I sit on the floor as I eat, leaning against the wall. I'm exhausted but my mind is buzzing with calculations, rehashing old math I've been going over for days and days now. Tallying up the numbers of my obligations is almost a ritual now, but I'm looking for a new angle, for something I've somehow overlooked, whatever will unlock the door to a solution for the problems that bloom out of the meagre figures.

Modelling. That's good for two gigs a month, not great pay. Half of that gets spent at all the parties I go to for the agency.

The dojo. I'm not taking any money out of that. Enrollment is steady, but costs are going up.

Unemployment benefits. Almost gone. My job as a maintainance electrician at DeHavilland Aircraft—not likely to call me back any time soon.

Other job prospects. Ones that don't clash with my training or my teaching schedule: basically none.

However I figure it, there doesn't seem to be any wiggle room in those numbers. I know this, of course, but my mind won't stop returning to them, like I expect the list to somehow rewrite itself. *Fat chance.* Where my mind balks is at projecting those numbers into the future—I'm already late paying most of my bills for the dojo. What happens when I can't pay them anymore? It's this point, a few months ahead, where my mind veers away, running into a giant wall of blankness. What lies beyond it? I know, but I can't say it, like I'm trying to explain to a child what happens to the family dog if the operation doesn't work.

Since Rico's proposal, the math has changed. My fee, twenty thousand dollars, would put an end to this incessant counting for quite a while. But my mind veers away from this too, repeatedly repelled when it comes to the word "smuggler." As the hours and days pass, roads are built towards the word, roads named "security," "adventure" and "what's best for the dojo." But none have reached it yet.

Thinking of the dojo helps build those roads. I knew from the time I was forteen years old that I wanted to dedicate my life to the martial arts, and share my knowledge of it, to help make a difference in the world. My training taught me what my life could become if I tried hard enough—bringing me into contact with many people I never would have met otherwise, and teaching me to "never give up," an attitude that no one had ever shared with me before. Everything good in my life up to now has come from my training—my health, my friends and colleagues, and many experiences that I would never have otherwise had. In "regular life" my options always seem limited—in karate, all seems possible.

It's that feeling that led me to begin teaching and open my school. It started as a way to give back, but now working with students and seeing them learn is one of my greatest joys. I learn at the same time they do—how to take the desire of another person, mould it through hard work, and then watch them reap the rewards. I cannot think of a greater satisfaction.

I look down at my empty plate—I can't remember what the food I just ate tasted like, or even when I finished eating it. I take the plate back to the kitchen and quickly wash up. The scrubbing of the pots is calming, activity being the best tonic for all my pent-up mental energy. My mind is still roaming, looking for something to latch on to that will point to the right road. I start thinking about Master Funakoshi's Twenty Precepts of Karate-do, which I'd just been reviewing with some students the night before. Two of the twenty jump out at me: *The mind needs to be freed* and *Trouble is born of negligence.* I shake my head: am I now twisting Funakoshi's words to justify dope smuggling?

In a few minutes I'm flicking off the light and falling into bed. Fatigue finally takes over and my body melts into the sheets. *Oh shit, I forgot to call Mia.* It's too late now, I'll have to call her tomorrow. I think of her lithe, soft body curled next to mine as I pull the blanket up under my arm and close my eyes. As I tumble towards sleep, I think of a story Rico told me about the last time he was in Pakistan.

He was in Peshawar, near the border of Afghanistan, walking through one of the old bazaars where weapons swiped from the Soviet army were traded alongside basic kitchen implements. He was there with a friend, a local, who had told Rico he had a friend who had something Rico would want to see. They reached a stall in the bazaar, built out of a large desert tent, and sat on a floor covered in beautiful carpets, sipping mountain tea, while the friend went to retrieve the item. After twenty minutes he returned with a long bundle of silk that he carefully unwrapped with great ceremony. Inside it was a sword, five feet long in the blade and honed to great sharpness, which the man claimed he bought from a Pashtun tribesman from deep in the northern mountains. The sword was from the eighteenth century and, according to the owner of the stall, had been used with great success in many wars since that time, cutting down foes in bloody local battles and separating a blonde head or two from its body in later skirmishes with the British and the Russians. It was a magnificent weapon, heavy but beautifully balanced, with a simple, rugged handle that bore an inscription with the name of the tribe that the various owners of the sword had belonged to. Rico begged the man to let him buy it, asking him to name his price, but the man refused, insisting it would be sacrilege to let the weapon leave the tribal lands. He had only wanted to show it to him, to demonstrate that his poor country had a rich and proud history. Rico left, dejected at not being able to own the fabulous weapon, but able to describe every inch of it.

Yes, I think before drifting into oblivion, *let's go to Pakistan.*

Rei
Respect, courtesy

Chapter 1

H<small>EAT</small>.

That was my first and only thought as the stewardess swung open the cabin door to the Pakistani night. *What heat!* It was night time, approaching 11 p.m., but I felt like she had just opened the door to a blast furnace. I blinked as the stewardesses secured the mobile staircase to the fuselage. *If it's like this now, what will it be like when the sun comes up?* I would have to wait until tomorrow to find out.

I was exhausted. I had now been at the mercy of the airline industry for nearly twenty-four hours, my five-hour flight here to Karachi being preceded by a six-hour layover in Frankfurt, Germany, and a nine-hour flight from Toronto. My six-foot-three-inch frame had spent most of the time pinned into a pint-sized economy row, unable to sleep much and running out of distractions after the first hour. I was restless—partly from excitement for the adventures I was about to have and partly from nerves about those adventures. Mostly I'd spent the trip impatient for the whole thing to get started. Now that I'd arrived in Karachi, all I wanted was a shower and a bed.

Three weeks had passed since I had woken up and phoned Rico to tell him I would accept his proposal. It had been a whirlwind of preparations since then, buying new clothes and building alibis, and all of it had left me feeling both nervous and energized to embark on the biggest adventure of my life. I promised myself two things before leaving: that I would put myself in

Rico's hands, leaving all the details to him so that if I were ever caught I could genuinely say that I didn't know very much; and that I would tell no one of what I was doing. It was a crazy, risky thing and I didn't want anyone to worry.

One person, though, had broken through my defences. Suzanne had discarded my vague excuses where no one else had, and pleaded with me not to do whatever I was doing. I'd brushed her off, trying to reason with her that she didn't need to worry about me anymore, that I just needed to get away for a couple of weeks, but our parting—full of tears and quiet promises—spoke to a deeper truth that rattled me whenever I thought of it.

I walked down to the tarmac carrying a portable typewriter Rico and I had bought the week before. When the time came it would carry several kilograms of hashish oil pumped into its hollow casing, but right now it was only a typewriter and was just a prop to support the story that I was a writer travelling through Asia to research stories about the martial arts. I held the case loosely in my right hand as I looked across at the terminal of Karachi International Airport. It didn't look like much at that hour, but I could just make out the silhouette of a slender dome rising from the middle of the terminal roof. Otherwise, it looked pretty much like any large airport as I followed the line of travellers, a mix of Pakistanis and Europeans, towards the entrance.

Inside, the first thing I noticed was the grime, thick and enveloping. The entire place was shockingly unkept, and I spied two uniformed airport workers slumped against a wall, sleeping in the open. There was no air conditioning and the humidity, combined with the weight of the suit I was wearing, was already making me sweat. *So this is what the subcontinent is like.* I was too tired to see the romance of it. I followed the crowd to the passport control, was processed quickly, and moved towards the baggage claim. I walked through a set of sliding doors, then stopped in my tracks.

The baggage area was open to the public and the room was

in complete chaos. Even at this hour it was a sea of people. They were shouting, embracing, craning their necks, calling out, jostling and generally acting as if an important football match were about to start. In addition to those waiting to greet friends and family, there were droves of merchants and beggars, all clamouring for attention. Everyone spoke in Urdu, so the entire scene looked to me like a symphony without a conductor, all sound with no meaning. I pushed my way over to the baggage carousel and before long spotted my two pieces of brown leatherette luggage churning around the bend towards me. I reached in to pull them out, but before I even had a chance to lay the bags down they were yanked from my hand! The dark leatherette disappeared into the crowd for a moment, then I spotted the bags surfing through the mass of heads, moving quickly away, two young boys underneath.

"Hey! Stop! Come back here!"

I started to chase the bags, which were already nearing the exit. Shoving my way through as best I could, I escaped the throng, but the two boys were out of sight. I ran outside and looked left and right, and there they were, just a few metres away, standing beside a beat-up Toyota like they were loafing on their front porch. An older man in a fraying polyester suit was tying down the trunk, with one of my suitcases inside, and had already put the other one inside the car. He seemed completely unfazed to see me.

"Where to, sahib?"

Oh hell, I need a taxi anyways.

"To the Sheraton, please."

"Oh, the sahib has good taste."

I piled in while the two youngsters ran back inside. The car was so tiny I had to sit scrunched in the back seat with one of my bags on top of me. We screeched away from the curb and were on our way into the city.

I remember little of the sights on that drive, since I spent most

Detour on The Path

of the time praying for our survival. My driver accelerated as if late for his own wedding and we flew down crowded city thoroughfares, barrelling through lane dividers, ignoring stop signs and red lights. Despite it being close to midnight, traffic was thick with all kinds of vehicles—including several people leading camels, a herd of goats and a man riding a donkey—and at one point we swerved to narrowly miss a horse-drawn cart. My jaw was clenched so tight my molars were beginning to hurt, but my host was calm and humming to himself, one hand on the wheel and the other leaning on the horn, punching it constantly to announce our arrival.

"You like Pakistani music, sahib?"

"It's one of my favourites." *How should I know?*

He took his hand off the horn for a moment to grab a cassette and pop it into an old tape deck swinging from the dash, held in place by a single, rusty screw. A new screeching began, and I decided that his use of the car horn was actually a tribute to local musicians rather than a safety device.

"Good music, eh sahib?"

"Yes, wonderful."

We blazed through traffic like this for about fifteen minutes, the stereo cranked to maximum volume, dodging crater-sized potholes before easing up to the back door of the Sheraton. I waited for my stomach to settle back into place before I got out, resisting an urge to kiss the ground.

"Ok, how much?"

"Fifty."

That's not bad, about three bucks American. I reached for my wallet and pulled out fifty rupees.

"No sahib, fifty dollars."

"Excuse me? Fifty dollars? Fifty U.S. dollars? That's crazy!"

"No sahib, that is what it costs."

"There's no way I'm paying that. I could buy five of your taxis for that much."

"But sahib, it's very important that you pay me that. I have many, many children and my poor wife is exhausted. Her mother is dying and has been forced to live with us, as well as two of her brothers. There are now eleven people living in my house and only me to support them. Hospital bills are very expensive and we don't want my mother-in-law dying in front of the children, and…"

Uh huh. "Look, I'll pay you twenty dollars."

"No, no sahib. Gas is also very expensive, and repairs, and if I don't keep my beautiful vehicle in tip-top shape, business will go down, down, down. It must be fifty dollars, sahib, or it wouldn't be fair to other customers, and…"

A wave of exhaustion came over me. "Alright, enough already, I'll give you fifty. Here."

"Thank you, sahib, thank you very much. I hope you have a very pleasant stay."

"Yeah, whatever."

I picked up my bags and walked around to the front door. The lobby of the Sheraton was bright and clean and I felt relieved to be somewhere with a western feel to it. My room had been booked in advance, so I made my way over to the smiling concierge and gave my name.

"Yes, Mr. Jones, your room is ready."

"Thank you. Tell me, what is the usual price for a taxi to here from the airport?"

The man blinked and waited one beat before replying, "Oh, I don't know, not too expensive, sir."

"Approximately how much?"

"Oh, I couldn't really say exactly, sir."

"About twenty dollars?"

"No, no, not that expensive. Maybe five dollars, at the very most. But we offer a free shuttle to and from the airport, sir, so you don't have to worry about that."

I thanked him and moved my things upstairs. I was far too embarrassed to tell him what I had actually paid, and too tired to care anymore. I'd barely dropped my bags and gotten out of my suit before collapsing onto the bed. I was asleep in seconds.

I awoke the next morning in the middle of a dream. A male voice was chanting rhythmically in a language I did not understand. The voice was beautiful and soothing, with a resonance unlike anything I'd ever heard. After several moments I realized I was not dreaming and the sound was coming from outside my window. I opened my eyes and saw that the room was starting to fill with light. Something, a memory of a sound I'd once heard while in Egypt, triggered in my brain—it was dawn and the voice was the Muslim call to prayer.

I got up and moved to the window. Across the street, perhaps fifty feet away, a thickly bearded man stood atop a slim tower at about the height of my room. His plain white shirt extended almost to his knees, standing out vividly against the orange horizon of morning. His voice—strong, rising and falling effortlessly while his body remained still—was projected across the neighbourhood by a bank of speakers pointed in four directions. The tower was attached to a modest mosque across from the hotel, and the street between us was quiet, the few people moving slowly, as if hungover from last night's exertions.

I watched the man, who did not see me, for another minute, enthralled by the beauty of his call. Then the song stopped and he shuffled below and out of sight, off to make the first of his five prayers to Allah that day.

I reached over to the dresser and grabbed my watch… 5:30 a.m. Smiling, I stretched, feeling rejuvenated despite the short sleep. *Now the adventure begins.*

With nowhere to go at that hour, I slipped back into bed and let my mind drift. It wasn't long before it settled on Mia. She'd given me quite a shock. I'd called her right after telling Rico I would go to Pakistan, not sharing with her what I'd just agreed to do, and she'd insisted on coming over that minute. Forty-five minutes later she was at my door, her beautiful almond eyes streaked with tears, her long, thick hair dishevelled. She walked in and wasted no time dropping the bomb—she was pregnant. We talked for many hours and days after that, but agreed that an abortion was the best thing. I'd gone with her to her family doctor and he'd set up an appointment at a hospital downtown. The date for the procedure was two days after I was to get back from this trip. I'd been vague with her about where I was going—just saying I had some work out of town—but I'd promised her I'd be back in time to go to the hospital.

Ah Mia, I miss you. I was struck by the irony of her not knowing that I was only a few hundred miles from the land where her parents had grown up. *How would this place look to you?* To me, it was full of possibility and promise, tempered by the lurking threat to my return to a normal life. *Ten more days*, I told myself, shocked to be already looking forward to my return home.

My plans for the day were modest. I was to meet Rico that evening in Islamabad, Pakistan's capital city, which lay more than 1,000 kilometres to the northwest, and I needed to arrange my flight. Otherwise, I was a tourist, free to explore the country's liveliest, bustling city.

I put on khakis and a golf shirt and went downstairs for the hotel's "American-style" breakfast. Stepping into the room brought back my sense of adventure. A rainbow of coloured floor cushions were strewn about the room, occupied by an equally strange assortment of foreign businessmen and well-dressed locals. The Pakistanis were all wearing vibrant, traditional robes wrapped loosely around them, a striking contrast to the sober tailored suits of most of the Western travellers. I must have been staring, as one of the local men smiled and motioned for me to join him.

Why not? I thought, and made my way over.

"Hello!" the man boomed, several people turning to look at him. "Thank you for joining me. I am a lonely businessman, visiting from Lahore. My name is Haroon. It gives me great pleasure to sit with you."

"Thank you, my name is Brad. It's my first day in Pakistan, so it's nice to have someone to talk to." I felt like we were both reading lines out of a book on how to learn English.

"Ah, wonderful. Where are you from?"

"Canada."

"Ah, I hear it is a spectacular country. You are here on business as well?"

"Yes."

Just then a waiter appeared, saving me from further explanation. I asked him to bring me an egg-white vegetarian omelette and a fruit bowl, part of my training regime.

"After that flight yesterday I could use a beer," I joked.

My host's face, a round, brown fleshy visage with crow's feet smile lines and an undefined jaw, went blank for a moment, then stretched into a thin smile.

"We Muslims shun alcohol, it takes us away from the best parts of ourselves."

"Well, that's not all ba—" I began to say.

"It is dishonest!" Haroon's pudgy hands came out from beneath his robe and started dancing around his head as he spoke. "Alcohol takes you further from your true self, even after a small amount it starts talking for you. To tell yourself otherwise is like sneaking around behind your own back…like you North American men do with your mistresses, lying to your wives."

"Excuse me?" The conversation was quickly getting away from me.

"Mistresses! Are you married?" I started looking around the room, worried that people were starting to stare at us.

"No."

"What?! You must get married, it is the most important thing a man can do. To not do so is a disservice to God. A man like you should have no trouble finding a woman."

I was becoming more than a little uncomfortable with his line of questioning. "What were you saying about mistresses?"

Here he began to smile. "That it is a poor habit of Westerners. Much better to have many wives, like we Muslims do, than to go around, what is the phrase, 'having affairs.'"

Ouch. As much as I was uncomfortable with what he was saying, it was hard to argue in favour of cheating. I weakly tried to deflect the attack: "You have more than one wife?"

He smiled broadly. "Yes."

"And you're trying to tell me that marrying many women is more ethical than marrying one?" I felt like I'd somehow fallen into his trap. He was starting to get to me.

"Certainly. We take care of all of our women for all their lives, rather than just tossing them away when we are bored."

"How lucky did your first wife feel about sharing you? How come she doesn't get to pick a new husband when she gets bored of the old one?"

"It's the natural way," he replied, unperturbed. "Both my wives are treated very well. Older wife is friend and confidant, but I spend as much time with her as with the new wife. It is just acknowledging the nature of male desire."

"What about equality?"

"They are treated equally! I am required by law to treat each wife the same. And by having several wives I rise up above other men, and my family rises with me. Our ways let us be fair to women, while making allowances for men's weaknesses."

I was getting frustrated, but I didn't have a comeback. Seeing my frustration, my new friend began to laugh at me.

"Don't worry, my young friend, it is not all roses for us Muslim men. We have a saying: 'One wife, one headache; two wives, many headaches.' It is not so easy for us."

I decided not to argue anymore. I was enjoying the conversation, despite my bewilderment, but I'd finished my meal and was anxious to get out and explore. The waiter appeared again, bearing a small bowl of rosewater so I could wash my hands, briefly making me feel like a sultan. I thanked Haroon for his company and excused myself, going back to my room to gather what I'd need for the day.

I stepped out of the hotel shortly afterwards, carrying only a 35mm camera. The heat, which I had been dreading all morning from inside the air-conditioned Sheraton, did not knock me over with the intensity I had expected, but I could tell that the heavy humidity would leach out my strength as the morning lengthened. It didn't seem to bother most people; the same chaotic rush of cars, goats, rickshaws, bicycles and crazed drivers were still buzzing around, and now several people standing on street corners seemed to think it was important to shout at the top of their lungs.

I decided the best way to get around was to hire a car, so I flagged down the most reputable-looking taxi I could find and, after establishing a reasonable price, asked for a tour of the city. My driver—this one a quiet man with no tape deck—and I spent most of the day driving and visiting the major sights. I was able to see a lot. Along the Lyari River I gaped at the "Great Laundry," where hundreds of people washed and dyed their clothes along a four-kilometre stretch of riverbank. I couldn't believe it when my driver told me that this was the best source of clean water for most people. After visiting the national museum I spent the early part of the afternoon staring at the Arabian Sea off Clifton Beach, enjoying a chapatti from a roadside vendor while being eyed by the lolling camels-for-hire and the homeless. After lunch I headed back to the hotel. On the way I noticed vultures circling in the air over a hill on the way downtown; when I asked my driver why they were there he explained that the Parsees traditionally exposed their dead to the heavens, so they could be consumed by nature. This amazed me, but also made sense. If we share our bodies with the worms and things that live in the soil, then why not share with the birds?

Throughout the day, I'd noticed a barely audible clicking noise coming from somewhere inside the cab. Finally I asked the driver if he knew what it was.

"It is me," he replied, breaking into a shy smile. "I am giving thanks to God."

"How's that?" I said, raising an eyebrow.

"Every time I think of God, and thank him for my existence, I click this counter," he said, holding up a two-inch-square black metal box that he'd been holding in the palm of his hand, with a mechanical counter triggered by a button underneath his poised thumb. "It keeps my mind on God."

"How many times a day do you click?" I asked, trying to be polite.

"Nearly a thousand!" he exclaimed, clearly glad I'd asked.

You spend your whole day clicking a bloody counter? I knew it wasn't a fair response, but for some reason I was annoyed by this.

"Don't you think you could thank God better by doing something more…productive with that time?"

"Ah, my friend, but I am doing quite a lot. Every time I think of God I become stronger. I am now a very strong man!"

I shook my head and bit my tongue; there was so much here I didn't think I would ever understand.

Back at the hotel, I packed up my things quickly and checked out, taking the airport shuttle this time. The departure area was not much different than the arrivals had been the day before, with hundreds milling around as if trying to find something they'd lost. There was no such thing as an orderly line, so I pushed my way through the crowd towards the Pakistani International Airlines counter. I was back in my suit, so people generally parted as if I were an emergency worker trying to get through.

"Hello. One ticket for Islamabad, please."

"I'm sorry, sir, but all the flights to Islamabad are sold out for the next several days."

What! "But I need to get there tonight."

"I'm sorry, sir. We can put you on a standby list for a 'chance' ticket if you wish."

What a great start. "Ok, sure."

"Please go though security to the departure lounge. Someone there will notify you if a ticket becomes available."

I sighed and picked up my bags again. Security was close by, so I elbowed my way through the crowd to the uniformed officer. He looked bored, but when he saw me he became suspicious, staring at the case in my hand.

"What in that?"

"A typewriter."

"Let me see."

The young guard, who couldn't have been more than twenty, took the case and eyed it critically, as if estimating the value of a precious gem. He then opened the case, took out the typewriter, and stared at it some more.

I did not like this at all.

Eventually he seemed satisfied enough to grunt and return the case.

"Raise arms."

The young man then conducted a thorough body search from head to toe, examining everything short of the caps on my teeth. I had nothing to hide at this point, but it made me reflect considerably on how I was going to get out of the country. I knew security was more interested in foiling hijackers than smugglers, but it was also true that bagging a Western dope runner (it was still strange to think of myself that way!) would make their day.

Eventually he nodded and let me go, and I moved on to the departure lounge. I put my name on the standby list and waited. And waited. While I knew that a few dollars slipped casually towards the ticket agent would have greatly enhanced my chances of getting a seat, pride would not let me do it. I could see on the board with the day's remaining flights that, after this flight, there was only one more departing that day. It left very late and arrived in Islamabad in the middle of the night, something that struck me as a very bad idea.

I became more and more agitated as I waited, my fingers occasionally drifting to two U.S. $100 bills that Rico had given me for emergencies. I cursed myself; how could the plan be going awry already? I was never going to make it as a smuggler if little hiccups like this were going to throw me off. I sat more patiently and, after forty minutes or so, my break finally came—the final boarding call was made, and then an airline attendant waved me over. I got the last seat.

The flight lasted only two hours and we were soon landing in Islamabad. The airport was much cleaner than in Karachi, but I still kept my bags close as I went outside to wave down a cab. I was learning—this time I asked about the fare and bartered him down to something more reasonable.

Driving into the city I asked the driver why everything up front looked so new. Turns out the city was not even twenty-five years old! Construction started from scratch in 1961 to make it the capital, and evidence of the bureaucratic mindset was everywhere. The streets were all laid out on a perfect grid and every building was rectangular and bare. I suddenly felt like I'd gone from a pre-industrialized country to a Soviet depot. According to the driver, however, only the politicians lived in Islamabad; everyone else lived in neighbouring Rawalpindi, its twin city, much larger and older and only fifteen kilometres away.

As we approached the hotel, I suddenly had the strange urge to turn back. This was my last chance—once I met Rico, I knew he wouldn't let me go. I imagined telling the driver to "Turn the car around!" and racing back to the airport, taking the first flight out of the country, then to Europe, and home. But even as I began to enjoy the thought, I knew it was nothing but a nice fantasy, as only Rico had the return ticket and the money I'd need. I couldn't go back if I wanted to.

— ★ ★ ★ —

The hotel was a Holiday Inn—a five-star affair in Pakistan. I didn't see Rico in the lobby, so I checked in and was told that he was waiting for me upstairs. I went up and knocked on the door. I looked forward to seeing a familiar face.

"Brad, man, good to see you!" Rico eagerly reached out with his good hand for one of my bags. "Welcome to Pakistan, man, isn't it great?"

I smiled and moved into the room, tossing the rest of my belongings on the empty bed. I'd known Rico for years, and had never been to his apartment in Toronto, but for some reason I'd imagined the room would be filled with drug paraphernalia and signs of last night's hooker. Instead, it was immaculate, all clothing and baggage hidden from view, as if he'd arrived ten minutes before.

"So how's the trip been so far? How did you like Karachi?" Rico flopped himself down on the bed and stretched out.

"It's, uh, pretty interesting." I didn't feel like telling him about how I'd been fleeced before I even left the airport, or how dirty and chaotic I found the city. "Pretty crazy. I've never seen anything like it before."

"Fucking right you haven't. This place is amazing. There's no rules here, man, anything can be done if you know how. You got money, and whatever wish you got will come true. And you ain't seen nothing yet. When you see the Tribal Areas, man, there's no fucking government! It's all just about who you know and what you got. And it's less than a hundred miles from here, the fucking capital! That's how afraid the government is of the warlords. Now that's pretty amazing."

He sat back to better appreciate the wonder of that fact. I had to admit, he looked pretty good, clearly a man in his element. His five-foot-seven-inch frame was draped in a casual, cream-coloured suit, single-breasted with an open collar. Even under the suit you could tell he was fit; he'd been training hard. His hair was black and curly and cut close, along with his usual tightly cropped moustache. With the help of a couple of days in the south-Asian sun his face was a couple of shades darker than I normally saw it, and few would have guessed that he wasn't Arabic.

"What have you been doing?" I asked, realizing I had never bothered to find out before I left how he was travelling here or what his plans were.

"Ah, you know, just checking things out, visiting some people. Having fun, man." He could be maddeningly vague when asked about his preparations for this trip. I suspected it was a professional instinct for discretion, a belief that nothing non-essential should be shared with me, more for his protection than mine. I didn't disagree; I still felt that the less I knew the safer I was, so I didn't push him.

Still, I was curious about what we were supposed to be doing in Islamabad and, admittedly, a little anxious to know.

"So how long we here for? What do we have to do?"

"Ah," Rico said, laughing as he pushed himself back to an upright position and leaned in.

"Just fun, man. We don't have to be in Peshawar for a couple of days, so we get to play tourist. Do some shopping, you know, see some sights." Here he actually winked at me. "Have a good time."

Have a good time. I knew from experience that our definitions of fun were very different, but I still wanted to believe him.

Mushin
Not thinking, no mind

Chapter 2

I ROSE THE NEXT MORNING, early, and went straight to the window. The sun was barely peeking over the buildings below, but already people were milling around the wide boulevards. It was a little after 5:30 a.m. and Rico was still sleeping soundly in the next bed; I realized I'd slept through the call to prayer and the day was well underway. Not wanting to wake Rico, I threw on a T-shirt and some track pants and snuck out, taking the elevator to the roof.

As I suspected, the patio and the deck chairs around the pool were empty. From here I had a 360-degree view of the city. The hotel seemed to float in an ocean of green—between the evenly spaced grid of avenues were tens of thousands of leafy trees, like a manicured forest stretching in every direction. A few kilometres to my right, hills sprung up from the plain, and beyond them I could see the silhouettes of mountains in the distance. Straight ahead of me, some kilometres away, the grid collapsed into a mess of tangled streets, and the trees disappeared and were replaced by a wide swath of earth-coloured buildings. *That must be Rawalpindi.* Rico had told me last night that we could spend the day checking out the old bazaars there, what he called "the real city, not this cookie-cutter government crap."

I was eager to begin the day, but first I wanted to slip in a quick workout. I decided on practising the kata *kank dai*, a Shotokan karate form that touches on almost all of the basic movements. Raising my hands to the sky, I began. *Bring hands down and apart;*

slide left, block; high back hand block; right turn and shift to block; turn to front, bring left knife hand up; right-hand chest punch; shift weight and block; left-hand chest punch; rotate hips, look right; raise right leg, move right fist to left hip; right fist strike and right-foot side snap kick; look left, make knife hand…

After twenty minutes of this I returned to the room, glistening in a pleasant sweat. Rico was up and already towelling off after a shower.

"Hey man, you out trying to cut a better deal with someone else?" he said, laughing.

"That's right." I laughed as well, trying to play my part.

We left shortly after breakfast, taking a cab. Stepping outside, I was smacked by the heat, which had already risen dramatically since my workout. *How do people stand this?* I didn't like the idea of spending the day outdoors, gasping like a roasting animal, but I really wanted to do some exploring.

Rico sat in the front of the car and started chatting away with the driver in Urdu, while I sat glued to the window in the back. As we moved from the square concrete government buildings of Islamabad into Rawalpindi, there may as well have been a time zone separating the two cities. Rawalpindi was less like an older sibling of Islamabad than it was a crazed ancient uncle who had given into senility. Cleanliness and order devolved into buildings that had given up the pretense of worrying about appearances. Walls were left to crumble, signs were hung askew, and the poverty that was so conspicuously absent in Islamabad suddenly poked through every available opening. As we drove, wide boulevards shrunk and became crowded by autorickshaws, minibuses, taxis, beat-up private cars, motorcycles, city buses, bicycles, pedestrians and the odd vehicle running on animal power, all jostling for the same two lanes of road. The driving space might have been sufficient if drivers didn't discard their vehicles wherever was most convenient, even if that meant parking on a sidewalk.

What hit me more than anything was the colour—while much of Rawalpindi was draped in the drab brown of the earth, and most of the people wore the traditional plain white *shalwaar kameez,* this simplicity was overwhelmed by the lavish decorations of the vehicles and signs. Minibuses and rickshaws were painted like moving shrines, with a blinding avalanche of reds, golds, indigos and violets mixing in an intricate detailing that rivaled the nicer mosques. Looming over the traffic was a sea of billboards that elbowed into the street like a low-tech Times Square. Many featured a swooping red Urdu script, and almost all bore the stern face of a man with a moustache or a beard, and a few women with covered heads were also present on the streets. In between the traffic and the billboards, on the wide sidewalks, I could see merchants selling out of stalls or the backs of vans, along with scores of people going about their daily business. Everyone seemed to have somewhere to go, and someone to argue with about whatever they were doing. I was enthralled by how *public* it all was, just so different from street life at home. The hills I had seen from the hotel roof were closer now, and even they looked older than they did from Islamabad. When I'd told Rico over breakfast what I'd seen from the roof of the Holiday Inn, he told me that nine of the thirteen highest mountain peaks in the world, including K-2, were just a few hundred kilometres beyond these hills. I felt like asking the driver to head straight for them.

We were headed for the Rajah Bazaar, the largest shopping district in Rawalpindi. The traffic got worse the closer we got, so we jumped out beside a taxi stand and began to walk. Alleyways and side streets shot off the main road like spokes, and Rico dragged me down one of the first. The already narrow roads closed in further, jammed with people selling mounds of cloth, produce, fish, tools, clothing and metal work. The space was claustrophobic, and we had to push our way through the crowds and vendors on both sides of us, but the energy of the place had me keyed up like a kid set free on a field trip.

Rico, motioning me over to one stall after another, wanted to show off his street smarts. Anytime I showed a passing interest in an item, he started bartering with the merchants in Urdu.

"Don't worry about it Rico, I don't need any of this stuff."

"Sure you do! How else are you going to prove that you were here?"

This shut me up. I had no intention of telling anyone I'd been here, ever. "No, I don't need it."

Rico turned his head to look at me, smiling. "Don't you think it would look a little strange to come all this way and not bring home any souvenirs?"

Of course. This wasn't just for fun; we were building "my character." I let him pick out a couple of trinkets for me. What I did want was a carpet. I'd read before leaving that Pakistan was known for its silk rugs and what I bought here for hundreds of dollars would go for thousands back home. We spent the next couple of hours looking at dozens of stalls, eventually finding a beautiful crimson carpet made from raw silk that I liked. After a lengthy negotiation we agreed on a price and to come back later to pick it up.

I began to notice that I was attracting a lot of attention. Not just from merchants eyeing my U.S. dollars, but from regular passersby. I'd gotten a few looks while wandering through Karachi, but it was an urban city used to visitors; here in Rawalpindi I stood out more. I noticed that sometimes people would stroll ahead of me and turn back to steal a look, walking like this for several minutes. If I stopped at a stall, I would look behind me and find two or three people staring, often children. At first I was slightly embarrassed by all the scrutiny, but people were more curious than threatening.

Rico, on the other hand, with his amputated arm and mechanical hook, got almost no looks at all. A missing limb didn't seem so out of place here.

By the afternoon my enthusiasm for exploring the markets had run out, so we picked up our purchases and hired a car to take us

Detour on The Path

back to Islamabad, the driver tying the carpet precariously to the tiny roof and took us to a post office to have it mailed home along with a few postcards. There was one more sight that Rico wanted me to see, so he had the driver take us to the edge of the city.

There, at the base of the foothills and separated from Islamabad proper by several hundred metres, stood what looked like a giant multi-faceted tent. Its peak rose almost fifteen stories, with sloping walls connecting at forty-five-degree angles. At each corner of the main building a slender, elegant tower rose up three hundred feet in the air, like a redwood built from ivory. As we drove up, greeted by green lawns and beds of roses, I could see hundreds of people milling around the entrance.

"What is this?" I asked, stunned.

"Welcome to Shah Faisal, the national mosque of Pakistan," Rico said with a flourish.

"They've been building it for six years, spending like tens of millions of dollars," he said, gazing up at it in open admiration. "Most of the money came from the king of Saudi Arabia, so that's who they named it after."

It was an awesome sight. We walked through the front gate of interlocking stone and past the bubbling of an elegant fountain, finding ourselves inside a sprawling courtyard. Here were many more fountains, and sitting areas and places for worshippers to wash themselves before entering the mosque. Scores of people wandered around craning their necks to take it all in, while others moved deliberately, reminding me of the Zen monks I'd seen when I was in Japan. The people seemed to come from all kinds of backgrounds: Afghans and Americans, Pakistani and Japanese. It struck me how harmoniously they shared the space, with no sign of the ethnic or nationalist tensions that they might face outside.

We climbed a long, broad flight of stairs to the platform on which the mosque sat. As we drew near, I was astounded to see that the building was made from marble, which is what made it so visible from a distance.

Taking off our shoes, we took a quick peek inside—it was filled with light and the whole floor was covered in a majestic blue carpet. Suspended from the ceiling was a gold chandelier at least thirty feet in diameter, studded with tiny lights. The effect was breathtaking, and the atmosphere throughout was peaceful and solemn.

The afternoon was beginning to fade, so we returned to the hotel. I was famished, my body still used to the frequent meals I ate during training. Our room was so cool and serene that I wanted to stay in and order room service, but Rico suggested a nearby place with good local food. We walked over and quickly got a table; Rico ordered for both of us and in a few minutes there were several steaming plates of curried meat, chapattis and rice.

"So, look, you've got nothing to worry about tomorrow," Rico said between mouthfuls. "I'll do all the talking, you just got to carry the case."

Yes, tomorrow. I'd almost forgotten. Anxiety started to get the better of me. "So, is there anything I need to do?"

"Nothing. Dress well, look confident, stay quiet. Nothing scares these guys, but you're a big strong guy. If you don't look worried, they'll respect you."

"Ok."

"Good. We got a flight in the morning and we meet them for lunch. You take the bus back, I fly. Then we'll be having dinner again here tomorrow night."

Piece of cake, I thought. Eight more days after tomorrow night.

Rico chewed thoughtfully for a couple of minutes, his eyes drifting lazily around the room. "So, there's nothing much to do between now and tomorrow morning. Why don't we go out and find some fun?"

Oh god. I knew what that meant. If I said the wrong thing, we'd be spending the night in a Rawalpindi whorehouse, smoking the local product and rattling off comparisons of kata to the kama sutra.

"I don't know, seems like an important day tomorrow.

Shouldn't we get some rest?"

"What for? All you got to do is show up. And I know these guys, there's nothing to worry about."

"Well." I cringed at how timid and Canadian my voice sounded. "Sounds to me like I'll get my share of adventure tomorrow."

"C'mon, man. Might be good for you to let off a little tension."

"No, really, I'm ok."

"Suit yourself." Rico dismissed the conversation with a wave of his hand. "A quiet night of poker it is."

I noticed that a few people from neighbouring tables were looking over in our direction. Maybe it was because we were speaking English, but they seemed disgusted about something, and one of them was shaking his head and clearly talking to his dining mate about us.

"What's with the attention from our neighbours?"

Rico scraped up some leftover curry sauce with his chapatti. "Ah, it's their fucking Muslim traditions. Look around—you see anyone eating with their left hand? No. It ain't because they're all right-handed. It's custom for them to wash—and wipe—themselves after they have a shit using only their left hand, so they consider their left hand 'unclean.'"

"But you don't have a left hand…"

"Which means I clean, eat and do every other fucking thing with my right hand, which a few of our close-minded friends over there seem to think does not meet their standards of hygiene." He looked over at them very coolly and stuffed the chapatti in his mouth, wiping it clean with the back of his hand. "Fuck them."

I looked down at my plate. I hadn't been paying any attention to what I was doing with my left hand. Were those stares meant for me? I shook my head. I didn't know if Rico was right or just paranoid.

— ★ ★ ★ —

At the hotel that night, during a long string of poker losses, I started asking Rico questions about Peshawar. I knew some things from stories he had told me before: that it was considered the "frontier" to the Tribal Areas; that there were men who walked around openly with Kalashnikovs; that the whole city was surrounded by camps for refugees who had been forced to flee the Russian occupation in Afghanistan; and that beyond the city the Pakistani government had given up trying to enforce its rule, and the law of the land was dictated by local tribal customs. This was the place that had caught my imagination during Rico's storytelling sessions at our favourite bar after karate class, and I wanted to know everything about it.

"So who are these people we're meeting tomorrow?"

Rico looked up from his cards. "I thought you didn't want to know."

"I don't want to know their names, but where are they from? Why are they selling to us?"

"To make money, like you and me."

"Are they from the Tribal Areas?"

"Probably."

"Why come into Peshawar and risk getting arrested?"

Rico sighed like he was being forced to explain something to a very small child, and laid down three queens. "They don't want us on their turf, and it's a hell of a lot safer for us. Look, man, they're Pashtun. They're not afraid of anybody. They fought off the *British Empire* and made them give back control over their lands. They're tough."

I prodded him more, wanting to know more about these people. "Ok. What makes them so tough?"

Rico pushed his chair back from the table and stared at me. "Ok. So the Pashtun live by a code, and they would rather die than go against this code.

Detour on The Path

"The code has four principles. The first is called *melmastia*, which means you have to be a good host to any guest, without expecting anything back. All Muslims are supposed to be hospitable, but the Pashtun take it way further than anyone else—they'd spend their last dollar if it would buy their guest a bowl of soup.

"Second is *badal*, which is their *obligation* to avenge any kind of insult you might happen to make about them, their family or the tribe. Whether you meant to do it or not. Some of them actually think they are direct descendants of one of the Lost Tribes of Israel, so "eye for an eye" has a lot of meaning for them.

"Third is *nanwatai*. This means that if you lose a fight, you are expected to go to the guy who beat you and *beg* him to forgive you for having bothered him.

"Last is *nang*. This means that a man has a duty to protect the honour of any woman in his family. And, in case you get any ideas, you can insult that honour by just looking at a woman the wrong way—you do anything more serious than that and they'll probably kill you without thinking about it.

"These people have been warriors for centuries. They have a saying 'We are only at peace when we are at war.' A lot of the Pashtun live in Afghanistan and they're the ones kicking the Russians in the ass right now."

I was amazed. I took a couple of minutes to think about what this meant. "So this code, it's kind of like *budo*." *Budo* is the samurai's code, the way of the warrior.

"Yeah, sort of," Rico said, getting up from the table. "But picture an entire people made up of samurai."

I thought some more. Clearly, these people demanded respect and deserved to be feared. It was easy for me to respect them, since I understood the discipline involved in following your beliefs so absolutely, and I admired it—they were fighting to defend their honour, nothing more. *Spirit and technique are one*, I thought, remembering one of the maxims delivered to us by

Tsuruoka Sensei. Those whose lives embody their spirit are the most deadly opponents.

"I'm going to bed," Rico said, heading for the bathroom. "Tomorrow's a big day."

The next morning I woke to a stomach full of butterflies. As I lay there, still half-asleep, I knew that something…just wasn't right. *C'mon, you're a nobody in this deal. This will be a piece of cake.* I decided that I was just hungry and rolled out of bed. Rico was already up and putting things into a duffel bag.

"Time to rise, man. We've got a plane to catch."

I showered quickly and put on my suit. Rico was dressed more casually, but still wore a jacket with an open-collared shirt. He told me to pack a small bag, as I'd look suspicious getting on a plane carrying only a typewriter. I packed and we went downstairs. He hailed a cab and we were on our way to the airport.

Rico bought us tickets and we went quickly to the gate, security not doing much more than grunting in our direction— it wasn't very likely that we'd be smuggling anything *into* Peshawar. The flight was under an hour and neither of us spoke the entire time; Rico spent the flight absently tapping his hook on the hard plastic armrest and looking out the window, while I leafed through an English-language magazine.

Upon landing, we got off the plane and, with no baggage to claim, were through the airport in five minutes.

"It's only 10 a.m.," Rico said, looking at his watch. "Our meeting isn't until noon. Why don't we have a look around?"

He flagged down a taxi and gave some directions to the driver.

"You're gonna love this place," Rico told me as the cab pulled away. "This is the real Wild West out here." His eyes were shining and he rapidly tapped his foot on the floor.

"This city has been invaded and conquered and occupied for two thousand years," he continued. "Fucking Ghengis Khan fought here. The Moghuls took it over 400 years ago and turned it into one of the great cities of Asia. Then the Sikhs came along and trashed the whole thing, until the British came along and trashed them."

As we left the airport, the few intrusions of modernity quickly dropped away. The landscape was barren and dusty, a land of stark hills and rock. As we drew closer to the city, vast clusters of tents sprouted up by the side of the road, whole plains filled with them. There were even mud-and-straw huts in some places, evidence that these temporary dwellings were maybe not so temporary. Groups of people, clad mostly in robes the colour of the land, walked around talking to their neighbours. They were mostly women and their children, there were few men, and while they didn't appear to be in poor health, they were clearly living with remarkably little. Occasionally we would see a cow, held by a rope attached to a stake, but otherwise these people seemed to have little more than what they could carry on their backs.

I turned to Rico, shaken. "What is this place?"

"These are the refugee camps," he replied, staring out the window as the little clusters kept whizzing by. "It's gotten crazy out here the last few years, the refugees keep coming and coming. I hear there's more than a million, maybe two million, and about sixty camps surrounding the city. Peshawar's doubled in size since the Russians moved in next door five years ago. There's people who've been living there for *years*. Most of the men are back in Afghanistan, fighting the Russians."

I tried to imagine what that life would be like, living in this parched landscape. It was difficult to wrap my head around it. "What do they *do*, stuck there all day?"

"They make carpets!" Rico started to laugh. "All fucking day! They sit in one place and weave these goddamn carpets, cuz it's the only thing they get money for so they can buy food. Their kids too! You'll see a whole family lined up there, weaving. Some of them eat opium so they can work longer. Man, I've even heard that they feed the kids opium so they don't get bored!"

I looked out again, trying to make sense of it. I couldn't get my head around why they were here. "What are these people fighting for? I mean, they have nothing."

Rico turned and looked back at me. "Pride. That's all they need."

I couldn't help admiring them, how strong they had to be to live in these conditions. It made me think that if I could only show this to people back home, their problems would suddenly become so unimportant.

I kept looking out the window as we moved into the city. I could see right away that there was something older about Peshawar than even Rawalpindi; the buildings, as shabby and unsteady as many were, seemed to rise out of the ground as an extension of the land. Every block presented a greater and greater juxtaposition of times and cultures. Most of the buildings were old, a monochromatic brown that had stood for decades, if not centuries; but there were also a few modern banks and shops. Some of the cars looked new, but they were overwhelmed by vehicles that looked salvaged from a junkyard, and our driver slalomed between clusters of horse-drawn carts. Even the people I could see looked as if they had been dressed in different eras—some wore Western-style pants and dress shirts, while most others were wrapped in long Afghan robes as if they had just walked in from the desert. Again, I wondered what I had gotten myself into, how desperate those people in the camps must be, what desperate people can do. I didn't think about it for long; doubt wasn't going to help me now, it would only make me nervous and confused. I just needed to get this done.

"Let's get out here," Rico said, signalling the driver. "We've got some time to walk around."

We stepped out and I froze—two men with assault rifles over

their shoulders were walking directly towards us. My face must have shown what I was thinking, because Rico cracked up laughing. The two men walked by us without noticing.

"Oh man, you're going to have to get used to that. Everybody carries those."

It was true, no one else was paying any attention to them. The street was filled with other drivers bidding for passengers, shouting after passersby. Beside them, vendors lured people down the many side streets to rows and rows of tiny, overstuffed shops. Almost everyone was dressed in a light-coloured *shalwaar kameez*, a few with an embroidered vest over top. And, almost all were men. I could see a few schoolgirls nearby, but otherwise there were few women.

We started walking along the main street and I saw three more men walking with guns slung over their backs and leather bullet belts across their shoulders. They wore Afghani topi hats and had the calm eyes of warriors at rest. I tried to be calm, but I could not take my eyes off the men. Rico saw what I was doing and gave me a little jab to the shoulder. "Hey, eyes ahead, man. You're just asking for it, staring like that."

I couldn't help it. "Where do all the guns come from?"

"A lot of them come from the Americans," Rico said, nonchalantly. "They want the Afghans to beat the Russians, so they supply the resistance fighters, the *mujahideen*, with weapons. All the weapons get delivered through here, right here in Peshawar, and get smuggled into Afghanistan through the Tribal Areas. Of course, the people working with the U.S. to get guns to the Afghans take their own cut of the shipments for their trouble.

"Then, these guys down these alleys you see, they like to make cheap knock-offs of the Russian guns. So, between the two, you've got a *huge* supply—which means the price is low for those people who aren't getting the guns for free. And everybody wants them."

Rico grabbed my arm and pulled me down a side street.

"We're here, man, you may as well see it first-hand."

Rather than seeing rows and rows of assault rifles, as I was starting to expect, I saw dozens of stalls selling everything else. Fruit, kitchen supplies, shoes, fabrics, artwork, all packed from ground to roof of each of the eight-foot-wide stalls. The stalls were packed together on both sides of the alleyway only about five feet apart.

"The Qissa Khawani Bazaar, AKA the 'storytellers bazaar,' the biggest in town. Everything here is made by hand, no one has money for machines…"

As I stopped to look at one stall—piled high with weathered-looking kitchen pots made from tin—several kids went running past us, laughing, turning to stare as they whizzed past, like they were afraid we'd snatch them if they got too close. We had been noticed and, while I was tense in the unfamiliar surroundings, they considered us the morning's entertainment.

A group of them gathered about ten metres further along, peeking out from behind a corner. Two of the older ones, perhaps eight or ten years old, stepped out of their hiding place, showing off their brazenness. They started waving at Rico and I, indicating they wanted us to follow them.

I looked at Rico, who shrugged. *They're just kids, what's the harm?* I thought. We started walking towards them and the whole group started to giggle, and some of the younger ones streaked out of sight. The two kids who'd signalled us waited patiently until we got there, then tugged us by the sleeve and started to pull us down the alleyway where the others had disappeared.

The alley was barely wide enough for me to extend my arms. The smaller kids ran ahead of us, while our guides chattered away in their Urdu dialect and tried to make us walk faster, pointing ahead with big smiles on their faces. The alley zig-zagged through some bends, and then opened up to a small plaza with homes on each side. There, a half-dozen adults sat cross-legged in a doorway working, several men in tan *shalwaar kameez* and two women clad head-to-toe in black robes, their faces behind a heavy veil. The kids danced around on the cobblestones of the plaza, playing with each other, their mission apparently accomplished. From what I could tell, they had taken us to meet their parents.

Two of the men stood up when they saw us and smiled. They opened their arms and walked towards us, speaking in welcoming tones, which neither I, nor apparently Rico, could understand at all. They shook our hands warmly, the one clasping mine with two weathered mitts smudged with black, and led us back to meet the group. No one could understand the other, but there was a lot of nodding, pointing, laughing and motions of understanding and agreement as we tried to learn about each other.

The man who'd greeted me cleared aside a box and some tools, which he'd been using to build leather shoes by hand. He waved at us to follow and gave us a tour of the house. As four kids ran ahead into every room, he stopped in each and explained (I guessed) the significance of each, sometimes talking for several minutes while Rico and I nodded politely. The house was poor, of course, with basic furniture and little evidence of electricity. The items that were there looked heavily used and nothing was new. The whole place was only five rooms on one level and we were soon back out in the sunlight.

I pulled out my camera and motioned to the adults, to see if it was possible to take a photo. They all nodded enthusiastically, and our host shouted at the children, who all came running over.

"Get in there with them, I'll take the picture," Rico said, taking the camera.

About fifteen of us stood in the doorway and smiled. My friend the shoemaker was missing one of his front teeth, but he and all the children grinned as if they were on an American game show. They all seemed happy and relaxed, despite what looked to me like overwhelming poverty. I could not help but wonder how these people, who had nothing, were able to seem so happy, when almost no one I knew in Toronto, child or adult, ever greeted me with that much pure joy. I held my smile for the photo, but inside I suddenly became unbearably sad—I realized, in that place deep within myself that never lies, how poor my own life was, and the lives of everyone I knew, compared to what these "simple" people knew. Their spirit, their understanding of what was really important in life, was so much more profound than I would probably ever be capable of, with a mind clouded by the minutae of affluence.

After several photos, we said our good-byes and went back the way we'd come.

Rico glanced down at his watch. "11:30, man. Time to get to our meeting place."

11:30! I'd managed to lose track of the time, and now it seemed like my holiday was over. In a half hour we'd be doing the exchange, and then I'd be starting the long trip back to Canada with my cargo. I pushed down a small wave of nausea in my stomach. *Let's just get this done and go home.*

We started walking west, through the bazaar. After a few minutes we were out of the narrow alleyways and onto bustling thoroughfares, city buses whizzing by our elbows as we jumped on and off the curb to get through the crowds. We passed a collection of food stalls teeming with kebabs, tomatoes, dates, melon slices and mangoes, side-by-side with a series of modern-looking dry cleaners. Nearby, carpet sellers tried to draw us across the street to the dozens of stalls selling local handiwork. We kept walking, railway tracks coming into view on our right, until we eventually came to a large brownstone hall across the tracks from the old city.

"The museum, this is the place," Rico said, very business-like. "We're about ten minutes early. Let's have a look around."

We walked in, paying the nominal entrance fee. I was tense and exhilarated at the same time—I was concerned by what was coming, which was just a business deal, but I'd been playing this meeting over and over in my mind for weeks now and I wanted to know what would really happen.

We walked into the first room and I stopped short. On each wall were huge, detailed paintings depicting enormous battle scenes. Rather than scenes from another era, the paintings all looked contemporary; the people in them looked like the same people I'd seen out on the street. Everything about these images—train cars, fashions, even weapons—could have been taking place outside this building, but the carnage—vast, sprawling, dripping from every inch of canvas—looked like something out of the Middle Ages. I turned to Rico, confused.

"What are these pictures of?"

"Partition."

Partition? What was that? "I don't understand."

Rico spoke evenly, looking straight ahead at a painting where a body lay hacked to pieces by a large crowd. "Partition was what happened when Pakistan was created in 1947. When the British decided to make India independent, the Muslims living in India wanted their own state. There were riots and killings until the Brits agreed and created Pakistan. When that happened, all the Muslims stuck in India decided it would be best to move to the new country, and all the Sikhs and Hindus living in what was about to be Pakistan decided they should get back to India. By that time, after all the riots, they hated each other's guts. Millions of people from each side had to move in a hurry. Each religion had its own militia, and they would just slaughter anyone they came across who was the wrong religion. More than a million people were killed."

A million killed? 1947? That was shortly before I was born, and I'd never heard of it. I couldn't believe it.

Rico was staring at a large painting of what looked like a train full of dead bodies.

"The militias would stop the trains of people trying to escape, hack everyone to death except the driver, and then send the train on ahead to its destination. People would be waiting at the train stations for their families to arrive and everyone would be dead."

I looked around the room, not knowing what to think. What a powerful, horrible memorial. It was hard to imagine a hatred that ran that deep.

"Alright, it's noon. Let's go." Rico began walking towards the exit.

Ok, this is it. I followed Rico and said nothing. I was alert, my senses elevated, like I was walking into a room where I might have to fight. I kept telling myself that there was no need, that this was just a business deal, but my instincts weren't listening.

We stepped back outdoors and there they were. Eight of them, all dressed in the usual baggy Pakistani clothing. They were lounging around the entrance, a couple of them carrying guns casually pointed at the ground, like teenagers with nothing better to do. Rico walked up to them right away, and everyone shook hands and exchanged greetings. Their manner was polite, but not warm. I stood off to the side, a few steps away, and no one paid me any attention. Each man sported a long, traditional beard, giving them a uniform look. They did not seem old, but they were lean and their faces had an etched, weathered look that added years. They looked like people I didn't want to piss off.

After the greetings were done, the group started walking and Rico signalled me to follow. I was carrying the typewriter case, but no one paid any attention to it. We started down the main street, then turned onto a smaller one, turned again and finally ended up heading down a small alleyway similar to the one the kids had shown us. After ten minutes we came to a door and one of the men motioned for us to go inside.

They led us up a flight of stairs, then through a curtain and into a large, spartan room furnished only with a large wooden table with chairs around it. To the right an opaque curtain hid another doorway; otherwise the room was bare. I sat down at the far end of the table, my back to the wall, facing the entrance. Rico sat next to me. He turned to me and gestured at one of the men standing beside him.

"Give him the case."

The man stepped towards me and extended his hand. It was worn and calloused, like it belonged to someone who frequently took part in manual labour. We made eye contact and held each other's gaze for a moment; his pupils were dark and hard. I couldn't help trying to read the story of those eyes, seeing if I could pick out any details of his past—was he a hardened killer or just an innocent farmer? He took the typewriter without changing expression, then left the way we'd come in.

Immediately afterwards, two new men entered through the other door. They put a huge bowl of dark meat down in the middle of the table and sat. Everyone immediately reached for the bowl, ripped off a hunk of meat with their hands and started eating. No plates or utensils! Rico was doing the same, so I reached in and tore off a piece. I couldn't tell what kind of meat it was—goat, lamb, ox?—but I didn't want to seem rude or unappreciative. It tasted OK, whatever it was.

The strangeness of the situation made it sink in just how serious things were. I was in an unknown room, in a country that no one knew I was visiting, sharing a meal with a roomful of dope smugglers, waiting for them to bring me a hollow case filled with hashish oil. If something unexpected were to happen...

I wasn't shocked or surprised or suddenly awakened to what I was doing, but my anxiety level was rising. *Just don't ask questions, what I don't know can't hurt me. This will all be over soon.* I said this to myself over again a few times. There was certainly nothing threatening happening in the room; the only time anyone had even looked at me was when I handed over the case. Rico seemed to be enjoying himself, digging into the meat with relish. The men mostly talked amongst themselves. Rico seemed to be half-listening, and would occasionally jump in with a short sentence in Urdu, but otherwise everyone seemed happy to eat.

I chewed my food and watched the room. The pile of meat was now a mound of bones and many of our hosts had slid back in their chairs, satiated. There was more talking now, but it was sporadic and unhurried. Even so, the words sounded like musical machine-gun fire to me with their guttural, expressive language. Rico was leaning back too, listening and jumping into the conversation here and there, often laughing at his own jokes. He was loose and doing a lot of laughing and nodding; he was like a guy hanging around a water cooler. I wondered how often he'd been in this room before.

"These guys have it rough, man," he said to me. "They were talking about how much the Russians have been hassling them, trying to destroy their crops near the border. Their harvest is half of what it used to be, and the prices for most things are three times as high. No wonder they want our money!"

Time passed easily like this for a while, a half hour or maybe an hour. Men moved in and out of the room and I just waited. Slowly, consciously, I tried to enter a state of *mushin*, or "no mind," emptying my awareness of everything unnecessary and clearing my mind so that I was only conscious of the room; not fixed on any one thing, but focusing on everything present, ready for anything. This is a common technique in Zen training that warriors have used for centuries before entering battle—with the mind no longer inhibited or distracted it is free to fully perceive and commit to action. Every time someone came near the door, or turned in my direction, I was aware. No one else paid any attention to these comings and goings, acting as if they were passing a Sunday afternoon in their living room. They may have been mulling over some religious point or a perplexing business problem—a couple of them ran their fingers through their thick beards and listened while three of the men engaged in a lively discussion, each obviously supporting a different side of the argument.

Then the man with the weathered hands walked back in, flanked by two men with Kalashnikovs, and the mood of the room changed. Immediately, conversation stopped and everyone was all business. The case bearer delivered the typewriter to Rico, who took it from him and handed it to me.

I held it on my lap and listened to the blood throbbing in my temples. *This is it.* I stared at it, but it didn't look any different. I lifted it a few inches off my knees, testing the weight, and was pleased to see the weight wasn't a lot different than it had been; someone looking for a difference would find it immediately, but someone oblivious to its contents probably wouldn't. *It's good, this will work,* I thought as I waited to find out what would happen next.

Rico pulled a wad of bills out of the front pocket of his pants. They were U.S. $100 notes, the same as he had given me for emergencies; he started counting them off individually, making ten little piles of three. Whenever he completed a pile, the man to his left would take it and count it again. When the last pile was counted, Rico looked at the man across from him—he was one of the three men who'd been debating earlier, but otherwise I hadn't seen anything special about him—and the man nodded assent at the count. Everyone at the table immediately stood up, and Rico shook hands with each of them.

"Time to go, man, we're done here."

Two of the men escorted us back down to the street and led us back to the main road. We shook hands again and Rico hailed a cab.

"What did I tell you, it was easy, you did great. A few more days and you'll be home counting your twenty grand." Rico was happy, slapping me on the back.

I was relieved, but still a little unsure about the case I had at my feet.

"I don't get it, how did they get the oil inside the case?"

"Ah, look closer my friend. There's a couple of rivet holes in the handle there that they drilled through. That's where the oil went, through the holes into the hollow part of the case. No one will notice unless they're looking for it. The only trick is that you have to keep the case standing upright, like when you're carrying it. If you lay it flat, after a while the oil will start to leak through those holes."

I looked closer at the handle. I could just make out two tiny holes, but I never would have noticed them if Rico hadn't told me. It wasn't foolproof, but it was pretty good.

"Ok, what now?"

"I'm taking you to the bus station and you head back to Islamabad. I'll meet you there."

I nodded, holding the case between my knees. "Hey, don't you want to test the case or something? I mean, how do we know what's in there?"

"I've dealt with these guys many times before, they're honourable men," Rico replied, smiling slightly. "Don't worry, we have what we came for."

I didn't say anything and in a few minutes we pulled up in front of the bus station. Rico shook my hand. "I'll see you in Islamabad. If anyone gives you trouble, use one of those $100s I gave you. Find out who's in charge, take them aside and have a chat, then slip them one of the Ben Franklins. After that, everything will be cool."

I got out and the cab pulled away. I'd begun my journey home.

Mizu no kokoro
Mind like water

Chapter 3

THE JOURNEY BEGAN with a lot of waiting. The bus wasn't due for another half hour, so I sat down on my own, ignoring the usual stares. I was nervous, and the two old men sitting in the corner eyeing me weren't helping, though they'd been collecting dust in that spot long enough to pass for family heirlooms. The station was equally decrepit, the grey walls caked with grime and the chair coverings old and ripped in many places. I tried to stay calm, but I realized that no one who looked and dressed like me would *ever* walk into a place like this—these people knew exactly why I was here.

Eventually the bus pulled up and I piled in. It was a minibus, bright blue, with room for about twenty-five or thirty people. The space on the roof of the vehicle disappeared quickly, men tying down their belongings at dangerous-looking angles, so everyone carried their remaining suitcases (and animals and children and other bags) onto the bus and crammed them into whatever space they could find. I folded myself into a bench in the last row and slid the typewriter between my feet, careful to keep it standing upright so that no incriminating liquid wouldn't seep through the rivets in the handle. I made myself as comfortable as I could and tried to adjust to the pungent odour of the close quarters.

Before we left, a young guy walked to the back of the bus with a round bundle wrapped in newspaper and twine, roughly the size of a softball. When he got closer to me he wrapped the whole thing in a white blanket and stuffed it behind the bench I was sitting on, sliding into the seat at the other end of my row. He was about eighteen, slight, clean-shaven and dressed in a dark blue *kurta,* with an intricately embroidered gold-and-silver velvet cap, a *topi*. I looked at him and he looked back without flinching, so I quickly decided that I had not seen his cargo and turned towards the window. Ten minutes later we pulled out and I tried to relax and watch the traffic compete for space in the narrow streets.

By this time I was already tired by the strangeness of the day, so I pulled the curtain across the window and tried to sleep. As it turned out, the bus driver was in a bigger rush to get out of Peshawar than I was, and spent the next half-hour braking, swerving and cursing at various mule drivers, making rest impossible. Once we escaped the city I finally contorted myself into a comfortable position and started to drift off. I had almost succeeded when the bus began slowing down.

I sat up and leaned forward to see out the front window. *Shit!* Lining the side of the road were at least six grey-green jeeps, each flanked by a burly officer in uniform armed with a semi-automatic weapon. I could see that two of them were motioning our bus to pull over. My heart, already on edge, exploded. My hands went cold.

We were about to be searched.

The bus stopped and two officers boarded, clad in dark berets with bullet belts over the shoulder of their powder-blue uniforms. The first began to question the driver while the second slowly walked down the aisle, scanning each person. He was muscular, with deeply sunken eyes and a wide, strong face, and he looked very unhappy. The brisk chatter that had been going on the whole trip died the moment the officers stepped on the bus. Most passengers just looked straight ahead, but no one escaped the officer's gaze, and he was working his way methodically towards me. I knew that the most important thing was that I

Detour on The Path

appear calm and relaxed, as if I could not care less about him, so I turned my head toward the window, opened the curtain and pretended to casually stare at the rocks outside.

Of course, calm was impossible. My insides were boiling with fear. I hadn't given much thought to going to prison in this country, but now all I could think of was what the approaching officer could do to me alone in a cell. Beat me? Torture me? I knew he could do whatever he wanted. I really had no idea what went on inside a Pakistani jail, but I was scared to death of whatever it was. Still, I knew I had to appear strong and confident to avoid suspicion.

As I looked out the window I could see the officer drawing closer. He still moved slowly, taking his time, and when he reached my seat he stopped and stared directly at me.

At this point I made a decision. I knew that if my eyes wandered or avoided his he would know that something was wrong, so I turned towards him and we locked eyes.

During my karate training, I had been taught many techniques to calm myself before a fight and control my fear. One of these was *mizu no kokoro,* or "mind like water." When looking at still water, the reflection you see is clear and the image has no distortion. When the wind disturbs the water's surface, anything you see becomes distorted and unclear. In the human mind, this wind can be any kind of emotion—fear, anxiety, exuberance or anger. To keep the body relaxed and the mind calm, I began to breathe with my lower abdominal muscles, the *tanden,* as I was taught to do by my Japanese teachers, so I could unlock the energy that flows from the body's centre. I also concentrated on relaxing the muscles in my face, neck and shoulders. Without appearing like anything unusual was going on, I tried to make my mind like a perfect pool.

The officer held my gaze for a long time. I was determined not to show weakness. Eventually, his eyes shifted to the floor and the typewriter case, and then back to my eyes. The fear rose up within me and I felt my resolve begin to waver, but I continued to hold his gaze. Finally, he grunted and turned to the man sitting at the other end of my row, whom I had noticed boarding the bus. The officer immediately pointed to the young man's suitcase and barked out instructions in Urdu.

This poor guy took the brunt of the anger that was meant for me. The officer attacked the man's suitcase with gusto, even though it was made out of cardboard and held together with a piece of twine. He rifled through its contents while firing questions at the petrified owner, knocking off his hat and getting right up in his face. I turned back to the window and saw that several other officers were checking the outside of the bus for secret compartments or anything else suspicious.

After a very long time, maybe half an hour, the police got off and the bus pulled away.

Thank god! I let out a huge sigh of relief and sunk back into my seat feeling a surge of confidence, even arrogance. *That's the best you can do?* I smiled and gave a surreptitious pat to the typewriter case.

Rico had let slip out—probably intentionally—that the Pakistani government at that time was under tremendous pressure from Western countries to curb the flow of drugs coming out of the Tribal Areas. After the Soviets invaded Afghanistan, heroin smuggling became one of the biggest revenue sources for the *mujahideen* fighters, and over time the land surrounding Peshawar had become the largest heroin-producing area on the planet. Because the region had been ruled by local warlords for centuries, the Pakistani government was powerless to go in and halt production. Unfortunately, I was travelling the only road out.

I knew that the road itself had a history of smuggling and trade that went back to the days of Alexander the Great. Peshawar was one of the original main trading centres on the southern branch of the famous Silk Road, and this route was the same one on which traders had been routinely assaulted in centuries past by

Detour on The Path

bandits on their way to India and China. Marco Polo travelled—and was nearly killed—on this road and complained in his *Travels* about how many men he lost to bandits. Drug smugglers had been using this route for more than a thousand years, transporting opium along with their silk and spices since the dawn of Islam.

Knowing this didn't make me feel any better. I had barely gotten comfortable in my seat when the bus began to slow down again. I leaned into the aisle to look through the front window—this time it was the Army. I couldn't believe it. Two military vehicles were blocking the path of the bus and several soldiers, in olive-green army uniforms with semi-automatic rifles, were waiting for us.

This was bad. While the police were not exactly renowned for their hospitality, I knew that the Army's reputation was much, much worse. It wasn't even legal for them to be stopping us, since drug enforcement was not their jurisdiction, but Rico had told me they often stopped buses to extort money from any smugglers they discovered, and the "authorities" turned a blind eye to this little side business. Having already taken a step beyond the law, the soldiers felt no obligation to follow it in their treatment of suspects, and beatings and torture were apparently routine. I began to shake and really get scared.

I reached for my breast pocket where I kept the $100 bills, confirming they were still there. Seconds later, the soldiers stormed the bus.

This was nothing like the first roadblock. The searchers spread out and were shouting at all the passengers. Women were screaming and the soldiers were going through *everyone's* belongings. One ripped open a suitcase, while another yelled into the face of a passenger from two inches away; baggage was being tossed randomly in every direction. It was bedlam, but I turned back to the window and again tried to calm my mind.

It didn't take long for a soldier to stop near me. He scanned me up and down—I'm sure he'd never seen anyone like me before—while I continued to look out the window. He grunted at me and I slowly turned to face him, as if to say "Who me?" He was pointing at the typewriter and giving some kind of instructions.

Oh no. I began to make a typing motion with my hands and say, "Typewriter, typewriter." He wasn't satisfied with this, and he motioned determinedly at the case, obviously wanting to look inside.

I could barely keep my hands from shaking as I reached down and pulled the case up and onto my lap. As I did, I noticed a smell. *Shit!* The scent of the hash oil was coming up through the rivet holes, where the oil had been injected. The soldier had to know what this was. I clamped my hands over the holes as I opened the case. I knew that I couldn't leave it open for very long when it wasn't upright, because the oil would ooze out through the tiny holes in the handle and coat my knees.

After the case was open for a few moments I spoke in a soft, calm voice and said, "There, you see, a typewriter." He looked at it for another moment or two and then he looked at me. Finally, he grumbled something like "Ok, ok" and moved on. I closed the case and slid it back down to the floor. I could feel the backs of my legs soaked with sweat.

He turned his attention to the next person—my young friend who had taken the brunt of the last search. That poor sucker. Once again his suitcase, already badly damaged, was torn apart and searched. He sat quietly, his slim face drained of all expression, as his belongings were strewn across the seat, as if this were a completely sensible and understandable thing for the searcher to do. Meanwhile, another soldier came and looked behind the seats at the back of the bus. He pulled out the small, round object in the blanket and unwrapped it. I could see him looking at the pieces of newspaper, and it made the soldier very agitated. He dashed off the bus and back to one of the Army vehicles. We waited for about ten minutes while the others continued to tear through our things.

When the soldier returned he was *extremely* pissed off. He screamed at all of us and gesticulated, thrusting himself into people's faces. I desperately wished I could understand what he was saying. When he thrust the package at anyone they shook their head vigorously. I certainly wasn't going to point the finger. What was in there? I guessed it was some kind of drug, but I really didn't know.

We sat on that road, baking in the heat that must have been close to forty degrees Celsius, for almost an hour. So many things went through my mind. I thought about prison and what it would be like to be tortured by men like these. I thought about Mia and the baby in her belly. I thought about my students and a flush of shame ran up my neck. Frustrated and afraid, I studied the men outside and tried to determine which of them might be the one in charge.

Finally, a woman dressed head-to-toe in a dark burqua went outside and began arguing with the men. She was furious, her voice thick with outrage as she chastised these men with guns, not at all afraid of them. This went on for several minutes, the conversation very one-sided. We sat and waited, me not knowing if we'd all be thrown in prison or if someone would be made an example of. I don't know what she said—my guess was that she was the wife of someone important—but she got back on the bus and we were allowed to pass. I could have kissed her, I was so relieved that we were moving again.

By now my nerves had been frayed to almost nothing and I began to curse myself. What was I doing here? What the hell was I thinking when I agreed to this? I cursed Rico too—this kind of thing had not been part of his stories in the dojo back in Toronto.

I breathed in and tried to relax. Slowly, gradually, the rugged beauty of the landscape helped distract me. The rock here was rough and exposed by the wind in many places, the forbidding countryside almost entirely devoid of signs of life. A river appeared alongside the road, unfurling for several kilometres in a murky-brown ribbon, the current strong and powerful. Abruptly, another river appeared; it was blue-green and looked clean and pure. The two ran parallel for a while, inching closer to one another, until they met at the base of a high bluff. When they connected, their flows did not mix, but ran parallel to each other for a long time, the blue-green on the far bank refusing to be tainted by the mud and silt running alongside it on the near side.

My ordeal was far from done. The bus was stopped at two more police roadblocks before reaching Islamabad. By now though, I was learning that the inspecting officers were often as intimidated by a well-dressed Westerner as I was by them. I kept my emotions in check, looked as calm and natural as possible, and the encounters passed without any more trouble. However, by the time the bus rolled into squeaky-clean Islamabad, my nerves were shot.

Rico arrived several hours later. I'd been looking forward to his return.

"Hey man, how's it going?" he asked me.

"I've been better."

"What's up, man?"

"I'm out! You can take your fucking dope and take it through the fucking roadblocks yourself. I'm done. I've had enough of this smuggling bullshit."

"Whoa! What happened? You just gotta be cool, man, you just gotta be cool!"

I didn't have my cool. I tore into Rico for half an hour as I told him about my harrowing escapes. He tried to calm me down, telling me to "be cool" as he waved his mechanical hand in front of my face, and explained that the inspections were normal and I had never really been in any danger—those $100 bills would have smoothed over any difficulties. I didn't really believe him.

"Look man, we have a deal. You carry the product all the way through and then you get your money. That's how it is. Now relax! It's no problem. In a few days we'll be laughing about this."

He didn't threaten me, but he didn't have to. I knew I was at his mercy out here.

I decided I needed a drink.

I called room service and asked for two beers. I quickly found out that having a beer in Pakistan is not for the faint-hearted. Alcohol being a foreign vice, the drinks arrived wrapped up in sheets so no unsuspecting Pakistani guest might be forced to look at them. Before they could be unwrapped I had to complete a two-page government form that asked for a dizzying amount of personal information. Not surprisingly, once I finally completed the paperwork, the beers were warm and tasted like camel piss.

Our plan had been to fly from Islamabad to New Delhi as soon as possible, but geopolitics threw us a curve.

When we showed up at the doors of the Indian consulate in Islamabad we immediately saw that getting a visa was not going to be easy. The office was filled with scores of people who'd been trying to get into the country for weeks. Many were backpackers and hippie types, usually with matted long hair and beards, looking to enter India to pursue their various paths to enlightenment. The whole consulate felt—and smelled—like a '60s commune.

After several conflicting conversations, we figured out that Indian security forces had recently stormed one of the holiest shrines for Indian Sikhs, the Golden Temple, in a counter-terrorism effort. More than 100 Sikh militants had been killed, leading to a wave of civil unrest that had killed hundreds more. Amritsar, the city where the whole thing happened, was just across the border from Pakistan, and the crossing was sealed to normal travel.

My heart sank as I realized I might have to spend weeks hanging out here, with a case full of hash oil in my hotel room. Rico assured me that this was really not a problem at all, that we just had to "be cool," but my faith in Rico had been whittled down to the thickness of an onion skin.

We settled in and began to wait. Before granting a visa, the consular officer had to interview you about your reasons for entering the country and decide whether or not you were a security risk. I was dressed in my usual suit and tie so I stood out from the crowd, but I had no interest in talking to anyone, afraid I would reveal something that would give me away. Mostly I sat quietly and rehearsed movements from different katas in my mind, doing what little I could to at least mentally keep myself in competitive shape. My frustration was building about that, as I could feel myself getting further and further from top condition with each passing day.

Hours passed this way, with little sign that anyone had gotten a visa. Eventually we were told to come back tomorrow.

On the short taxi ride back to the hotel, our driver was watching us in his rear view, and decided to make conversation.

"Where are you from?" he asked in halting English, smiling encouragement at us.

"Canada."

"Ah, parlez-vous francais?"

I was about to offer a polite no, being hopeless in the language, when Rico jumped in with a "oui" and started peppering our driver with questions. As I looked at Rico in surprise, they chatted amiably for a couple of minutes.

"I didn't know you knew French."

"Ah, yeah, I was in Belgium for a while and picked some up there, you know."

This was news to me. I'd known Rico for years and I didn't remember hearing about any extended stays in Belgium. "Oh yeah, what were you doing there?"

Rico flashed a wolfish smile and scratched at his left shoulder with his hook, turning to look out the window. "Ah, you know, I got busted there a couple of years ago with a bit of stuff on me. I did about a year inside. Picked up the language pretty good."

"You what?"

"Ah, you know, nothing serious. Just a bit of bad luck."

What the hell? I ground my teeth and looked out the window of the cab. *Bad luck? Whatever happened to your foolproof system?*

The next day at the consulate we finally got our interview. An official escorted us into a large, clean office, dominated by a massive oak-panel desk. Behind it sat a young Indian man in his early thirties, well-groomed, with his jet-black hair neatly combed back. He rose and offered us two seats.

"Good day, gentlemen. My apologies for the wait, but we have quite a number of people to speak to these days. Now what exactly is your reason for wanting to visit India?"

As usual, Rico did the talking.

"Well, sir, I am a travel agent and I'm just doing a little research for my company on some trips we'd like to do to your country."

This was his usual cover story—and a good one, since his mother actually was a travel agent and he knew enough to fool anyone who wasn't one. It also had the advantage of explaining the large number of stamps on his passport. The young consular seemed satisfied with this and turned to me.

"And what is your reason?"

"I'm a teacher."

"Oh, what kind of teacher?"

"A martial arts teacher. I travel quite a bit for competitions, and I like to visit different schools around the world whenever I can to learn about their different training methods." All of which was technically true.

The officer perked up and leaned in towards me. "Really! What kind of martial art do you teach?"

"Shotokan karate."

"That's extraordinary! I'm a student of Shotokan karate!"

He launched into a series of questions about my training, and got very excited when I told him I had trained with Nakayama, Tanaka, Asai and other masters in Japan.

He seemed interested, so I decided to tell him a story about training with a Zen monk in rural Japan.

"I and a couple of other foreigners were invited by Tanaka Sensei to join Nakayama Sensei and other head instructors from the Japan Karate Association (JKA) to train at a martial arts college four hours northeast of Tokyo. At the end of one particularly gruelling ninety-minute session, a side door to the dojo opened and a Zen monk in traditional Japanese clothing and *geta* (woodblock shoes) walked through. His head was clean-shaven and his gold-wire-rimmed spectacles heightened his serious look. We were told that the man had come to help us with our training. He was an old man and I couldn't see what he could teach a room full of advanced students and masters.

"What followed was a lesson in pain. First, he made us sit in the lotus position and remain completely motionless for one hour. We sat in rows facing each other, Nakayama Sensei not far from me. My legs hurt so much that I wanted to scream, but I did not want to show weakness in front of Sensei. As we sat in concentration, the old man walked amongst us, carrying this four-foot-long thin wooden paddle. As he walked past, a student raised his hands in front of him, palms together in a prayer position, and nodded; he then leaned forward with arms crossed to accept the blow. The monk stopped in front of him, bowed to him, then smacked him twice on each shoulder, hard. I mean *hard*. Then he bowed again and continued walking, while the student returned to sitting silent and upright, until another student nodded.

"He did this several times, and eventually my curiosity got the better of me. I raised my hands in prayer as the monk walked by, and he stopped before me and bowed as I leaned forward. Then he brought the paddle down sharply on my left shoulder. The crack of it was like a gunshot going off in my ear, and I thought I was going to vomit all over the dojo floor. It was unbelievable! Before I could prepare myself, the second blow landed on my right shoulder, and I gritted my teeth against the pain and to keep from screaming. The point of the exercise was not to flinch, to remain motionless and detach yourself from the pain, to *examine* it. While I wanted to jump up and shout and touch the fire raging along my shoulders, I remained still. Slowly it subsided, and I learned something about what I could handle.

"The guest bowed then continued to walk and, while I was still marvelling at how much pain such an elderly man could inflict, Nakayama Sensei raised his hands in front. The paddle came down twice in quick succession, with no less force on the bony shoulders that were past their seventieth year, and Sensei's face remained completely impassive. His participation and grace in the exercise struck me deeply."

The young officer's eyes were like saucers as he listened to the story.

We spoke for another fifteen minutes, the consular laughing and fawning over us as if we were movie stars. Eventually, he glanced down at his watch and signalled that our time had come to an end.

"I have another appointment. What did you want again? Visas? Here, give me your passports."

We slid them across the desk and he stamped and returned them, rising to shake our hands and show us out. We left the consulate laughing to ourselves at the benevolence of the universe. We had secured our passage to India.

We were already leaving later than we'd planned, so we wasted no time getting out of Islamabad. Rico didn't even try to hide how eager he was to sink himself into India's notorious red-light districts and he left for the airport almost immediately, aiming for the next flight to New Delhi. Since we couldn't travel together—no point in us both getting busted if something went wrong—I made arrangements to fly out the next morning, making myself comfortable in the plush hotel room, happy to be alone. Despite being only hours away from getting out of Pakistan, I was no more relaxed than the moment the typewriter case had first been handed to me. I tried to think of the money and how much easier it would make my life, but I still had a hollow feeling in the pit of my stomach. I looked for Voice of America on the radio for a while, then drifted off to sleep.

The next morning, I checked out early and booked a taxi to the airport. I was flying first class, since this was not too expensive and tended to make people ask fewer questions. In front of me was a long counter with smiling airline staff checking bags for several lines of passengers. Two rows of potted plants and a well-kept red carpet led to the separate first-class check-in on the far left and it gleamed with a hospital-like cleanliness that I hadn't seen in too long. A clean-cut young man in a crisp airline uniform waited patiently for me to approach the counter with my bags.

"Good morning, sahib."

"Good morning."

"May I check your bags please, sahib?"

I handed him my suitcases, keeping a small shoulder bag and the typewriter case with me as carry-on.

"Did you enjoy your stay in Pakistan, sahib?"

"Yes, thank you."

"Very good. You may proceed directly to the gate on your far right, sahib. Please enjoy your flight."

I picked up my bag and the typewriter and walked past the lines of burquas and kurtas and Western business suits. It was still very early and I wondered if first class included a cup of complimentary coffee. I was starting to look forward to visiting India, feeling more like a tourist. I rounded the corner and stopped.

Military.

I don't know if it was because I'd been taking internal flights so often or if it was just too early in the morning, but I really hadn't given any thought to customs. I did now. There were three surly-looking soldiers, probably not too happy to be doing this kind of work at this hour, behind a waist-high stainless steel counter about ten feet long. They were going through each passenger's bags. Unhappy as they looked, they still took their searches quite seriously and were opening each bag and unpacking its contents, running their hands along the lining of many bags to make sure they missed nothing.

The muscles in my stomach tightened like I'd taken a punch to the solar plexus and a wave of sweat appeared on my forehead. There was no avoiding this. I had to pass through here and it would look suspicious if I turned around to regroup now.

Taking a deep breath, I steeled myself and sidled up to the soldier on the right. He motioned for my shoulder bag, grunting something in Urdu, not even bothering to look me in the eye.

He rifled through it fairly quickly, tracing his hands along the bag's interior and poking through my toiletries. Satisfied, he nodded and motioned for me to hand over the typewriter case.

Pushing down a mounting panic, I handed it over. He immediately opened it and pulled out the typewriter, leaving the case prone across the table. I knew the oil had started its slow march towards the rivet holes in the handle. He held the typewriter in both hands and looked at it, sceptically. He started to shake it, then hoisted it up above his head and shook it vigorously, eyeing it for anything suspicious. I later guessed that he thought it might be hiding jewels, or some other hard substance that would make a noise or fall out when the typewriter was shaken hard enough. Seeing and hearing nothing, he started to put the instrument down.

This was a critical moment, because if he picked up the case he would immediately know that it was three kilos heavier than an empty case should be. I held my breath—he tossed the typewriter back inside the moulded plastic and motioned for me to move on. I tried to get the machine to slide into the form-fitting interior but I couldn't because the sliding part of the typewriter was protruding from the left side at an odd angle.

By now I was petrified. It took a massive act of will to stop my hands from trembling as I tried to get the typewriter in place. I couldn't get my hands to manoeuvre the machine so it sat properly, and I was shaking the entire case. Finally, after a struggle, my eyes half on the case and half on the soldier's weapon, the typewriter snapped into place and I brought the two halves together in the upright position and snapped the case shut, unsure of how close I had been to wiping hash oil across the countertop. I hurried on to the departure lounge, trying hard not to break into a run. I sat there, pretending to be as relaxed as any other business traveller, my heart pounding in protest as the adrenalin flowed. Gradually, after some minutes, I was able to calm myself.

Thirty minutes later I boarded the flight. It was Pakistani International Airlines, or "Prayer In Air" as I overheard someone call it, and I took my seat next to a man in his late forties. His dark hair was set off by his light skin and he wore neatly pressed clothing—clearly a Westerner. We introduced ourselves and began to make small talk. His accent struck me as familiar, so I asked him where he was from—Toronto! I started laughing. Seven thousand kilometres from home, we found that we lived twenty minutes away from each other.

Having a taste of home so close released some of my tension and we began an animated conversation. His clothing was that of a minister; he'd been working in the area for several months for his church, relocating Afghan refugees to new homes in India. I asked questions about his work and why he did it, which he answered in a quiet, steady voice. His calm and serenity impressed me tremendously, seeming to come from a place deep within him.

Naturally, he wanted to know what I was doing in Pakistan. I told him that I was a writer, travelling through this part of the world to research some stories I wished to complete. He found this very interesting, and pressed me further on what sorts of things I liked and what I planned to write about. I tried to stick as close to the truth as possible, worried about sounding like I was avoiding his questions. I found myself tapping distractedly at the typewriter case between my legs. He didn't seem to doubt my alibi and I gradually turned the conversation back to his work.

We continued to chat as we disembarked. I was quite relieved, but when we entered customs the familiar fear came back. Apparently the Indian customs officers did not trust the work of their Pakistani brethren, so *their* military personnel were enthusiastically inspecting each piece of luggage carried by every passenger. They were still afraid of terrorist attacks, and the inspections were being conducted with a meticulousness and thoroughness stricter than anything I'd come across so far.

I couldn't see any way out, so I got in line and waited for the inevitable.

"Aw, these guys don't need to see what kind of toothpaste you're carrying. I come through here all the time, they know me. Just come with me and we'll grab a cab," said my new friend, taking me gently by the elbow.

Somehow not noticing the sudden lack of colour in my face, he walked up to the nearest customs agent and flashed his passport. The guard recognized him and waved him through, barely bothering to turn his head to give my own identification a cursory glance. We left the frustrated travellers behind us and walked straight out of the airport, my friend chatting away about the sights I had to see while I was in Delhi.

We shared a cab into the city centre. I tried to listen as the minister gave a running commentary on the sprawling city, but my mind was still buzzing. I was again exhausted and starting to learn how little my martial arts training had prepared me for this kind of subterfuge. I knew it was this continuous fighting against what I knew was right that left me feeling so emotionally trampled, and I resolved for the hundredth time to forget this chapter of my life as soon as possible and resume my training with new intensity.

The minister dropped me at my hotel and wished me safe passage. I thanked him and never saw him again.

Go no sen
Seizing the initiative later

Chapter 4

"Let's go! Let's go! Let's go!"
Rico was rapping the bedside table with his hook, already fully dressed. I looked over, groggily, at the alarm clock. 4:30 a.m. Rico darted around the hotel suite like he'd already had three coffees that morning—he made a big show of putting his suitcases by the door, then he opened my suitcases, miming surprise that they weren't packed, all the while merrily giving a running monologue on the dozens of reasons to get to Bombay ASAP, along with a few mild threats to my health. I couldn't imagine what had put him in such a mood, but I was too exhausted to ask. I felt no relief at waking up in a new country; it still wasn't the country I wanted to be in.

Much of the day before had passed quickly. The taxi dropped me at the hotel Rico had picked, and he met me there later in the afternoon. I'd spent the time inbetween walking around the more affluent part of New Delhi where we were: listening to the subtle difference in the street chatter, the machine-gun patter of Urdu replaced by the sing-song wailing of Hindi; admiring the deep-red dots on the foreheads of the head-scarved women in the markets; and salivating at the smell of curries bubbling up from the food stalls.

Later, Rico and I had eaten a simple dinner and turned in soon after to be ready for this ungodly early-morning flight.

Once we made it to the airport we whizzed through the security checks—I was getting used to the usual wave of panic at the sight of the soldiers—and were shortly thereafter hailing a cab in Bombay. The airport was well outside the city, and separated from it by a gulf of corrugated tin, disintegrating brick, sewage and blank-eyed people stretching as far as I could see on either side of our car. The shantytown crowded both sides of the road, and seemed to stretch for miles.

"You won't find this in your in-flight magazine," he muttered as he rolled down the window.

It looked like—and probably was—a disaster zone. A whole city had grown up along the roadside, as people, for reasons I could only guess at, had pitched flimsy shelters wherever they could find a couple of square metres. Most of them were women and children, and many looked like extras in a famine relief video; their eyes were glazed over, and even the young ones seemed unnaturally lethargic. Most were poorly clothed. Any order that had ever existed in the shelters looked like it had been trampled by a marauding elephant. There were, in fact, a number of goats and water buffalo wandering through the camps and on to the road—I couldn't figure out how people maintained these animals.

"There are probably four million people like this outside the city," Rico said, watching me. "Twice as many people as in all of Toronto. Almost as many people live in the slums as in the city itself."

I could only shake my head, my mind numb at the numbers. It was so much worse than any other place I had ever been or heard of that I couldn't even think of anything to say about it. Our car had slowed enough that children had started to chase it. Rico looked at me a moment longer, then threw a few rupees out the window for the children and told the driver to speed up.

Soon we'd left the shantytown and were arriving in the heart of Bombay. Rico had booked us into the King George Hotel, an icon of old British India. The massive six-storey brownstone took up most of a city block, capped by a domed tower that

Detour on The Path

gave excellent views of the Indian Ocean just across the street. Inside was like entering an English time capsule—big leather wingback chairs, cherry wood panelling and ivory wherever possible. It was also an oasis—the air-conditioning fought off the searing heat and the doors protected us from the relentless poverty on the street and the stench of open sewers.

Rico had told me that our only reason for spending time in Bombay was to extend our trip and add credibility to our alibi about travelling through the region. By noon, I was tired of staying in the hotel, so I convinced Rico to brave the heat with me and do some exploring.

A giant stone archway stood behind a ribbon of cars across the street, so we walked towards it. The historical plaque stated that the arch was erected in 1911 to welcome King George V and Queen Mary to their distant colony.

Next to us, a few people were gathered around a stocky man squatting and playing a foot-long flute. I looked at the man's feet and did a double-take: there was a cobra, head swaying slightly, coiled and staring intently at the flute, looking very much like it was entranced by the music.

I tapped Rico on the shoulder and we walked closer. The snake charmer held the reptile at bay for a few minutes, guiding it back and forth. I noticed that the distance between the cobra and the flute rarely changed; if the snake moved closer, his keeper pulled back and if the cobra's head retreated, the man's would follow. This way, it seemed to me, the charmer kept the snake constantly on alert—it was not just the reptile who was dancing.

After a while he stopped playing and the cobra relaxed. The handful of tourists with us applauded politely and tossed a few rupees in the hat; we were about to walk away when the man turned towards us.

"Do you want to see something interesting?" he said evenly.

Surprised, Rico and I looked at each other. "Sure."

"Ok, come with me then."

The man quickly swept up his snake and basket and hurried off the main street to a side alley. Without the snake, he would have looked like any ordinary Indian, dressed in beige khakis and a light cotton dress shirt, his white hair cropped close. We followed him until we were out of sight to traffic. There, he produced a cloth bag and dumped from it a slender, short-haired brown animal that looked like an otter, putting it on a leash. Then he turned the wicker basket upside-down and grabbed the snake by its tail as it fell, holding it a few feet from the leashed animal. The cobra's head rose up, alert, and began hissing at the strange-looking bundle of fur.

My curiosity was piqued—this *was* interesting.

"I know what this is," I said, turning to Rico. "That brown, slinky thing is a mongoose. Sensei Stan Schmidt in South Africa teaches a lesson about this, the story of the mongoose and the cobra."

"Teaches them what?" Rico grunted, looking suspicious about what was happening.

"*Go No Sen*. We're about to see a demonstration."

By now, the man had taken the mongoose off the leash and was comfortably holding the cobra by the tail.

"You want to see what happens?"

"Oh yes."

He released the cobra, which immediately coiled itself, staring directly at the mongoose, now about three feet away. The mongoose seemed unconcerned. With its head low, sniffing the ground, it started exploring the area. Casually, it moved towards the cobra, which rose up to strike. As the mongoose moved to within two feet the cobra lashed out, but the mongoose, surprisingly agile, jumped back out of range.

The snake charmer caught my eye; I nodded appreciatively.

Within another minute, the mongoose was encroaching on the cobra's territory, and again the snake's venomous fangs shot out for the furry exposed neck, and again the mongoose darted out of harm's way in the nick of time.

"This doesn't look like a very bright mongoose," Rico grumbled.

"Just wait."

A third time, the mongoose sniffed it's way into the territory of the snake, and a third time the reptile rose up to deliver the killing blow. When it struck, the mongoose again jumped back to safe territory, but this time it counter-attacked, springing forward in one fluid motion and taking the cobra's head in its own suddenly formidable jaws. It clamped down hard and shook the snake as hard as it could; the battle was done in a matter of seconds.

"It's interesting, nature, isn't it?" the man said triumphantly. "Sometimes the mongoose is too slow and the cobra wins, but usually the mongoose is the smarter animal."

I agreed, still amazed at the contest. It was an almost perfect demonstration of martial arts in action. I had taught the tactic—translated as "take the initiative later"—many times as the strategy of stepping back from an attack, blocking, and counter-attacking your opponent. The mongoose had been risking its life to determine its opponent's timing, using what it learned to plan its assault. I'd taught the movements as a good technique for beginners, but I felt like the animals had just given me a master class. I had been reminded that anything on this Earth that must fight to survive understands, at some level, the techniques that are imparted in the dojo—how to observe and understand your opponent, like any good hunter.

The man suggested we might want to make a donation to cover the cost of replacing the snake, so I paid him twenty dollars and walked off with Rico, still thinking about the lesson.

We were right in the heart of Bombay's tourist area, with dozens of camera-toting travellers walking underneath the archway (billed by the men hustling to be our tour guides as the "Gateway of India") down steps that led to the ocean. People streamed through to catch the ferry for a tour of the harbour, stopping to pose before the city's skyline, but I felt the urge to get away to somewhere quieter. Rico had seen all this before so he went back to the hotel to have a drink, but I decided to keep walking.

While the Gateway had the usual sellers of tourist trinkets, only a couple of blocks away I was nearly knocked over by the reality of desperate poverty. I'd been walking more or less aimlessly, still thinking about Go No Sen, when a beggar's hand pulled me out of my daydreaming. It was a woman's hand, withered and cracked, stuck up under my nose. I recoiled—I couldn't help myself—and followed the line of her outstretched arm down to a face wrinkled and wrapped in a fraying head scarf. Cradled in her other arm and laying against her ochre sari was an infant, maybe three months old. The woman was pointing at her mouth with her free hand, and then pointing at the infant.

Rico had told me, as we were driving into town, how some older female beggars would rent babies from younger women, to increase the pity others would take on them. Now I was seeing it. The woman was way beyond child-bearing years—I guessed she was in her fifties—and my first reaction was revulsion at how predatory and cynical she must be. But then I felt a wave of pity, not for the woman with the starving baby, but for the woman who needed to do this to get noticed. To have reached that age, with all its perils and infirmities, and still be forced to beg for your daily existence was just horrible. I grabbed a few rupees from my pocket and shoved them at her, almost knocking her over in my hurry to get past.

As I kept walking, I began to notice the surroundings. There were beggars on nearly every block; some crowded me as I walked, pleading for help, others prayed, and some didn't bother to raise their heads or swat the flies that buzzed around incessantly, a tin can in front of them their only sign of need. What amazed me the most, besides how many of them there were, was how they had colonized the sidewalks and turned them into living spaces. The street wasn't just where they earned their living, it was where they did everything—slept, ate, defecated. Many had built shelters out of discarded cardboard, and a lucky few had cooking stoves and sheets. It didn't seem to matter if they were in front of a store or a home; they had created another Bombay along the sidewalks.

I walked quickly back towards the King George. The people at my feet were of all ages, including entire families living out of boxes. A few seemed content, but most were suffering; many were missing teeth or digits or even limbs. I felt frustrated and angry and could only think of getting back to the hotel where it was quiet and cool and I could think.

I was almost there when I stopped short. A man was lying across my path and he didn't seem to be breathing. Flies buzzed around his head and there were several other homeless sitting nearby, but I was sure he was dead. I stifled an urge to vomit and crossed to the other side of the street, desperate now to be in my private room.

— ★ ★ ★ —

The next night what I'd seen was still bothering me, so I asked Rico over dinner how he was able to enjoy himself in India when faced with so much poverty and disease.

"It used to bug me," he said, picking at the curried goat he'd ordered. "So I asked a guy who lived here, a well-off guy, how he did it. He told me, 'I give to one person every day.' You can't help everybody, it's impossible, the country has too many problems—it's overcrowded, there's not enough food, not enough jobs, it gets hit by an earthquake or a tsunami nearly every other week. It makes sense to me—otherwise you just get overwhelmed."

I thought about that for a minute, thought of all the hundreds of homeless I'd walked past just that day. "But how do you choose who to help?"

"Just pick one, it doesn't really matter who, they all need it.

But you've got to stick to one, you can't start feeling sorry for people—you gotta be firm, but not cruel. This guy I was talking to told me, 'If you have a soft heart, you will give away everything. If your heart is hard, you will become a cynic.' You have to find the place in between."

It might not always have been obvious, but he did care about these people. *Maybe Rico does have a heart.*

A sly grin crept across his face. "I've got one more thing to show you before you leave this country."

We finished our dinner and hailed a taxi soon afterwards; Rico gave instructions to the driver that I couldn't make out. We drove for twenty minutes, leaving downtown behind.

"You're not going to believe this, this is gonna be the craziest thing you've ever seen." He was drumming his fingers, looking out the window.

Eventually we arrived at a somewhat rundown stretch of roadway and Rico told the driver to slow down.

"I present to you," he said with an overly dramatic flourish, "the Cages."

It was, as I should have guessed, a red-light district. I'd seen red-light districts before, but this one was different.

"You name it, they got it here," Rico enthused. "Boys, girls, women, men, one, two, three, four, as many as you want, in whatever combination. Man, you just got to dream it up."

He looked at me sideways, judging my reaction, and I made no effort to hide my disgust. I was deeply shocked. As we drove I saw row upon row of small buildings of different heights, jammed together along both sides of the road, each with large windows on most of the floors. But in place of a glass window there were *bars*, and behind them people of all description. Most were women, of all types. Almost all were young; in the worst cases, there were children who looked to be as young as six. Before long, several other children, perhaps a dozen, started running after the car, begging for some change. (By this time we were moving at about ten kilometres an hour, giving us time to get a better view.)

My jaw tightened; I didn't know where to look or what to do. We were passing hundreds of these "cages," probably thousands. I didn't even know what to call this, whether it was sex slavery or something even more perverted. It didn't look like a terrible place at first glance—the women all wore saris that were clean and well-kept, and many were lounging in open doorways or on little porches, gossiping with their neighbours. In some ways, it was like something you might see in a working-class neighbourhood in any big city. But here the doors had bars on them and it was obvious that none of the residents strayed far from those porches.

Rico was now staring out at the passing wares with open appreciation. "See anything you like?"

I could only shake my head. Surely he'd known I wouldn't be interested in this? What was he trying to prove to me?

We'd been cruising along the strip for several minutes now, the sun was down, and we had not yet come to the end of the "displays." I heard shouting and saw that the children who'd been running after us had been chasing our car all this time. *How desperate are you?* They must have been chasing us for at least a mile, maybe more. *What can I do to help you?*

Rico glanced at me, then tossed a few rupees out the window at the children and motioned to the driver. To my great relief, and Rico's disappointment, we sped away.

I slept only a couple of hours that night, since I was booked on an early-morning flight to Paris leaving at 5:45 a.m. I couldn't begin to describe how much I looked forward to leaving Southeast Asia; I didn't plan to return for a long, long time. But I knew there were still several security checks to pass through before I was home. Only when I arrived there could I truly enjoy anything.

I quickly packed and climbed into my business suit again. Rico was still sleeping since he wasn't leaving until the next day. I planned to meet him in Belgium then and, after a day or two, go back to Paris and fly on to Toronto. He rolled over and mumbled, "Have a nice trip," as I shut my suitcase, and then I was downstairs and hailing a cab for the airport.

Even at that hour it was sizzling hot, so I rolled down the window. As we drove along, I took in the last sights, hundreds of people sprawled sleeping on the sidewalks. Part of me was still amazed I was in India at all.

We stopped at a traffic light and I looked out the window to my left—sitting on the corner was a man with no legs. No legs! He sat on a makeshift skateboard and pulled himself along with his hands. I couldn't imagine a person living on the street like this back home. I felt like throwing the man enough rupees to at least buy him a bloody wheelchair. At least then I would feel like I'd helped someone.

Just as I was wondering how much that would cost, a dark, putrid object was shoved in my face through the window on my right. I recoiled before I realized what it was—a human arm, spindly and pock-marked, attached to the body of a boy who could not have been more than twelve. There were open sores all over his skin, many of them damp as if they were fresh, and the face of the boy bore the same terrible marks. *My god!* He was silent, but you could tell with a glance that he was weak from hunger. I thrust my hand in my pocket like I was putting out a fire and grabbed the few rupees I had left and gingerly put them in his outstretched palm.

A leper. A fucking leper.

I chastised myself as the light changed and we drove off. I couldn't keep losing my cool every time I was confronted with a hard part of life that was new to me. It was overwhelming, how to react to these hard truths and how to do something good, but

Detour on The Path

I had to learn to accept this as reality.

I wasn't too worried about the security check at Bombay airport, since I couldn't see why they would care about what I was taking out of the country. So I was fairly relaxed in the lineup for the X-ray machine. I put the typewriter case on the conveyer belt and waited my turn to go through the metal detector.

A sleepy security guard motioned towards me. "Next, please."

I walked through without incident, since I was wearing no metal.

"Behind the screen please, sahib."

While in line I'd seen that security was asking every passenger to step into one of several booths they had setup, closed off from public view by a sheer curtain. I figured they were worried about hijackings. I stepped inside and a uniformed officer pulled the curtain closed behind me and began to frisk me very thoroughly, without saying a word.

I was shielded from public view on two sides by the curtain, but I could see the officer monitoring the X-ray machine off to my left and a little ahead of me. From where I was I could actually see the screen he was looking at, at a slight angle, and I was watching it when the officer pushed a button to bring the next item on the conveyor belt into view. The officer frisking me had moved from my feet to up above my knees when the typewriter case came onto the screen.

Oh my god.

On the monitor I could see a distinct line near the top of the case, with the area below the line being a slightly darker shade than the area above it—it was like looking at water in a nearly full glass. It was obvious that there was something unusual about the case.

Oh god, not here, I can't be caught here.

The officer in front of the monitor continued staring at the case, while the man frisking me worked his way up to my waist. I was afraid to move—afraid to breathe—or do anything that would tip them off. I knew that once the frisking officer got up to my chest I was a goner, because my heart was beating like I'd just run all the way to the airport.

The officer had been watching the monitor for at least ten seconds. I was sure my heart was going to explode right there. It was over, there was no way out.

Then he pushed the button. The typewriter case moved along the conveyer belt and nothing happened.

How did he not see that?!

I slowly, slowly exhaled. The officer in the booth was patting down my arms and shoulders.

"Ok, sir, thank you."

I walked out, picked up the case, and moved on as nonchalantly as possible to the departure lounge. I sat down, not shaking, just in a state of shock, as if I'd walked away from a car wreck without a scratch. Then a huge wave of relief washed over me. I'd made it. I was past the last checkpoint in South Asia. The worst was over. From now on, I'd be travelling in countries where things made sense, where I knew the rules. I was looking forward to having a beer, to seeing Paris, and to fitting in. From now on, things would be easier.

As I waited to board the plane, I began to overhear the chatter of other passengers. My luck had been better than I thought. Several people had been forced to go through a full strip search, women as well as men, apparently at random. It sounded very thorough. I don't know what the security people were looking for, but I hope they found it.

— ★ ★ ★ —

As we began our descent into Charles de Gaulle airport, I

Detour on The Path

reviewed the plans Rico had given me. I was booked on a connecting flight to Brussels for later that day, but I was to leave the airport in Paris and go to Gare du Nord train station and book a train to Belgium. That way, said Rico, security in Paris would be less thorough in their checks, since I was not staying in the country. Rico and I would meet in Brussels the next day. There, the hashish oil would be transferred into several balloons. The balloons would then be attached to me with a body pack, since in North America customs officials rarely did body patdowns, but often searched people's luggage. I would be given my ticket to Toronto, then I'd go back to Paris and fly home.

I was in a fantastic mood as we taxied into the gate. I could see the green grass twinkling in the morning sun and I knew the late summer warmth would be comfortable instead of crippling, and my clothes already felt better on me.

Then, out the window, I saw what looked like a temple of modernity—the Concorde. It was sleek and angular and amazing in its simplicity. It was my first time seeing it and the sight put me even more at ease.

I went through passport control without incident and went to retrieve my luggage. I put my bags on a cart, with the typewriter case at the front in plain view. Then I headed towards the exit. There were two doors, one for Items to Declare and another for Nothing to Declare. I stopped and thought for a moment. I had bought very little on the trip, just a couple of souvenirs worth no more than a few dollars, so I walked towards Nothing to Declare.

I was about halfway through the doorway, about to enter the arrivals lounge, when a man in a dress shirt and tie stepped out of an office immediately to my right.

"Excusez-moi, monsieur. Ticket, s'il vous plait."

I reached into my jacket pocket and handed him my ticket. He glanced at it casually and looked up.

"Passport, s'il vous plait."

"Ok."

"Parlez-vous francais, monsieur?"

"No."

He continued in a heavily accented English. "What do you do for a living?"

"Teacher."

I was trying to keep my answers short and simple, to avoid tipping my hand or showing any nervousness. But now my mind was beginning to race. Teacher. As he continued to leaf through my passport, he saw stamps from Egypt, Venezuela, Hong Kong and Japan, all from my travels in recent years for competitions and training for the national team, and none of them with dates during which a teacher could travel. And, of course, stamps from Pakistan and India. I didn't want to backtrack and stumble through an explanation of what kind of teacher I was; I was doubly nervous when I realized that many of those countries had significant connections to the drug trade.

"Can you step into this room, please?" He motioned me into the office behind him, following me as I pushed my cart into the tiny room. There were two chairs, a table and a French flag. He pointed at the case.

"What is this?"

"A typewriter."

"Open it, please."

I laid it on the table and opened it to show him the typewriter, aware that I couldn't leave it in this position for very long before hashish oil would start seeping out of the holes. The man, who was slender and middle-aged, with a pair of severe glasses and a trim moustache that gave him a serious look, walked over and picked up the typewriter, putting it on the table next to the case. He then picked up the case in both hands and hefted it, feeling its weight.

"I will be back in a moment." He and the typewriter case left the room.

Suddenly, every breath of air was sucked out of my lungs at

once, and my insides collapsed into a tiny ball in the pit of my stomach. *Oh my god, he knows.*

I sunk into a chair and closed my eyes. It was over, really over, this time. I could think of nothing to do but sit and wait for the inevitable. I felt nauseous. I gave no thought to slipping out the door and losing myself in the crowd of the arrivals lounge, only a few metres away. More than anything I was overcome with relief, like a house had been lifted from me, and I felt something close to gratitude that I wouldn't have to pretend anymore. It was total surrender.

Within two or three minutes the man came back, his face flushed, flanked by two men in uniforms with pistols drawn and pointing at me.

"What is this! Opium?!"

He was holding the typewriter case in one hand, and had torn a gash in the middle of it, from which amber-coloured hashish oil was spilling out.

I made an effort to sound calm, but I had no fear or fight left in me anyways. "No, no…it's hash oil."

"Hash oil? What is this?"

"Cannabis."

"Cannabis? Oh." He seemed to relax at this news. He put the case down and one of the men holstered his gun and pulled out a pair of handcuffs. He pulled me out of the chair and I let him force my hands together in front of me, as he quickly applied the cuffs. I offered no resistance. I had sunk into the strangest fog since being left alone in that room. It was like watching myself in a dream; I had given up all volition about what would happen next, I just waited with detached curiosity.

I was marched through the terminal—still in cuffs, with the two guards—in full public view. I imagine people were staring at me, but I didn't notice. After a couple of minutes they led me to a hallway and down several flights of stairs. The march ended in a nondescript grey office with only a desk, chairs and a large steel ring mounted to the wall. I waited. One of the men told me to sit, then undid the cuff on my left hand and snapped it to the ring. His partner had brought my bags and these were carried into the room. No one spoke; every movement the men made was brusque and all business. After I had been "secured," the two officers left.

The official in charge put one of my bags on the table and opened it. As he began to pore over each item, the questions came:

"Where are you going?"

"Canada."

"Is that where you were delivering the case?"

"Yes."

"To who?"

"I don't know."

"Why not?"

"They haven't told me that."

"Who is they?"

"Rico."

"Rico who?"

"I don't know."

"Rico is your contact?"

"Yes."

"But you don't know his name?"

"Just Rico."

He found my business card holder and started to go through it with interest.

"Karate—you do karate?"

"Yes, I run my own school."

"Hmph."

He picked up the telephone and spoke briefly in French. In a few moments, two new (and very large) plainclothes officers walked in and stood by the door. In better times, I would have laughed.

My interrogator's attention turned to the typewriter case.

"Where did you get this?"

"Pakistan."

"Where in Pakistan?"
"Peshawar."
"From who?"
"I don't know."
"You don't know who you got it from?"
"They were Afghan, maybe. I don't know who they were."
"How did you get it?"
"Rico made the deal."
"Where is Rico?"
"India."
"Where did you go?"
"All over. Karachi, Islamabad, Peshawar, New Delhi, Bombay."
"Is this your first time smuggling?"
"Yes."
"Who else was involved?"
"Just Rico."
"What is his last name?"
"I don't know."

And so it went. Rico and I had made a deal before the trip began that, if I was caught, last names would not be used. In exchange, he would help me out after the law was finished with me. I planned to honour that agreement. I would otherwise answer all questions honestly, but I would keep my word to Rico too.

Questioning went on like this for a long time, probably a couple of hours, before nature intervened—I had to piss.

"Is there a washroom I can use?"

Everyone just looked at each other. You could see the worry written on their faces—that this was all part of my nefarious plan, and I was suddenly going to turn into Bruce Lee.

After a hurried discussion in French, the handcuffs were re-applied and I was escorted by the two men in plainclothes down another hallway to an empty washroom where I could relieve myself. My two friends stood very close behind.

When I was returned and re-attached to the ring the questions went back to Rico, but they still led to the same dead end.

"Where does he live?"

"Toronto."

"Where in Toronto?"

"I don't know."

"What does he look like?"

"About five-foot-six, olive skin, dark curly hair, moustache." Of course, this could describe several million people. I didn't feel the need to mention that he had one arm fewer than most of them.

"What does he do?"

"I don't know."

"How do you know him?"

"I met him at the dojo."

"How long have you known him?"

"Not that long."

"Did he talk about anyone else?"

"No."

I could see that my interrogator had actually begun to feel sorry for me. He tried to downplay the situation, making it clear that he didn't consider it serious.

"You know, these things happen. It'll be a year. Bad luck for you. We only catch about twenty percent of the stuff that comes through here."

In another place, in another time, I might have felt thankful for his good intentions. As it was, I'd become like someone who'd spent too many hours on the couch watching bad television—I was listless, unfocused, only half-interested in what the next plot development would be. I didn't even think about what would come next; I just wallowed in my apathetic stupor.

I didn't have to wait long for the next twist in the story. The questioning soon finished and two new officers in plainclothes showed up. It was time to go to jail.

Mokuso
Meditation

Chapter 5

AS STUNNED AS I WAS by my situation, I quickly realized that even cops in France are a little different than everywhere else.

The pair who walked into the room were dressed like they were popping into a stylish Left Bank bar after their shift was done. Both looked only a few years older than me, and they moved with the casual arrogance of men who felt that there was nothing the world could throw at them that they couldn't handle. They were fit and each sported a trim moustache. One was dark and the other fair-haired, and they wore their hair just long enough to flout convention without crossing the line into counter-culture. The dark-haired one even wore a leather jacket. Both had handguns strapped to their belts.

My interrogator stood up and nodded at them in a formal way, speaking to them rapidly for a couple of minutes; I could pick up enough from my poor grade-school French to know he was explaining my case to them. The fair-haired one nodded absently as he spoke, while his partner chewed gum and checked out the room. After a couple of minutes the blonde cop said "OK" and one of the guards came over and unlocked me from the iron ring, clasping my hands together in front of me.

"Let's go," the gum-chewing cop said in heavily accented English. "Time for a drive."

We walked back up the way I'd come in, this time crossing the busy arrivals lounge and heading outside, one of them guiding me by the elbow to move in a particular direction, neither speaking as they walked easily on either side of me. A few people stared but I didn't care, it was good to be out of that damn dungeon.

Their car, unmarked, was sitting near the exit, and the dark-haired one opened the back door for me. There was no barrier between the front seat and the back, but neither of them seemed worried.

"We're taking you to the *prefecture*," the driver said as we pulled away. "You'll like it better."

"Ok." I couldn't think of anything else to say.

We pulled out of the airport and had soon left the highway to wind through the streets of suburban Paris. We hadn't driven for long when we pulled up in front of a modest two-storey brick building.

"Scenic tour is over." My door opened and I was escorted through the front door.

It was a small station with offices around the perimeter and a large front desk where a uniformed officer nodded at us as we went by. Behind it, in a corner, were two floor-to-ceiling panels of plexiglass. This is where we were headed; the blonde officer stopped in front of the open glass door, removed my belt and my tie, then took off the cuffs and motioned for me to step inside. There was only one piece of furniture in the room, a long metal bench along the left-hand wall, so, not knowing what else to do, I went and sat on it.

This was it. I was in jail.

I looked around to see what I could see. My cell was the only one in the station; the rest of the place was occupied by officers, some uniformed and some not, sitting at desks, talking on the phone and bustling off to unseen destinations. No one looked in my direction. My cell looked to be about fifteen feet long and perhaps six feet wide, with a concrete floor and no windows; besides the bench I was sitting on, which was bolted into the wall, it had no adornments at all.

I still hadn't shaken the disconnected feeling I'd had since I first got pulled into the customs office at the airport, like I'd been watching everything that had happened since on television. I was having trouble focusing on anything—my mind wanted to race off in a hundred directions at once, and the moment I settled on one thought I sped off to another. I sat like this for a long time, not really thinking of anything, just letting all these thoughts bounce around inside my head—Mia, Rico, the dojo, my friends, my family. This must have gone on for a couple of hours, because when I heard someone opening my cell I looked up and could see through the front door of the station that it was dusk. An officer walked in and handed me a coffee and a baguette with ham and cheese. I realized that I was starving; I hadn't eaten anything since picking at the meal on the plane more than twelve hours ago. I wolfed down the sandwich.

I must have lay down afterwards, because the next thing I remembered was lifting my head from the bench to see my cell door opening and another man being shoved inside. He was obviously very agitated and said something I couldn't understand back to the cop as he stumbled, which was ignored.

"*Fait attention*," the officer said, speaking to me. "He has beatten a man to death." Then he turned and shut the door.

I sat up straight and looked at my new cellmate. He was pacing back and forth along the far wall, very keyed up. The space was so small that he would take about five paces and he'd be three feet away from me, then he'd turn abruptly on his heel and take five steps in the other direction. He was talking to himself the whole time, under his breath, very emphatically but not very loud.

He looked like he had spent some time on the streets: his clothes were dirty and ragged, and a few days' growth on his cheeks along with long, curly, filthy hair made him look a bit wild. I wasn't too worried that he could hurt me—I was about six inches taller than him and at least ten years younger—but I didn't want to turn my back either.

He was starting to talk louder now, chastising himself and pacing faster. He was waving his arms as he walked, his whole body involved in getting out what he had to say, and then he yelled something and paused, turning to look at me. I looked back with a blank expression, having no idea what he'd said, and then he turned and drove his fist into the plexiglass—the wall shuddering under the force of the blow—and started walking again, his muttering back down to a loud whisper.

I just watched. I knew that a normal man would have cried out in pain after hitting a wall that hard, probably would have injured himself, but this guy kept on pacing as if nothing had happened. It was hard to tell if he was on drugs or just surging with adrenalin, but either way I didn't want to cross him.

I was looking for signs as he paced back and forth. I had worked for several years as a bouncer, and I knew that if he wasn't being aggressive *towards me*, I would probably be ok. Right now, he wasn't even looking at me, more distracted by his own internal monologue, so he probably didn't mean me harm. Eye contact was key—so many times in training I'd learned that if someone couldn't look you in the eye they weren't ready to fight you. I'd won many matches armed with this knowledge.

I watched him like this for several hours. Sometimes he would stop pacing for a little while and sit down at the other end of the bench I was on, maybe six feet away, but then he'd get up start walking again, always talking. He was like an animal, all reaction and instinct. It was the middle of the night by now and I hadn't slept more than a few minutes since waking up in India the previous morning; I was exhausted in every way, but didn't dare sleep while he was still so hyped up—the space was so small that when he paced he came within two or three feet of me, close enough that he could be on top of me in less than a second if he wanted. So I stayed in my corner, looking relaxed, keeping myself alert and not letting down my guard. Eventually, I slid down and lay on the bench with my back to the wall and gently let my eyes close, listening for the slightest indication that he was getting aggressive. I'd open my eyes every few minutes to check on him, or stare at him through half-closed lids, but he didn't have any interest in me. His monologue didn't need an audience and he kept it up with no sign of tiring.

I drifted like this for I don't know how long, dozing, but not getting any real rest. Gradually, I could hear the sounds of the station getting busier as the calm of the early morning hours passed into a new day and officers began showing up for their shifts. Giving up hope of getting any proper sleep, I rubbed my eyes and sat up on the bench, watching the pacer because there was nothing else to do.

Not long afterwards the fair-haired officer who'd picked me up the day before popped his head through the door. "You want to join us for breakfast?"

"Sure."

He motioned for me to follow (my prowling cellmate just sat on his end of the bench, pretending we didn't exist) and led me up a flight of stairs to the second floor. His partner was there, sitting at a table in their staff cafeteria.

"Bonjour," he said, without getting up. "I'm Luc and this is my partner Léon. You want some coffee?"

"Ok."

I sat down across from Luc while Léon went to get my breakfast. No handcuffs, no warnings against trying to escape. I almost felt like a guest in their home.

"So, you are from Toronto? I have a cousin in Montreal. I have always wanted to go to Canada. Go out to the woods. Maybe hunt a bear." Here he brought his hands together in front of him and made a shooting motion, making a little "pow" noise as he pulled the trigger.

"Really."

"The bears do not need to worry, he is a terrible shot," Léon said as he put a tray down in front of me with a steaming mug of coffee and two croissants. "Have you done any camping in Canada?"

I started to tell them about canoe trips I'd taken in Algonquin Park, describing the lakes and the animals I'd seen. They had heard of Algonquin and asked about portages and if I'd been to other places in Quebec and the Rockies. It was all a bit surreal. I still had no idea what was going to happen to me, so I tried to steer the conversation back to my situation.

"So what kind of sentences do people usually get for smuggling dope?"

"Ah, you know, not so bad," ventured Luc. "It is your first time, so maybe a year."

"Yes, a year is about average," said Léon. "You are just unlucky, we do not catch that many people."

Great. A year in prison didn't seem like much to them, but my mind balked at the thought. I asked more questions about how to get bail and what prison conditions were like, but they were vague and blasé in their answers. They were more interested in talking about Canada, so we had a gentle tug-of-war about the conversation's direction, both of us trying to answer the other's questions while politely changing the subject. This went on for ten or fifteen minutes until Luc looked at his watch.

"Ok, we need to take you to court. You are scheduled to meet the judge this morning."

I wasn't sure what this meeting was for, but apparently a judge had been assigned to evaluate my case before I went to trial. Luc and Léon stood up, all business now, and Léon re-applied a pair of handcuffs. We walked out of the station through the back door and got into their car. A few minutes later we were pulling up in front of a large stone building with a sign that read *Palais de Justice* and I was being escorted inside.

I was taken straight down to the basement, where there was a series of holding cells. Luc and Léon handed me off unceremoniously to the officer in charge, a broad-shouldered man who copied down my registration details with tiny handwriting before removing my cuffs and leading me down a dank, fluorescent-lit hallway. The place stank, but I couldn't tell from what. We walked past a number of cells with heavy steel bars, until we stopped at one and the officer opened the door and motioned me inside.

This was more like the jail cells I had imagined. Everything other than the bars was made of concrete, while a long bench that ran along all three walls was the only furnishing. There were about a dozen men in the room, all sitting down. They all looked up at me as the door opened, then went back to studying the floor or whatever they were doing to kill time once they saw the door wasn't opening for them.

I sat down as far from everyone else as I could. I was still very, very tired and my head was buzzing. I thought about lying down, just for a minute, but having a nap amongst a gang of criminals seemed like a bad idea so I just rested my forehead in my palms. *What the hell am I doing here?* All the relief of my capture was gone, replaced by a rising fear of the future.

After a few minutes, a name crackled over a PA system speaker in the hallway and a man across from me got up and stood by the door. Before long, an officer came and let him out. A few minutes later it happened again and I figured out that everyone here was waiting to be called so that they could get their meeting with a judge. I couldn't guess how long it would be before my name was called, but I became more alert knowing it could happen at any time. The last thing I wanted to do was miss my name.

As I waited, I looked around the room. It was a real mix of cultures that had landed here. About half of the men looked European—mostly French, but also someone who appeared Italian or Greek—while the other half were North African and Middle Eastern. No one spoke much, so it was hard to tell. I assumed they were all like me, nervous, defeated and unsure of what was coming next. It wasn't a place where making friends was a priority.

Before long though, someone did try and strike up a conversation with me, a bearded Frenchman a couple of seats over. He asked a question in French that I didn't understand, so I just shrugged, then he asked another, which I guessed was where I was from, so I said "Canada" and he said "ahh" like that explained something. He didn't try to ask me anything after that, but it made me wonder *How am I going to explain myself properly to a French judge?* The more I thought about things the worse they seemed to be, as I couldn't see anything but a long stretch of barriers between me and getting a handle on my situation, never mind gaining my freedom.

I sat there for a long time. It was the first time I was undisturbed since my arrest, so questions began to slip into my mind: How would anyone at home know where I was? Did I need a lawyer? How would I find one? If they gave me a phone call, who should I call? There were so many things to think about and so many things I didn't know, it made me feel sick to concentrate on them. So I didn't. I let my mind buzz around like a hummingbird from thought to thought, not resting in any one place, and waited.

I don't know how long I waited for, several hours was my best guess, but more than half of the men in the room when I arrived had heard their names and left. I was sitting very still with my eyes closed when the PA system came to life and spit out "Bradley Jones!" My eyes popped open and I was on my feet, waiting by the door.

I was led back the way I came and up and out of the basement. It felt good to get out of the damp air and the depressing lighting, to be around normal people again. There were many of them, scurrying to different appointments and courtrooms. The guard took me through the lobby and down a hallway into a large office. The first thing I saw was a big mahogany desk, then several plush leather chairs, a French flag and one entire wall lined with books. There were two women in the room; one sat behind the desk, surrounded by a stack of files, while the one nearest me got up from one of the leather chairs when she saw me and walked over.

"I am here on behalf of the Canadian embassy," she said in a business-like way, not offering me her hand. Her clothes matched her manner, a conservative dark blazer and knee-length skirt. "My name is Julie."

"Hello."

"Please be aware," she said quickly, "that my main role today is to listen. We are unable to interfere with the French legal system, so I am not here to defend you. But if we can help in some other way we will do our best to do so."

"Maybe you can tell me what is about to happen? No one has told me anything."

"Of course. You will talk with the *juge d'instruction* here and she will evaluate your case."

"Evaluate what exactly?"

"The evidence. Her job is to find out all she can about your charge and about you. When she feels there is enough evidence your case will proceed to trial."

"When will that be?"

"That depends on how long it takes her to gather enough evidence for your case."

"Do I get a lawyer?"

"You will have the opportunity to hire legal counsel before you go to trial."

"What happens until the trial?"

"You will be retained in custody until enough evidence has been gathered." Here she cracked a shadow of a smile. "So it's in your best interest to provide as much evidence as you can."

No kidding. I could see that they didn't mess around in this country; if you didn't talk you could spend a long time sitting in a cell somewhere. So much for innocent until proven guilty.

"Whenever you are ready, Mr. Jones." The judge looked up at me from behind her desk and motioned towards a chair across from her.

"The purpose of this interview," she continued, her English flawless and only lightly accented, "is to determine the nature of your crime so that I can recommend a course of action to the prosecutor. Not answering any of my questions, while it is within your rights to do so, will only lengthen the amount of time it will take for me to make a recommendation. It will be best for you if you answer as honestly and completely as possible."

"I understand." I could already tell from her demeanor that this was not the kind of woman who tolerated games. Her face, framed by a swoosh of chestnut-brown hair pinned up at the back, was placid and expressionless while her eyes were dark and gave no hint of her emotions. She was, in her way, like a well-trained warrior who gives nothing away before going into battle.

"So, Mr. Jones," she began, looking down at the file folder in front of her. "Where did you get this hashish from?"

"Hashish *oil*," I interjected.

"This hashish *oil* from?"

"Pakistan."

"Where in Pakistan?"

"Peshawar."

"Who did you get it from?"

"Some locals…I don't know who they were."

"How did you find them?"

"I was taken to them."

"By who?"

"Rico."

"Who is Rico?"

"Rico is…the person who got me to do this trip."

"What is Rico's last name?"

"I don't know."

She stopped and made a note in the file. Had I just made a mistake? I still planned to keep my word to Rico, but was this a "lack of evidence" that could delay my trial? I studied the judge's reaction, but it was unreadable.

"Where were you taking the hashish oil?"

"Back to Canada."

"What were you going to do with it?"

"Deliver it to Rico."

"What do you do in Canada?"

"I'm a teacher."

"A karate teacher?"

"Yes."

More than anything, I wanted to sound like an educated person, like a good person. A normal person who had just made a really bad decision. I told her about how I needed the money for my school, how I wanted to help my students. How I'd only planned to do it just this once. I told her everything I could think of that made me sound good. She listened impassively, occasionally making a note in my file, but not giving anything away. I tried not to let it bother me, but I really wanted to provoke some kind of reaction from her, a hint of sympathy.

The questions kept coming.

"Where did you visit on the trip?"

"Lahore, Islamabad, Rawalpindi, Peshawar, Delhi, Bombay."

"Nowhere else?"

"No."

"What about these stamps on your passport—Egypt, Venezuela, Hong Kong?"

"I was travelling for competitions."

Where did I get the typewriter case? What did the people look like who sold us the hashish oil? What had Rico said about them? There were a lot of questions about Rico, most of them the same as I had been asked at the airport. The problem was that I had been in such a stupor when I was first questioned that I couldn't remember now what I had said then. How much detail had I given describing Rico? Had I said how much we'd paid for the full typewriter case? I knew I'd answered honestly then and now, but was I saying exactly the same thing? If not, what did that mean? What was the best thing to say? The sleepless night and the constant scrutiny were beginning to take their toll. I felt like I could damn myself with something I said and not even know it.

It continued. We had been talking for about forty-five minutes, the judge referring back to the file, repeating some questions, asking for more information about others. As it went on and on, I caught myself squeezing the armrests on the chair looking at the clock. The more I had to say, the more likely it seemed that I would say something wrong. *Doesn't she know enough?* She continued to copy down notes, betraying no emotion.

Finally, she looked up. "Thank you Mr. Jones, I think I have everything I need."

"What now then?"

"You will be returned to your cell."

"When do I find out about a trial?"

"Someone will let you know when the time comes."

"How long will that take?"

"That will be all, Mr. Jones."

"That's it?"

"Yes, Mr. Jones, thank you. The guard will take you now."

I mumbled thanks and followed as the guard, who I hadn't noticed behind me, guided me out of the room. Julie nodded at me as I left but said nothing, only meeting my eyes for as long as was polite before looking down to study her notes.

I was taken back by a different route than I'd come, reaching the basement by a set of back stairs behind heavy doors. The smell hit me again; I could almost identify it now as part mould and part sweat, a stew of damp cells and unwashed men.

The guard paused at the bottom of the stairwell. He pointed at an empty room and down the hall towards the cell where I'd waited for the judge. "Içi où içi?"

I hadn't been alone for days. I pointed at the empty cell.

He opened the door and motioned for me to enter. The

room was all white and very small, with just a narrow bench built into the wall. The door closed behind me and I sat down.

I was very still. I kept going over my answers to the judge in my head: Had I described the men who sold us the oil the same way as I had at the airport? Had I given Rico away somehow? The judge had looked like she considered the matter to be serious—had the cops at the station misled me on how I'd be sentenced? How long was I going to be in here?

My mind went around and around in circles looking for these answers until I ran out of questions to ask. It was futile. The future was a black hole that was dragging me relentlessly towards it. I knew absolutely nothing about it.

Slowly, I awoke to the room. Where was I? I knew I was somewhere in Paris, or just outside of it, but where would I be next? When would that be? And how could I tell anyone where I was?

Yes, how would I tell other people? Never mind *how* I would tell them, *what* would I tell them? For the first time since my arrest I began to seriously think about people at home. Mia! *Oh god.* I was supposed to be home in a couple of days so that I could go with her for her abortion. What would she think when I didn't show up? That I'd run out on her? God, she was going to hate me. Would she still go through with the abortion when I didn't show up? I thought of us lying together back in my apartment, her head resting lightly on my shoulder. Would she ever speak to me again?

And the dojo! Who would run it? No one else had access to the bank accounts—how would the bills get paid, who would pay the rent? I could see my students, each of their faces, as they showed up for class the day I was supposed to return, confused when no one came. What was I going to tell them? I was their teacher—how could I instruct them anymore after they found out I was caught smuggling dope?

From there, the floodgates opened. How was I going to explain this to my mother? I could already hear her heart breaking. What would my friends think of me? At the same time, I was lost trying to figure out how to take even the most basic steps to help myself: *Who do I call to explain what's happened to me? How do I get a lawyer? How do I pay for one?* There wasn't a single person I knew who knew what was happening. I was utterly, completely alone.

You asshole! How could I have been so stupid? I'd thrown my whole life away, for what? There must have been some other way I could have made some money, if only I'd thought hard enough about it. How many times in the dojo had I shouted out the karate creed: "Seek perfection of character! Be faithful!" Did those words mean nothing to me? I cursed myself over and over again, holding my head in my hands. *Stupid! Why was I so stupid?!*

I started to think about Rico, and I started to get angrier. Somehow, this was his fault too. It was he who had talked me into this trip, had persuaded me that it would be safe. Where was he now? Still, he was also my only lifeline to the future. Before we left he had said to me that if anything happened he would take care of me once I got out—get me "set up," put me back on my feet. That was all I had right now.

My eyes began to fill with tears. *The dojo.* I was going to lose the dojo. I had set out to save it, and all I had done was kill it. At first I stifled a sob, then another, then I gave in to the fear. My body shook, and I was wracked by sobs and cursing, wailing in utter hopelessness, not thinking if anyone could hear me or what they would think of me. I began to punch the walls over and over and over again, but the pain in my hands only reinforced the cold reality of where I was. There seemed to be nothing below me, nothing that could catch my fall. The whole world fell away and it was just me and my fear, and the fear won hands down. I wept until there was nothing left in my body, except emptiness. If I had had a gun I think I would have killed myself. I was utterly destroyed.

I lay on that bench for a long time, catatonic, empty, thinking of nothing. I wasn't waiting for anything, or planning, I was just a blank. So it was impossible to know how long I'd been there before the door opened and a new guard stood in the doorway. "On y va," he said, motioning for me to move. He put a pair of handcuffs back on and pushed me ahead of him.

I was led through another series of hallways that went to the back of the building, where a police van was waiting. Two more guards opened the back door of the van so I could get in. I sat down next to five other men, all of us wearing handcuffs, as the door slammed shut. There was no light inside the van and no windows. The engine roared to life and we pulled away, all of us leaning into the corners as the vehicle swerved so that we wouldn't land in our neighbour's lap.

We drove through the night (it must have been night, with the length of the day and the grumbling in my stomach) for about an hour. There was a ferocious storm outside, the rain pelting the top of the van like tiny firecrackers, and I could hear peals of thunder every few minutes. Finally the van slowed and reversed to a stop. The doors opened to rows of armed guards and we were led out one at a time down a long hallway, each of us watched by several guards, to yet another small, smelly holding cell, where we sat for a while longer. It was obvious we were all exhausted; no one spoke the entire time.

Eventually someone showed up and said my name. I got up and followed him to another room, where I was photographed several times then taken to a small cell by myself. It had a tiny window and I could hear the storm still boiling outside. I had only been in there a few minutes when the room went dark; I could see there was no light coming in from underneath the door so I guessed the power had been cut. I sat there in the dark, listening to the roar of the thunder, when another sound ripped through the night—screams. I couldn't tell where they were coming from, or even what language they were in, but a chill ran through me at the sound.

After what seemed like days but was probably only minutes, another guard showed up and took me to a large room to be processed. A long counter ran across the width of the room, a steel grey very close to the drab paint on the walls, and my suitcase (which I hadn't seen since the airport) was sitting on top of it. The guard told me to strip and all of those clothes were put on the counter; another guard then looked up my ass to make sure I wasn't carrying anything there. The man behind the counter had been waiting for me, and immediately unzipped my suitcase and silently examined each article with great care. Most went into a box next to him; a few items were slid across the counter towards me. Two T-shirts. A pair of jeans. Underwear. Socks. A couple of times I asked the man if I could keep something, a watch or a notebook, but I just ended up staring at the shine of his bald head, since he didn't look up from his job to give an indication he'd heard or even understood. This went on until he had emptied my suitcase; the basic items I was to keep were slid across the counter to me.

Next I was directed to an adjacent room and told to take a shower. God, it felt wonderful. When it was done I dressed and the guard handed me soap, a set of sheets and a towel, and then motioned for me to follow.

This time I was taken down a very long passageway, dimly lit with floors, walls and ceiling all made from polished concrete. That passageway led to another, and then another, all occasionally dotted with doors, but I couldn't guess what might be behind them. The guard and I walked for several minutes, the halls quiet except for the hum of the electric lights and the slap of our own footsteps. Then we passed through a door and there were voices, loud and animated but none in English, like entering the tunnel of a carnival fun house. About thirty metres down that hallway the guard stopped and unlocked the door in front of him. This time he did not go through, but stood aside for me to pass in front of him.

I took three steps into the room and stopped, unable to see

anything until my eyes adjusted to the darkness. The door clunked shut behind me, the lock clicking into place, and there was a moment of quiet. A bunk bed emerged out of the darkness on my left, a toilet on my right, and the silhouette of a table and chair underneath a small window ahead of me.

I stood perfectly still in the middle of the room for several minutes, listening as sounds began to appear, looking for my cue on what to do next. The voices from the hall came back quickly, guttural shouts and a constant, bitter laughter. From the bottom bunk I noticed a heavy, rhythmic breathing and saw there was a body curled up there, his back to me.

This was it. My new home.

With nothing else to do, I climbed up to the top bunk and lay down. The old adrenalin was pumping through me again, and I knew sleep would not come. I couldn't think of anything to do, so I just listened to the shouting. The shouts seemed to be getting stronger; every few minutes a scream was added to the mix, what I can only describe as pure anguish, like someone's soul was being torn out of them at that moment. *Where am I?* I got up to look out the window, which was open, but couldn't make anything out beyond more walls and concrete. Terror was building from the pit of my stomach now, my mind brimming with questions that only fed my fear—how will anyone find me here? Who is making those sounds? How will I ever get out of here? How long until I'm the one screaming?

At some point exhaustion must have won out, as the next thing I remember is the sound of the door clicking open and a tray being slid along the floor, and the door closing again. It was light now and the voices were quiet.

I would have rolled over and given myself back to sleep, but my stomach leaped as the smell of the coffee reached me. Twenty-four hours had passed since my last meal, so I hopped down and gulped down the coffee and slices of baguette like an animal stumbling on an unguarded picnic. The shape in the bottom bunk was still snoring undisturbed and I was in no mood for introductions—I climbed back into bed the moment the last drop was drained from the tin mug and slipped back into oblivion.

Next memory: awaking into darkness. The shouting was back and there was snoring below me. Then I turned over and was gone.

— ★ ★ ★ —

The next time I opened my eyes the room was again filled with daylight. I lay still for several minutes, blinking and assessing: I felt more like myself than I had in many days; I was hugely hungry; I could tell from looking at the ceiling that I was still in the same room and had not dreamt the whole nightmare; and I thought I might have the willpower to get out of bed.

A yawn came up from below me and the groan of a body stretching. I turned my head towards the room to fill in the details of what I'd seen in my exhausted semi-delirium. The table and chair were as I'd seen them, bare and functional, and on either side of the table was a little wooden cupboard. The porcelain toilet had no seat, and was separated by a half-wall from the bed. A laden tray identical to the one from the day before sat inside the door.

The man below rolled into view and went for the tray. He was very pale, and alarmingly thin. His hair was oily, near shoulder-length and scraggly, and he wore a half-grown beard. He sat on the bed and chewed his baguette slowly, taking an occasional sip of coffee, not looking right or left as he ate but staring into the middle distance. Each move was slow and deliberate, as if completing it only brought on the problem of what to do next.

I must have shifted my weight, as my metal bed frame gave a little pang. The head I'd been staring at snapped around, his eyes immediately latching on to mine. They narrowed for a moment before he broke into a broad grin.

"Bonjour!" he exclaimed, putting down his coffee and turning to face me. A long string of animated, rapid-fire French followed, but, of course, I had no idea what he was saying. I could only smile weakly and say "I don't speak French," while looking apologetic. The first thing I noticed when he turned towards me were his teeth, which seemed to take up half his face. He looked crestfallen for a moment, but kept chattering in his herky-jerky way. Not knowing what else to do I feigned interest until he gave up with a shrug and went back to his bunk.

I let my head fall back down on the pillow. *Great. I'm living in a 120-square-foot space with someone I can't even speak to.*

I thought about what to do next. I could eat my breakfast...and then what? Piss. Look out the window...my brain balked at what came after that. Wait till I got fed again? *Like a bloody farm animal being fattened up for slaughter.* Was this what my future was? For how long?

My eyes closed. I lay still.

The PA system crackled something unintelligible and suddenly the lock on my cell clicked and the door swung open. My bunkmate swung his feet to the floor and sauntered out, and I could see a steady stream of men walking casually through the hallway. I watched for about thirty seconds, then jumped to the floor and followed. The doors to all the cells were open and some prisoners were chatting as they walked down the hall. It almost looked like a street scene from Karachi—all kinds of male styles of dress were represented, from jeans and T-shirts to sand-coloured tunics and flowing pants from the Middle East.

We went down some flights of stairs and after a couple of minutes the line entered into mid-morning sunshine. We were inside a rectangular enclosure, stretching about sixty metres in width, with a simple flat roof sheltering a patch of concrete at the far end of the yard. There were guard towers at either end of the opposite wall, with coils of barbed wire running between them, and a diagonal pattern of cables crisscrossed overhead. In front of me, a small asphalt track circled an expanse of grass where it looked like teams were being selected for a soccer game. Others paced the track while further small clumps of men dispersed themselves around the grounds. A few people eyed me suspiciously, but for the most part I was ignored.

I began to walk. It felt good to stretch my muscles, clamouring for attention after so many days of being ignored, and feel sunshine on my skin. What I was exercising the most was my eyes—drinking in every detail, watching every person, keeping my guard up. I felt wary and charged up all at once, with that now familiar readiness for the unexpected. I walked slowly and kept to the perimeter.

"Do you speak English?"

The voice came from my left, strolling towards me across the green. A round-faced, puffy man with a receding hairline bounced towards me. He was smiling; when he got up next to me he extended his hand and started walking alongside.

"Yes." I smiled and shook his hand. "It's good to hear some English."

"My name's John Blair," he spoke with a clipped English accent. "I'm the welcome wagon around here. Where are you from?"

"Canada. My name's Brad."

"A Canadian, eh? There's another of you in here; I'll introduce you later. How did you manage to get yourself into this place?"

I hesitated for a moment. "I...got caught with some hashish oil."

"Common story. I was trying to liberate some cocaine from Columbia. There's all kinds of stories in here—we've got your murderers, your rapists, your bank robbers, your drug runners, your petty thieves, your immigration 'problems,' pretty much everything under the sun. You'll learn all about that. There's a certain way to do things in here that you'll figure out."

Detour on The Path

"None of it's obvious right now."

"Not to worry, all will be explained. You talked to anyone in here yet?"

"No, the other guy in my cell doesn't speak English."

"That's alright, I can tell you what you need to know. You'll have to get yourself a lawyer, you'll have to see if someone can send you some money. Anyone know you're here? I didn't think so. You can't get them on the telephone—this ain't like the American system you've seen in the movies, there's no phone call you're entitled to—so you'll have to write them a letter and get them to organize some things for you from the outside."

As we walked, he told me a bit about the prison. Its name was Fleury Merogis and I was on the outskirts of Paris with several thousand other prisoners from all across France. What I saw was just one small section of the prison—there were other exercise yards like this one, as well as a hospital and a factory. The prisoners were a rainbow of nationalities; there were criminals here from all across Europe, and a broad collection of immigrants to France, especially Arabs from different parts of North Africa. Some had been here for months or years, some for decades.

I asked the question that was most on my mind. "How do I get out of here? I mean, don't I have a chance to apply for bail or something?"

"Ah, like I said my friend, this is not America—the French do things their own way. Before they can decide on whether or not you deserve bail, they have to build their entire case against you. That's why you need a lawyer. Once you get one, bail could be set next week, if you're lucky, or it could take months. There are guys who've been in here for three years while the system collects evidence on them and decides whether it's worth putting them on trial."

I didn't know what to say to that. I couldn't imagine three years.

A few men had started to head back towards the entrance to the prison.

"Look," John said. "Let me run in and get you a welcome kit. We can talk more this afternoon."

With that, he jogged off towards the door. I lingered outside, watching a few men playing cards, using cigarettes for poker chips. *Three years?* Could what the cops had told me before be wrong? I had a lot of work ahead of me to get my case heard. But how do you rush the system? Where do you even begin?

A bell went off and men began slowly walking back inside. Just then, John jogged back out with a shoebox under one arm.

"Welcome to Fleury. We'll have a chat a bit later and I'll see if I can help you out." Then he jogged off to talk to some other men, so I headed towards the door, the shoebox under one arm. My roomie was already back in bed when I got to the cell, so I sat down at the little table and opened my package.

In it were all the essentials I didn't even know I needed, plus a couple of luxuries. Writing paper. Envelopes. Stamps. A French-English dictionary. There was even a novel and Sony Walkman with a couple of cassettes. It was amazing how good it was to see these simple items.

I looked up from the table to see a pair of eyes trained on me from the lower bunk. He said something when he saw that he had my attention and let loose a cackle. I smiled and shrugged. This had to stop. I must remember *something* from all those grade-school French classes.

"Je m'appelle Brad."

"François."

He grinned and then rolled over to face the wall. That was enough conversation for one day.

I climbed back up to my bunk. At last I felt a sliver of hope about what lay ahead, or at least that I could put together a plan.

I closed my eyes and tried to clear my mind, a meditative technique known as *mokuso,* trying to find my equilibrium again. I decided to try a breathing exercise, inhaling deeply through the nose and holding the tension in my abdomen, then exhaling slowly from the mouth, repeating the movements over and over. It felt good.

Back out in the yard that afternoon, I made a beeline across the yard towards John. He was talking to what looked like a slim older man, perhaps fifty, with a trim grey beard.

"Brad! Glad you found me, this is Jim, the other Canadian here."

"Hey," I exclaimed. "I know you!"

"Don't think so, friend…"

"No, from yesterday, at the Palais de Justice jail. You walked by my cell wearing a tweed jacket, with elbow patches." I'd caught a glimpse of him walking by while I was waiting for my name to be called and, for some reason, he'd stuck in my mind.

"Yes," he said, bemused. "That was me."

"Jim, as well as being a fellow Canadian, is also an ex-hash importer," John said, as if introducing us at a cocktail party. "I'm sure you two have much in common," he added, leaving us with a wave.

"How long you been in here?" I asked.

"A little more than a month." He was wearing a short-sleeved dress shirt over top of dark blue canvas pants; something about him was quite distinguished. He was calm to the point of being serene, like being stuck in prison was the most natural thing in the world.

"Do you have a lawyer?" He leaned towards me as he asked the question.

"No."

"You must do that first. Nothing gets done without a lawyer. It's a terrible scam, but it is the way it is. Get one of the guards to give you a list—it will take weeks for them to get around to it if you don't ask. Or I can give you the address of mine. You will have to write to him to request a meeting."

"Ok, thanks."

We walked a little longer, watching two men yell at each other over the soccer game going on.

"I left home when I was seventeen, and have travelled and lived all around the world," he began to say, looking at me out of the corner of his eye as he spoke. "And I've learned that there are some very hard places to live. I can tell you that this place is not like anything you know, and you can't expect the same level of…reason from people that you are accustomed to. So keep yourself small and out of people's way. That is the best way to survive."

I nodded solemnly, not knowing exactly why I was nodding. But I knew he was right.

When I returned to my cell I was too jazzed up to lie down, so I stood by the window and looked outside. At least now I knew what I had to do. It was time to write some letters.

Dojo
Place to practise your path

Chapter 6

Thursday July 26, 1984

My dearest Suzanne,

I have been sitting here for two days trying to think of how to start this letter.

Even though we are no longer together, I really need your help.

I am in jail in France. I don't know yet for how long, but it could be a couple of years. You are the first person I am writing to because I feel closer to you than anyone in this whole world and right now I need to know someone cares about what will happen to me. I'm sitting here with your picture in front of me, you remember the small one from my wallet? They let me keep it and the tiny heart you gave me before I left. Everything else is gone.

I realize that I am about to ask a lot of you because I trust you. And after what I have done to you in the past, and what I have put you through, I would understand if you simply told me to piss off and dismissed me from your life forever.

But Suzanne I <u>need</u> you. Yes that's right, I need you. I am in a very desperate situation. I have sunk to the lowest level of my life. And now I need help. I will explain a few things, but the mail coming in and out of here is read.

I was approached by a man who offered me some money to carry something from South Asia to Canada. I said no the first time. But when my unemployment ran out and my dojo stopped making money and I couldn't find a job, I was backed into a corner.

After saying this I feel inside that my whole life is over. First I lost you, through no fault but my own. Then I lost my money. And now I have lost my pride and dignity. Here I sit in prison among criminals of all sorts, wishing I could turn back the hands of time to when life was simpler and you and I were so very much in love. It is only now that I realize that I still must love you. I am such a fool!

But I must keep my head about me and keep a positive attitude or I will go crazy here.

I must be careful who I tell about this. I will write my parents a letter and you can phone them. But you must not tell them why I am here. If they persist tell them I used my karate when I shouldn't have.

Be especially careful with people from my dojo. I must try to preserve my name or I will be ruined forever. You are the only person who knows this. Please keep it that way.

The letter went on for a couple of more pages asking for the many things I needed: money so I could buy food and soap and stamps; more money to hire a lawyer with; documentation to prove that all the other stamps on my passport were for karate competitions and training (and not other smuggling trips); instructions for who to talk to at the dojo so that the rent and the bank loan would be paid on time; and finally to pass on my credit card bills to my mother and ask her to pay the minimum balances until I returned, somehow explaining to her the charges from various hotels around the world.

Detour on The Path

The words spilled out of me quickly after having been pent up for so long and I felt like going on for pages and pages about everything that was on my mind. But I imagined the shock, the many shocks, Suzanne would have already had—receiving the unexpected letter with the foreign postmark, learning I was in jail, learning how much I still needed her—and decided not to overwhelm her any more than I already had. I folded the letter and put it in the envelope John had included in his welcome package. Once that was done, I just sat still for a moment. It was late, and I could hear the catcalls of the other prisoners screeching back and forth in their nightly sing-song. François was in his bed, turned to the wall, maybe asleep or maybe not. Soon it would be lights out, but I didn't have anything to occupy me until then. I sat there, listening to the night sounds for a few minutes, then climbed up to my bunk and turned to the wall.

Would she reply? Would she help? Or would she rip up the letter and say I'd gotten what I deserved? I thought of all the terrible things we'd said to each other in the fiery breakup of the eight years of our love and each insult struck me now like another nail sealing my fate. Standing at the edge of a precipice had fanned the flames of love in me, but were there still enough sparks within her to save me?

I knew Suzanne was the person I had to turn to. Certainly Mia deserved an answer as to why I was not there helping her through what she needed to do, but she was too young to take on all this, and we'd only known each other a few months. My mother would have gone to the ends of the earth to help me, and might still need to, but I was too overwhelmed with shame to break the news to her yet. And my friends at the dojo were competent and trustworthy, but I would already be asking a lot of them to keep the school running in my absence. The more I thought of Suzanne the more I missed her, the more her strength and compassion came back to me, and I knew she was the one. While our lives were on different paths now, a thread still bound us together, and I just hoped the memories of our love and what was good in us was strong enough to keep that thread from breaking.

I heard a rustling below me. François was getting up to go to the toilet. I could hear him laughing softly to himself, a snivelling, under-the-breath kind of laugh, like an abused servant who has snuck away with food scraps stolen from his master's kitchen. God knows why he was laughing. When I rolled over towards the room I found he was looking right at me.

"Comment ça va?"

"Ok."

He spoke again, rapidly, pointing at our little window and taking a couple of steps towards it, then a couple of steps back towards the beds, swaying like he was a bit drunk or trying to dance. Someone was screaming, a constant high-pitched wailing like a cat being tortured, and I guessed that François was trying to explain the sound to me. I'd heard the screams, or ones like them, every night since I'd arrived and still had no idea where they came from. I shook my head and said something in English like. "Yes, they're terrible," while François continued his pantomime. Maybe he was trying to organize an escape. Just then the lights went out and the room was pitched into blackness. I heard François lie back down below me and I turned to face the wall and continued to listen to the screaming. *Just another night in paradise.*

Friday July 27

I have decided to keep a diary while I am in here, if only to pass the time. I'm using the notepaper from John's care package for now, but I will write to Suzanne and ask her to send me a proper journal.

I was anxious to get out in the yard this morning and talk to John and Jim. They were already there together when I stepped out, standing off to one side chatting, Jim taking long drags from his hand-rolled cigarette. We began to walk, slowly, around the perimeter of the yard while the two of them explained how things worked here.

"Now to the untrained eye, such as yours," began John, "it looks like about eighty percent of the lads out here are Arabs, which is true. But they don't all fall from the same tree. Those boys over there playing cards are Tunisians, but they don't get along too well with the fellas playing footie, or soccer as you probably call it, who are mostly Algerians. Likewise, we have some Egyptians here on this side of the yard, and over across the way are the Lebanese, which is the usual distance they like to keep from each other. There are also quite a few Moroccans about, who tend to go their own way, and Turks, who are just happy to be here rather than in their own prisons back home. Then you have a smattering of Saudis, Syrians, Libyans and Jordanians who tend to glom on to whichever team seems to have the most players at the time. And of course some French-raised Arabs who tag along with whatever country their parents came from. It's a good idea around here to know who's on what team, in case you find yourself in a spot of trouble."

We'd walked about halfway around the yard in the time it took for John to explain all this, and Jim stopped to chat with a group of Asians, maybe Thais. I was happy to see that at least a couple of them spoke some English—Jim seemed to know a bit of their language as well, so the conversation jumped back and forth between the two tongues. After a minute, Jim patted his friend on the shoulder and we continued walking.

"The non-Arabs tend to stick together," Jim said. I noticed he had a habit of looking away as he spoke to you, just keeping you in his range of vision so that he was looking at you from the corner of his eye. "There's not enough of any nationality to form a large group, but there are quite a few Asians—Thais, Cambodians and Filipinos, mostly—and a clique of South Americans, some Africans, and a few unlucky Westerners like ourselves."

Just then there were some raised voices from the soccer field. A couple of players were shoving each other, shouting and flailing their arms. Within seconds one had thrown a punch, the other replied, and in almost an instant there were five or six men in the melee. Eventually the groups were pulled apart, but not before one combatant had the beginnings of a black eye and another had what looked to be a broken nose. John and Jim kept walking without even looking over. I saw guards standing at the doorway to the prison, but they were chatting amiably as if nothing had happened.

"It's the ones who don't hang out with anyone that I try and stay away from," Jim continued. "They're probably not dangerous, but you know there is a very good reason that no one talks to them."

We walked in circles like this for over an hour while the conversation ambled along, stopping our paces only long enough for Jim to pull a tobacco pouch from his pocket and roll another cigarette. Jim, who hadn't been back in Canada for over a decade, asked me if I knew this or that place; John told a story about a time he'd gotten drunk with some British rock band and ended up getting a job keeping them supplied with hash for a week while they toured Germany; I peppered them with questions about what they knew about the French legal system. Before long I was back in my cell, thinking of the next time I would be in sunshine.

Saturday July 28

If I can say one good thing about being locked up (which I can't), it gives you lots of time to write letters. A real change for me, since I always disliked writing in school, and haven't had to do it much since. Yesterday I sent off a letter to Jim's lawyer, Dominique Tricaud, asking him to represent me and meet me as soon as possible. I wanted to tell him the whole story, but I kept it short and very professional. Thank god he speaks English—it's probably better than mine. I must have reread the letter a half-dozen times to try and catch all the spelling mistakes, so I wouldn't look like another uneducated lowlife.

Today I've written to Jon Juffs and Joan at the dojo, explaining where I am and that I'm ok, and yes, I'm an idiot. They'll understand. Hopefully between them they can hold things together until I get back. I gave them all of the instructions I could think of on what they'll need to do while I'm gone. They're good people, so as long as the money holds up, things should be ok. I will owe them big, though.

The much harder letter was to my mother. That was tough. How do you tell a mother that her son is locked up in a foreign jail as a criminal? I kept the tone as positive as I could and was vague about how I got here. *Feeling fine, hope to be out of here soon. Love you.* I know she'll worry like crazy, but I'll need her help to organize things for me back home.

The mail doesn't go out until Monday, but I'll put the letters into the shabby cardboard box taped to our cell door tomorrow morning for the guards to pick up. That way the bastards can have lots of time to read and photocopy them.

François is being particularly creepy today. I guess since I've been sitting at this table in front of the window all morning, he's been standing in front of the cell door looking out through the peephole (which is covered on the outside, meaning he's looking at blackness). The freak keeps chuckling to himself every few minutes with that nauseating, wheezing laugh of his. He might be on to something, though—leaning on that steel door is about the only way to cool off in this stuffy little room.

I know Suzanne hasn't gotten my letter yet, but I keep imagining what her face will look like when she reads it. I can see her shoulders sagging, her cute little mouth dropping open. This is the worst part; I am putting the people I love through all this pain because of my stupidity. I am such an idiot. I can only hope they are big enough to forgive me.

Monday July 30

Some welcome news from Jim today.

"I found out this morning that my cellmate is being transferred," he said as we paced slowly around the yard, trying to keep from sweating in the mid-afternoon sun that bounced back at us off the asphalt track. "The powers that be have deigned to allow me to request who will replace him, and I was wondering if you might be interested."

"Yes!"

"Conditions would be rougher than what you have now—my room was only designed to hold one person, so you'd have to sleep on the floor. And the entire space is only ninety-six square feet."

"I don't mind. I slept on the floor for months when I was living in Japan." That was at the Hoitsugan, Nakayama Sensei's private dojo, where there was no heat and they just threw old mattresses on the floor for us, which we shared with the cockroaches.

"Good. I'll tell the guard. Also, I think you should join the French class I'm teaching. You'll get along better if you can understand what people are saying to you. We have a class tomorrow morning, it's twice a week for an hour. It will give you something else to think about, and it gets you more time out of your cell."

"Ok."

I'm excited about moving in with Jim, even if it means giving up a proper bed. You just feel more human if there is someone you can talk to when you feel like it, someone who knows what you're talking about when you talk about home. Hopefully it won't be very long before I'm out and back there.

Tuesday July 31

There's one letter I've been putting off a long time: Mia. I finally worked up the courage today to write, but it was very hard. By now she has had the abortion—assuming she went through with it when I didn't come home.

It turned out to be not a very long letter—there are only so many ways you can say "I'm sorry," no matter how true it is—and I don't want to scare her with stories about what it's really like in here. Just "This is what happened, and I don't know how many months I'll be in here." I tried to be simple and honest. What really made me sick was asking another person to wait for me, and to know I've disappointed them. That's worse than whatever they put me through here.

Still no mail.

Wednesday August 1

Dear Suzanne,

It has been over a week since I wrote to you and I haven't yet received your return letter. But I couldn't wait to write you again.

After the day I've had I needed to write Suzanne immediately. Finally, some progress to report.

Dominique Tricaud, the lawyer Jim had recommended for me, showed up unannounced in the afternoon. The meeting was brief, maybe about ten minutes, and was one of several he had at the prison that day, but for the first time I saw the path that would lead to my release. I was surprised to discover that my lawyer was not much older than I, a preppy, slightly effeminate man with a pageboy haircut and a well-cut suit. His English was good and he seemed to know his stuff—he was familiar with my case beyond the few details I'd included in my letter and he got right down to business.

The key to my defense is paperwork. I need to get as much documented proof as possible that I have been a good, upstanding citizen before this little brush with the law. This means proof that all the trips on my passport have been paid for by either the government or the National Karate Association. It means retrieving newspaper clippings on my previous competitive successes. It means supplying copies of my paid income tax forms for the last several years, business registration forms, insurance forms and even my resume. It means getting reference letters from prominent people who know me and making copies of all the awards I've won. And all of it needs to be couriered to Tricaud as soon as possible. There is only one person who can do all this: Suzanne.

The other thing I'll need is money. The lawyer's fee is 4000 French Francs, about $600 dollars. But if this all works and Tricaud is able to work out a deal for bail, that could be another $2000. I asked Suzanne to ask my mother to try and get this ready. But I can't hold my breath—bail is only a possibility, I might have to wait until I am put on trial, whenever that is.

I was so jazzed up from the feeling that something was finally happening that, after several pages explaining in great detail everything I needed Suzanne to pull together, I kept writing.

> *It is now just after 8 p.m. and the noise has already started, as every night after supper the inmates have nothing better to do than hang out of their windows between the bars and scream and shout threats and obscenities until after midnight. So you don't get much restful sleep. They keep you locked up in your cell twenty-one of twenty-four hours a day. You eat, sleep, shit and stink in the same room as someone else. I can't eat most of the food they give us, and you know I can eat just about anything. That's why I need money right away—to buy some good food supplements, like fruit, sugar and peanut butter.*
>
> *For the first time in my life I have just let myself go. I can't work out because if I do I'll stink for the whole week. You see, we are only allowed one shower a week, and that is our treat on Saturday.*

There are no words to describe my thanks to you. My life is in your hands. You could let me slide right through your fingers, but I know how much you like stray creatures. At the moment that is about all I am.

I will make it up to you in the future. I promise. In the meantime don't worry about me, I am fine. Say hello to everyone and with any luck I might see you in a few months instead of years.

Saturday August 4

Moved in with Jim yesterday. We are really crammed together—there's less than three feet separating his bed from my ratty little sleeping pad, plus a toilet, sink, writing table and chair in our little cubicle. Still, it is a great improvement on living with François. The little bugger didn't even say anything when I told him I was moving out, just smiled his toothy grin and rolled over on his bunk, and I know he understood me. Now I can breathe easier, just shoot the breeze when I feel like it, actually have a conversation with someone. A lot better than lying around thinking all day.

Now I know that the wheels are in motion, that there are people outside of here working to get me out. At least now there is a reason to hope.

No mail yet.

Sunday August 5

Made a new friend today in the yard.

"Brad, this is Paul," said John, as he turned towards a skinny kid who looked about nineteen. "He's another of the Queen's wayward subjects, like me."

Paul stood out because he was one of the few men in this place taller than me. He looked about six-foot-six, but all bone and sinew, and he was probably thirty pounds lighter than I. His leanness and bleach-white skin just accentuated the intense blue fire in his eyes, which looked me up and down with a distrust that showed he expected trouble. We started the slow lope around the yard, falling into the now-familiar "getting to know you" line of questioning.

"What are you in here for?" he asked.

"Smuggling hash oil. You?"

"I was with me mate Derrick—he's the blonde one standing in the corner over there—and we'd been picking grapes for a bit of coin, but the bastards didn't want to pay us. We was broke, so we tried to hold up this guy for his wallet. The stupid bloke didn't want to give it up, so I accidentally stabbed him and now they've got us on these trumped-up charges of armed robbery."

My eyebrows shot up. "Accidentally stabbed him?"

"Yeah, I didn't mean to, but I was holding the knife in front of his chest like this, see." He pointed two of his fingers at my sternum. "And he got so excited he started jumping around. I just gave him a little poke to make him calm down, it didn't hurt him any, but when he told the cops about it he made it out like I was trying to kill him or something."

Uh huh. I decided to keep my comments to myself and changed the line of questioning. We talked for a bit about work we'd done. He'd studied some judo and was keen to hear more about the martial arts. We'd stopped to lean against the fence, next to a circle of six Arab guys sitting on the ground playing cards, while I told him the story about the time I'd competed in front of an audience of police and military officers in Cairo, when four other Arabs stepped between us and the card players.

I can still hardly believe what happened next. One of the four, without saying a word, snuck up behind one of the card players, a heavy guy with blonde, shaggy hair. Then he just kicked him in the head. His two friends quickly joined in, raining kicks and punches on the guy's head, chest and stomach as he rolled around on the ground. None of the other card players moved. The attackers were not pulling their punches either, they were hitting the guy with full force. This went on for at least twenty seconds, the four men shouting God knows what as they beat the man. Then, after a final kick, they stopped and walked away. A couple of seconds later, the card player slowly sat up, wiped his bloody nose on the back of his sleeve, and started playing cards again. No one said anything. There was blood on the guy's face and clothes, and one of his eyes started to swell shut.

I was four feet away the whole time.

"This place is fucked up," Paul said, watching the backs of the attackers move away. "I've just been in here three days and I've already seen more violence then I did in three months anywhere else I been locked up."

"How many places is that?" I was still staring at the card player, wondering what he must have done to deserve an attack like that.

"A couple, just juvenile pen back home."

Nothing like this place, I'm sure.

Thursday August 9

Today I found a brief taste of regular life during exercise period.

I was walking through the yard, shooting the breeze with John Blair about how much we missed edible food, when I noticed two guys at the far end. They were sparring, their shirts off, a lean, well-defined young man circling an older, stocky brick of a guy, both of their black bodies glistening from effort. Kickboxers. Roundhouse kicks flew within a few inches of each other's heads, and a punch thrown to the body would make a resounding smack when it connected with a sweaty abdomen. They were going at each other hard, controlled but holding little back, the older one clearly offering instruction to the younger. I nudged John and we walked towards them, stopping about ten feet away to watch.

It was good to watch combat again, to feel the old instincts come alive as I studied how these two men moved, gauging their tactics and searching for openings in their defences. I'd fought a kickboxer once before, in Japan, and had enjoyed it. When they paused to break I stepped forward, and asked in halting French if I could practise with them, mimicking a couple of shadow punches as I spoke. The younger one was eager, and his partner shrugged and nodded to his trainee. I removed my shirt and gave it to John, and the student and I began to circle one another.

The two men had been using one sock rolled up within another as gloves, the more experienced fighter giving his to me. The kid was agile and very anxious, with fast hands, and he attacked right away with a great flurry of blows; he had no knowledge of tactics, though, so it was easy to defend myself. When he punched, I would parry and step to one side, opening up his flank for a reverse punch; I could see him set up for his roundhouse kicks early enough that I could block with my arm and take him down with a foot sweep.

After a few minutes of this the older man, who was actually roughly my age, indicated we should stop, then looked at me and said, "OK, you and me" in French. He appeared pissed off that I was making his boy look bad, but he was careful and patient: he'd leave openings for me to attack, then be ready with a quick counter-attack; when he blocked he was in good position and prepared for the next blow. Although he was much smaller than I, and at a significant reach disadvantage, he wasn't afraid to stand toe-to-toe and step in to make his punches count. We were fairly evenly matched, and I knew right away that I could test him without holding anything back. He knew this too, and we were soon enjoying a rapid exchange of strikes, each of us grunting in equal parts of pain and pleasure when someone landed a solid hit. My senses, already in that heightened state of battle readiness that makes me feel most alive, were doubly alert since I was facing someone whose style of movement I didn't know well. We danced around like this for several minutes, kick-block-punch-kick-punch-block, until I finally stepped back and we both bent over to try and pull some air back in our lungs.

"I'm taking you with me next time I want to go pub hopping in the bad part of London," John said, handing me my shirt. "That was fantastic."

My sparring partner came over and shook my hand, very solemn. He only spoke French, but was able to get across that I was welcome to train with him and his protégé any time. It was only then that I noticed the regular soccer game had stopped and everyone in the yard was watching us—a group of about fifteen or twenty had gathered around, mostly Africans. Five or six immediately walked over to talk to me. In very halting English, they asked what kind of fighting technique I had used; when I said karate, several nodded their heads. Then one asked me would I teach him, and a round of "yes" and "me too" spread through his companions.

Why not? I told them to meet me there the next day during morning exercise period. I don't know how this will fly with the prison officials, but it will be good to teach again.

Saturday August 11

Today I launched my other coaching career—as an English teacher. Once again, I have Jim to thank. He has taught English abroad for many years to help fund his travels to places like Japan and South America, so when he arrived here it wasn't long before he found himself teaching a Saturday morning class to people who wanted to better themselves while they're stuck in this hole. The class has grown to more than a dozen students, so he asked me if I wouldn't mind going around and helping some of them while he taught. It's not like I have other plans! He's even managed to get his hands on a textbook and notebooks for everyone. I'll have to write Mom and tell her I'm now teaching English, she'll never believe it.

It's been raining the last couple of days and it's starting to affect my mood. Or maybe this place is starting to wear me down. There's just so little to look forward to. The highlight of the day for most people is when the mail is delivered, and that always comes around breakfast time. If there is no mail—and I haven't gotten any yet—then your hope for the rest of the day is already extinguished, and all you have is a plate of crappy dried bread and bad coffee. And the whole day to wonder why there was no mail and if some will come the next day, which it probably won't. I thought I would have at least heard something from Tricaud by now, but I have no news of any kind from the outside world.

On days like this, when the weather is bad, you don't even feel like going outside for your exercise period—but what else do you have to do?

I've started to think about trying to escape. I don't know how yet, but there has to be a way. I think about it a lot, when I'm not writing letters or talking to Jim. I think it would have to happen during exercise period, perhaps on the way in or the way out. If I could catch one of the guards not paying attention as we were walking between the yard and the cells, I could slip down a side hallway and sneak around until I found an exit, fighting off any other guards I came across if I had to. Once I'm locked up in my cell there is no way out. The floors, walls and ceilings are all made of cement, the door is thick steel and the window is covered with bars. While I'm out walking around, though, it's possible. I am keeping my eyes open for any opportunity.

Monday August 13

My new karate school seems to be taking root. This morning was our third day of classes and I now have a group of eight willing and very able students waiting for me when I step out into the yard.

To my surprise, it is turning into a great way to learn French. Almost all of my students are French speaking, so I am learning the command words I need to make the lessons go smoothly. At night, while the other prisoners are yammering away at each other through their windows, I will ask Jim how to say "faster" or "backward" or whatever I need in French, then I'll write the words down on paper and use them the next day. Before long I should have a substantial vocabulary of verbs and commands—who knows, I may soon be able to teach karate in three languages!

Most of my students are Africans, large, muscular black men who were very fit before coming here, almost without exception. The British kid, Paul, has also decided to train with us. All of them are very eager and looking for somewhere to direct the pent-up energies that build more and more within them each day. I had them strip down to our blue prison-issue pants, no shirts or shoes. The first day, I started with very basic things—a couple of the important stances, how to make a fist properly, good breathing technique—but many of them have fought before, even if they've never been trained, and they grasp much of it intuitively.

Now I am already able to give them a full, strenuous beginner's class, and try things with them that I would normally only do with more advanced students. Today we did a full thirty minutes of *kihon*, working them through basic sets of punches and kicks at high tempo, as well as *go-hun kumite* (five-step sparring) attack-and-block sequences and basic kata, all with very little rest. They ate it up, loving the chance to push their bodies, belting out their *kiais* so that their shouts rang across the yard.

For kata training, I decided to test them with some of the traditional methods I'd learned in Japan. I had them separate into pairs, making one person in each pairing sit on their partner's shoulders. Then they would have to do the kata *heian shodan*, the bottom person moving into all the deep stances, the man perched on his shoulders performing all the punches and blocks.

"*En bas!*" I shouted, pushing them to go lower in their stances. I made them repeat, repeat and repeat, going all the way through the twenty-one movements several times before the person on the top became the person on the bottom.

We practised our kata for another half hour, the partners reversing position a half dozen times, so that by the end the legs of these powerful men were shaking like twigs in the breeze.

They do not complain, but compete silently with their last drop of sweat, powered by pride and a fear of appearing weaker than their neighbour. In many ways they are dream students—motivated, able and determined not to show weakness.

When I bark out commands my students reply in their deep, growling baritones like soldiers, ringing out across the exercise yard. By now we usually have a crowd two to three deep to watch. I'm sure it can't be hurting my reputation—hopefully it will mean that any potential troublemakers will have the good sense to leave me alone.

Thursday August 16

Tricaud finally showed up today.

Even though two weeks have passed since I last saw him, it seems like very little has been done. The first thing he told me was that he only had ten minutes. We were sitting in a room with a half-dozen other men, all waiting to talk to him. He still hasn't received any of the paperwork I need from home, so he started rhyming off all the things that I needed to get; I was watching the clock out of the corner of my eye the whole time, not wanting to waste a second, but he kept talking and talking, telling me things he'd already told me the last time we'd met. Before I knew it, five minutes had passed! I needed answers.

"Do you know any more about how long I'll be in here? Once you get the paperwork, how long until we can apply for bail?"

He looked at me and smiled, a thin, humourless smile. "You are like someone with a cancer in your little finger," he began, raising his pinkie in a way I imagine he thought was dramatic. "Maybe it will be cut off clean, and the problem is cured, or maybe it will spread to your entire body." He finished with an emphatic shrug, as if these were mysteries beyond human comprehension.

What the hell did that mean? He then tried to give me a little pep talk, assuring me that things would move quickly once my documents from home arrived and he had something to present to the judge. Then, with a smile like one gives a small child told there is no more dessert, he told me he had to move on to the next person.

Later in the yard, I walked around with Jim, saying little, lost in my own thoughts. *What if Suzanne doesn't reply?* It seemed impossible, I couldn't imagine she would cut me loose that way, but why hadn't she replied? And if she didn't, who would help me then? I'd written to everyone who needed to know where I was and had yet to receive a single reply—what was taking them so long? Was someone at the prison holding my mail?

I had been taking particular pains the last few days to study the exercise yard, looking for a crack, an opening, some kind of advantage I could exploit to help gain my freedom. There was a web of cables that ran across the top of our enclosure, a good forty or fifty feet in the air, running in parallel from the top of one wall of the courtyard to the other, every five feet or so. I'd been looking at them for days now and couldn't figure out what purpose they served.

"Jim, do you have any idea what those cables are for?"

He nodded once, pulling himself away from his own thoughts. "Yes, the story I was told was that it's to prevent an escape from the air. Apparently a few years ago someone important, a big figure in organized crime, had a helicopter land in the middle of this yard during exercise period. He was expecting it, and the copter wasn't on the ground more than two seconds before he was inside and it was taking off again. It caught the guards by surprise so much that they never even fired a shot. The cables went up the next week."

"Did they ever catch the guy?"
"Don't think so."
Wow. That was a plan.

Friday August 17

I don't know what's happening to me, I really seem to be falling apart. I ran my fingers through my hair today and ended up with a clump of it in my hand; over the last week I've noticed blemishes starting to appear on my back and thighs, probably from not being able to wash properly. Thankfully, our weekly shower is tomorrow. A good thing too, since I'm really beginning to stink without having any deodorant. And my gums are beginning to hurt. Why? I don't know.

Part of it has to be the food here. Lunch today looked like something a dog puked up. Powdered potatoes mixed with bits of ham fat and some sort of plum sauce that was basically purple sugar. And three slices of dry white bread. Even that was better than last night—a disgusting pile of slimy over-boiled spinach with—guess what—powdered potatoes. They looked like what you find in a baby's diaper. And a slice of ham with bits of fat in it and…three slices of dry white bread.

If I just had a little money I could buy a few things to make life bearable: fresh fruit, jam, coffee, toothpaste, deodorant. Soap! I just lie here and think of what life would be like with these simple things and it feels like I'm on the threshold of heaven. But what's the point? Until someone sends me some money it just hurts to hope.

My body is beginning to turn to flab from lack of use. The prison karate school will help a little, but I am still locked in a cage twenty-one hours a day. And doing anything in here is useless—there's not enough room for proper training and I would just stink for the next week anyway.

I'm terrified to think of what I'll be like if I'm in here a few more months. People try and commit suicide in here almost every day—and some of them succeed. I think that might be the source of some of the worst screaming at night, prisoners trying to slit their wrists. A couple of days ago I saw the guy who was in the next cell over from me when I was with François. A nice little guy. Just twenty-one and he'd already been in jail eight times. When he came into the yard both his wrists were heavily bandaged. Not hard to figure out what happened.

Sometimes I find myself lying on the floor on my piece of foam rubber and daydreaming. I'll think of Suzanne, how nice it was to come home to each other, and to cuddle together on a cold winter night. And then I realize two hours have passed.

WHY HAS NO ONE WRITTEN TO ME?

Monday August 20

It finally arrived! Suzanne's first letter came this morning, almost four weeks after I wrote to her. It is beautiful and everything I expected when I first wrote to her—supportive, concerned, fearful, resolute and determined to help. No, it is more than I could have hoped for—she says her love and appreciation for me are still very strong, and she sent me a little photo of herself from back when we were together to keep my spirits up. All of my doubts have been put to rest. There is someone in my corner.

Besides all of the emotion, there was much good practical information in the letter. When she replied she had clearly not yet received my second letter, but already she had made concrete steps. A power of attorney form was included so that she could begin to administer my financial affairs; questions on how to keep the dojo running smoothly and what to tell the other instructors who will need to take over the teaching; even a great idea about subletting my apartment so that I don't lose that too. It gave me so much hope that I even told her to hold off sending me a few things to make life more comfortable here in case Tricaud is able to work out an arrangement for bail in the next couple of weeks. I wrote back immediately, not only answering her questions but starting to describe the stark conditions here—it is impossible to describe how a part of me is already released now that I have someone to confide in. I shall put my reply in the mailbox tomorrow morning and send it out into the world.

Now I am expecting not only letters from Suzanne, but from all the others I wrote to after first writing her. I do not understand why a month must pass for a round of communication to take place, but it seems like it must. Yes, I have now been in Fleury almost a month. How much longer it seems!

Still, there are other small reasons to be optimistic. On Saturday one of my karate students gave me some shampoo for our weekly shower and I was able to wash my hair for the first time in twenty-six days. The hairs practically jumped off my head! I have cut my hair very short, like most people here do, but being clean still makes a fantastic difference. I have also, for the first time, begun to think of my future beyond these walls and make important plans for my life. I spent much of the weekend creating a five-year plan for the dojo, expanding the school as soon as I can, then putting in gym equipment, paying everything off and saving towards a down payment that will let me purchase a bit of land and build my dream—my dojo and house combined. It seems a very long way off, but being here has started to make me focus on where my life is going and what I want from it. I guess it is being immersed in the dark side of what could happen that has spurred this new thinking, but if it puts me on the right path it will be worth it.

Zanshin
Remaining spirit, continuing alertness

Chapter 7

Friday August 24

An avalanche of mail today. Four letters—a second from Suzanne, another from her mother, and one each from my mom and my dad. Combined with the letter I got yesterday from Suzanne's sister, Sheila, it feels as if I am suddenly swimming in support. I can't begin to describe how much it means that they have all decided to stand by me. Of course they all worry, and want me to tell them more about my situation, but each in their own way said that whatever I had done wasn't important and I must work hard to get myself home as soon as possible. What a difference it makes to hear that! I feel sorry for the men here who don't have that kind of love waiting for them—some don't, and it must be a whole other level of hell to not be able to look forward to what lies beyond these walls.

I am guessing that the reason for the delay, and why all the letters came at once, is that the judge is reading my mail. Several people here warned me about that and everything I receive has already been opened. So much for rights.

I've already begun to respond to everyone. I wrote Sheila a long letter yesterday, thanking her and filling her in on some of the details on how I got here. She can handle it. She is such a sweetie, she even sent along writing paper and envelopes. Dashed off a quick note to Suzanne, just to thank her for all she's done. Tonight I'll write my parents and let them know that I am still ok. What a disappointment this must be to them. Much writing to do today, so I'll stop here.

Saturday August 25

Today the mail brought a turn in the tide. It was the letter I was dreading, the one that has given me a look at the darker side of the truth I have feared. Mia's reply.

> My darling Brad,
>
> I received your letter today and it has taken me five hours to get myself to sit down and reply. I received the postcard from India on Friday August 3. There is so much to say but I don't know what to write down.
>
> I expected you back July 26. When you didn't get in, I started to worry. By July 29, worry turned to panic. What to do, where to start, who to ask—you left me in the dark. The dark is a very lonely place. I managed to get Sue's phone number (on my own too) and rang her up Sunday night (the 29*th*). She asked me if I had heard from you and in turn told me that she had not heard anything either, and if she did, she would phone me and let me know. Well, nothing up until August 1. Wednesday night Jon Juffs phoned me to ask if I knew anything of your whereabouts. I told him I was going crazy as well. Then he said that Sue had given him a message (from you) that the school was to keep on running. Thus I would assume that Sue got a message (perhaps on your machine) from you. She also failed to inform me that you were alive! I phoned her Thursday to ask if there had been <u>any</u> word from you and she said NO!!

Two of the most important women in my life. Fighting. I would have made sure *that* never happened if I were home. Her letter was dated August 8, so she must have received my letter a week after Suzanne received hers.

> *I haven't spoken to her since. The only thing your postcard did was tell me that you were indeed alive. You cannot imagine what the past four weeks have been like for me (though I do realize it hasn't been a picnic for you either). The abortion was very difficult to go through without you (or anyone) there for me. It was on Friday July 27. I was very depressed for a very long time afterwards. I have a list a half page long of all the things that have gone wrong in the past four weeks, the worst of all happened about a week ago. I ended up in the hospital again (overnight) after some maniac tried to rape me. I managed to get away, but not before he did some damage. I have to see the doctors again in about two weeks. No one understands why I'm so upset these days—I was almost raped! And because no one knows how badly I need you. Nobody knows anything (about me or you). Only my brother knows that I'm very worried about you. He called me at work today and told me that I received a letter from you. I was so anxious to read it, yet I was scared. I <u>knew</u> it was not good news. On the way back home I had the feeling that I wouldn't see you for a long, long time. I've felt that since July 29 or 30. When I opened your letter I didn't want to read it, but forced myself. I sat on my bed and cried and cried and cried. I'm having a hard time hiding these red, swollen eyes from my parents.*

Good god! What a horrible, horrible person I am! Tears began to well up in my own eyes as I read this, and I turned towards the wall to read so that Jim couldn't see me. So she had the abortion. I felt a mix of relief and a deep, deep sadness as I read that, trying to imagine what it must have been like for her to go through that on her own. And that animal! I couldn't help but think that asshole wouldn't have gone near her if I'd been around; if I ever find out who it was he'll be learning a thing or two about what it feels like to be torn up. My poor Mia. It shatters my spirit to think of her lying in a hospital bed, terrified, wondering why there is no one there to comfort her, to protect her. I have failed her.

> *I spoke to Jon tonight (he phoned) and he is rather upset. I didn't tell him anything and I promise to you tonight that I will keep your secret to myself, I swear it on my love for you. Sue was at the club Tuesday (Jon said) and has obviously heard from you. What you wrote her I don't know, but tell me if she knows as much as I do (for fear of running into her and having her question me). I also don't know what arrangements you've asked for regarding your club. However, everyone is a little upset (again, Jon says) since Sue has asked for the cheques to be made out in her name yet says that George is to take over the club. Why George does not also take care of the finances is why everyone is upset. No one has seen your books and Jon feels like a little "rug mat" (his quote). It is all so confusing. I only hope that Sue is running things as you requested. Please don't think I'm going for her throat, I'm not. It is just that I don't have a good feeling about all this (and you know I get very strong feelings about things). <u>Don't</u> think I'm going to move in on Sue and take over. I just want you to have some faith in me and in anything I can do for you. Sue told everyone that you would be away for many months (up to a year). Sue also does not know that I speak to Jon. She doesn't like me and I don't want that to have any effect on Jon.*

More pain. More people hurt. And again, it's all my fault. The shame of all this is going to last so much longer than the time I spend here. All of this over one bad decision to smuggle some dope to help people have a good time!

Oh Brad, my dear Brad, what happened? Please tell me.

Please tell me why you went away, what did you do? You owe me that much. You can't leave me here wondering when all that is happening. Wondering why I won't see you for so long. Have you received your sentence yet? What happened? Please tell me <u>everything</u>. I beg you Brad, please! I promise you I will never tell a soul anything. You know you can trust me.

But you're so young Mia—I don't know why, but I'm just afraid you can't handle this. Your life has been so sheltered; how can I tell you I've gotten involved in smuggling and then ask you to lie about it to keep my secret? It doesn't seem fair.

I will not play games with you, I will not say one thing to you and think another. What tomorrow brings, no one knows. I cannot promise that you will be the only one in my heart a time from now, but I can tell you this: I love you Brad. I love you and only you, with all my heart and I do <u>not</u> think that it is best to forget you. I cannot forget you. My heart and soul belong to you... Please don't think that I am going to "dismiss you from my life." I could not say I love you if I could forget you like that... And don't ask my forgiveness until you've told me what you did wrong.

Sometimes late at night I phone your apartment, just to listen to your voice on the machine. I even wait for the beep before hanging up. I got some of your photos from the agency. I pull them out and talk to you. I tell you how much I miss you and how much I love you.

There were several postscripts to the letter, and they were sealed by a rose-red kiss of her full, beautiful lips. I stared at that for a long time. She also sent two pictures of herself, tall, confident and sexy, ones from a modelling shoot. I put them on a little shelf we have next to the window. It broke my heart to hear Mia's pleas ("Is there any way at all that I can phone you?") and I was grateful that she chose not to abandon me, even if I thought that was what I deserved. But what could I offer her? We'd only been together three months, and while we'd become incredibly close in that time, I didn't know when I'd be able to see her again.

I also received another letter from Suzanne today. Her spirit has started to falter. She complains of other little worries that are dragging her into depression, but I know it is me she is concerned about. She is complaining about Mia contacting her; that cannot have been easy for her to have to talk to her. And yet, she still says she loves me. It is simply amazing, after all I've done to her. Why is it that we can't live together? It is probably my selfishness. I know, deep in my bones, that if we had still been living together she would not have let me take this trip.

I continued to think of all this all afternoon, staying in from exercise period so I could be alone, wondering how I had earned the love of women such as these and yet had managed to cause both of them so much suffering. Perhaps my arrest was the universe calling me to judgment for my actions. I had a hard time arguing with the punishment—should I not suffer if others had?

To make matters worse, Tricaud has not shown up all week. Where is he? With his frustrating philosophical sermons, I have no more idea of the state of my case than I had three weeks ago. Has he received the papers I needed from Canada? Is he nearly ready to apply for bail? Has anyone sent money yet? It would make such a difference to know these things, even to send a note with an update on my case, but instead I know more about what is happening in Canada than I do here. But what can I do?

Sunday August 26

I think I may be starting to lose it for real.

Today was movie day, the one time in the week that we get treated to a bit of normal life and are allowed to watch a film. I didn't understand a lot of what was being said, as it was a French film, but it was a story about a woman who is suffering from lung cancer. She had a lover but was also still married; there was a scene partway through the movie where she is having dinner with her husband and they both become very emotional.

When the woman looked at her husband I thought of Suzanne—the actress even looked a little bit like her. When I thought of Suzanne, tears immediately began to well up, and once they began I couldn't stop them. I sat there, quietly sharing the darkness amidst rapists and murderers, with these tears streaming down my cheeks and a feeling like someone had stuck a knife in my heart and turned it. I didn't even know why, but I think it was because when a crisis came the woman realized who she really loved.

At least I hope it's that—I'd hate to think I was acquiring a taste for French films.

Monday August 27

I'm learning the value of having friends in here. For one, I've been eating much better the last few days, thanks to Jim. He's been helping out one of the little Chinese guys who works in the kitchen and serves up the food (So Ping). The poor guy's lawyer screwed him—So Ping was implicated in a heroin case and given eight years. When he launched an appeal, the court gave him another four years! And he has a pregnant wife on the outside. So Ping doesn't speak French, and very little English, so Jim has been helping him write letters to another lawyer and translating other letters for him. In return, he's been slipping us extra food—yesterday it was a whole bowl of boiled chicken, and another of mixed vegetables (vegetables!). Today at lunch it was an extra helping of macaroni and sauce and a big bowl of apple sauce. It certainly helps.

I've been doing a basic workout now too—nothing that will make me too sweaty, but it's better than nothing. I wait until night when it's cooler, then I do 125 push-ups, 100 leg raises and

200 sit-ups. There's a bruise the size of a pancake growing on my tailbone from doing the sit-ups on this concrete floor, but it's better than letting myself go completely.

John has loaned us a shortwave radio, and Jim and I now spend our evenings trying to find interesting stations to listen to. Most of the time it is the BBC, since London is close and the reception is strong, but other times we fiddle with the dial and pick up Voice of America or even Radio Moscow. They are really too much—it's all wall-to-wall propaganda, from both of them, but the Russians are by far the worst. If they're not talking about how evil the Americans and the West are, then they're saying how the people of Afghanistan are lining the streets to greet the Russian soldiers with open arms. Now I know just how much of a lie that is.

If we can't find anything interesting to listen to I'll try and study my French, or Jim and I will just chat. It's not terribly exciting, but it's a hundred times better than being left alone with your own thoughts. It's thinking in here that gets you in trouble—thinking about home and what's waiting for you there, or what you'd be doing on a late summer night in Toronto, or anything at all that's happening outside these walls. That's a recipe for disaster.

Tuesday August 28

I'm feeling almost human this morning. I think my body is adjusting to sleeping on the concrete, so I slept almost all through the night. And just now I got back from the exercise yard and the sun is shining for once. It felt extra good, since we were allowed to take a shower this morning (no reason given)—usually we just shower on Saturdays—but the water was ice cold. I didn't mind. I had a shave afterwards and then stepped out into the sunshine. Wonderful. It really takes so little to be happy.

I think I'm in an extra good mood because as I was coming back from the yard one of the guards told me that some money had arrived for me and I could buy something from the canteen.

Thanks, Suzanne dear. I'm going to order some good soap and shampoo—I've been washing my hair with a bar of hand soap, and I think that's why my hair keeps falling out in golf-ball-sized clumps. I've also applied for a job—yes, you can actually get a nine-to-five job, working in a factory that makes car parts here inside the prison. It is considered a privilege, something you earn through good behaviour, but I want it because I can earn a little money (a dollar or two a day) to buy things from the canteen and it will give me something to do. The factory has been closed for the summer, but opens again in a couple of weeks.

One of the guys from down the hall gave us a copy of *Time* magazine yesterday and there's a story about the Canadian election, which apparently is happening a week from today. It must have been called while I was in Asia. I guess I won't be voting.

Thursday August 30

Ugh. It's the morning after the night before, and it isn't pleasant. My head feels like there is a little man inside it, using my temples as a punching bag. Yes, I'm hungover! Jim and I were up late, talking loudly and drinking beer, and my poor neglected body, unused to alcohol after so many weeks, is now rebelling against the mass invasion of it into my bloodstream.

Everyone in here is allowed a beer a day, but since they only deliver the canteen orders once a week, it all arrives at once. So Jim and I ordered six beers each and drank them all last night. The occasion was both a celebration and a wake. The good news was the fact that my money had finally arrived, and I didn't have to eat like a beggar anymore. And that first beer, even though it was as warm as bathwater, tasted pretty damn good. It only took one and a half for me to get a glow on, and before long Jim and I were both rambling on about Japan; he'd spent a year teaching English there about ten years ago, and he claims that his daughter was conceived in Tokyo. We were comparing the racism you find there with what we see here—I was arguing that Japan was far more racist than anything we saw here. At least here, I argued, people were open about the fact that they didn't like you because you belonged to such-and-such group that was in conflict with their group. In Japan, there was an unspoken prejudice towards foreigners of all kinds, especially Westerners, but it was hidden behind the façade of Japanese politeness.

"I've seen it," I said emphatically after my third beer. "When I trained, they had a special class for foreigners—you had to prove you were as good as a Japanese, and it wasn't easy. The Japanese would fight you extra hard. And god help you if they saw you with a Japanese girl; they hated that."

"Yes, I can understand," Jim mused, still composed and thoughtful despite the booze. "I always found that there was the official story in Japan—what you were supposed to think, how you were supposed to act—and then there was the truth, which could be very different. I think that's why I always found it difficult to get a straight answer from my students, because they were always saying what they felt was the 'proper' response."

Just then a voice rang through our little window, screaming something in French that I could tell involved sexual acts with monkeys. (I understood not because my French vocabulary had suddenly become very advanced, but because it was not the first time I'd heard it.) "You see," I said with a wide, warm grin. "Here at least they tell you exactly what they think of you."

The bad news that came out soon after was that Jim was leaving. He'd known it was possible for some time, but they had just given him confirmation. Why bad news? Because he was not walking to freedom, but to the operating table and a long convalescence at a prison hospital. The poor guy has a nasty case of hemorrhoids, and apparently surgery was the only way to cut them out of him. It's complicated enough that they can't do it here, but will be sending him to a facility an hour away. And it's bad enough that he could be gone as long as two months, since they want to keep an eye on him during his recovery.

Which probably means a new cellmate for me, if not a new cell—you can't expect to get away with just one person in one of these ninety-six-square-foot palaces. He leaves next week—I expect life will be a lot tougher without him here to coach me through things.

By the end of the night, after we'd polished off our half-dozen beers and were drunk enough to join in the name calling between the cells, I made the mistake of letting my mind wander back to my case. I started to get angry. What happened to that little shit Tricaud? It's been nearly two weeks since I've heard a word from him. As far as I can tell, he's been on the case for a month and nothing has happened yet. Have my papers arrived yet? Do I have a bail hearing scheduled? How long am I going to be in here? I get the feeling that things haven't progressed an inch.

Friday August 31

The little shit showed up today. And the news isn't good—he hasn't received any of the paperwork and money I need from Canada yet. I don't understand what the hold-up is—it's been twenty-nine days since I wrote to Suzanne with the list of what I needed. Even if you figure it takes a week for my letter to get to her and a week for her reply, that is still two weeks to collect everything.

So after all that waiting there wasn't much to say. Tricaud just threw up his hands and tossed his hair and told me not to worry. Ha! He asked if someone from my family, such as my mother, could come over for the trial, as that will make me look better to a judge. I don't know how I can ask that—I've already put her through so much, never mind the money she's already spent.

They put me in a holding cell after my ten minutes with Tricaud to wait for someone to escort me back to my cell, and I could hear a radio that someone was playing. Suddenly a Phil Collins song came on, sappy and familiar, and the words hit me like I'd been sucker-punched:

> *There's so much I need to say to you,*
> *So many reasons why*
> *You're the only one who really knew me at all*
> *So take a look at me now, well there's just an empty space*
> *And there's nothing left here to remind me,*
>   *just the memory of your face*
> *Now take a look at me now, 'cause there's just an empty space*
> *But to wait for you, is all I can do and that's what I've got to face.*

The words hit very close to home.

Sunday September 2

Today was a good reminder about just what kind of place this is.

I was in the yard with Rolf, a tall, loud Dutchman in his early forties, weighing in at a stout 250 pounds. or so, who John introduced me to a few weeks ago. He was the perfect antidote for my foul moods, always ready with a joke on his lips and a laugh that could shake trees, and I would look for him in the yard when I was feeling lousy. He'd been at Fleury longer than I, but from the way he acted you'd swear he thought he'd gained admission to an exclusive country club. He'd been caught with a large quantity of hash lining the doors of his car, and I always assumed from his attitude that he had a large stash of cash waiting for him when he got out.

We were standing over in one corner of the yard, loitering in a sliver of shade, when there was a commotion behind me, about fifty feet away. By now I didn't even turn around at the sound of a fight breaking out—it was so common that it had become an expected part of the landscape. There would be about thirty seconds of fury, then friends of the fighters would break it up, then the guards would show up and someone would be taken away for medical attention and someone would be taken to solitary for two weeks, the standard punishment for a fight in the yard. I kept talking, but then there was a scream and I could see that Rolf's attention had gone over to the group of people who were gathering.

"Let's see what's going on," he said, tapping me on the shoulder. We walked over slowly, moving to the back of the group of a hundred or so that had gathered in a circle around the combatants.

The fight was already over. I had to crane my neck to see who had been involved, as the loser was sprawled out on the grass. Two of his friends were standing over him, and they were frantically waving for the guards' attention. I stood up on my toes to see who it was, and only then was able to see that the body was covered in blood.

I saw Paul a few feet away. "What happened?"

"Sounds like the guy got stabbed. A fight over a watch apparently. Not sure if he stole it from the other bloke or just hadn't given it back to him yet. But he gave it to him pretty good—my mate over there says the bugger knifed him seventeen times before somebody pulled him off."

Christ.

By now the guards had shown up with a stretcher and I could get a better look at the victim. He looked to be a pale-skinned North African or something, not more than twenty-two or twenty-three; with all the blood he'd lost he was as white as a glass of milk. There was some taunting back and forth in Arabic between the friends of the two fighters and then the bell rang to tell us that exercise time was over and everyone began to disperse.

"How the hell did that guy get a knife?" I asked Rolf as we walked in.

"Who knows, he might have got someone to steal it for him from the kitchen, or he might have had a visitor smuggle it in for him. If you really want something, there's always a way."

Thank god I haven't made any enemies in here. If someone

wants to get you, they don't have anything better to do than figure out how to make it happen. I thought of one of Master Funakoshi's precepts: *Once you leave the shelter of home, there are a million enemies.*

Monday September 3

Today I was able to show my students a little bit of the value of karate.

Training has gone well these last few weeks, and it is wonderful how hard I'm able to push my protégés—they don't bat an eyelid at sets of knuckle push-ups or kicks repeated a hundred times. This morning I was pushing them to really throw themselves into their katas. Like most beginners, they don't realize that a kata is meant to prepare them for battle—that they should be imagining an opponent lunging at them when they move through their blocks and punches. I was yelling at them to *plier plus loin* (bend deeper) into their stances, to get themselves lower and more stable, when I saw an opportunity.

While our workouts still attracted a good-sized crowd, which I didn't mind, for the past week a man had appeared who had begun to test my patience. He was a huge mountain of a man, probably 350 pounds, with ripples of fat rolling down his pear-shaped body. He was an Arab of some kind, and for the entire lesson he would talk incessantly, taunting us in his language, giving a running commentary on what he saw, quite obviously speaking and gesturing at us. He would get so worked up that his bald head would sometimes be sweating almost as much as my students. I ignored him, not wanting to show that I noticed him and not being able to say anything he would understand anyway. But today, I let my frustration get the better of me and decided to do something about it.

We had been practising kata with partners on our shoulders again, and I lowered the man I was paired with and put one of my best students at the front of the class to lead the movements, allowing me to walk around on the pretense of critiquing each pupil. Our commentator was standing in the first row of onlookers, having a good laugh at something only he saw, and I strolled closer to him while observing the class. When I got to within five feet of him, I suddenly swooped in behind him and in one fluid motion bent down and thrust my head between his thighs and then stood up, lifting his shocked mass up on my shoulders. He immediately stopped talking and froze; I stormed to the head of the class as my students gaped.

"Arrete! Vous faites comme ça! Allons-y!"

With that order I launched into the beginning of *heian shodan* kata, my baggage suddenly silent. It was absolute hell bending into the deep stances, one leg suddenly wobbling to support 350 pounds of weight, but I didn't want to show weakness to my students or the critic on my shoulders. There are twenty-one movements to *heian shodan* with several stance changes, and it takes forty seconds to complete; by the time I got to the fifteenth movement my legs were burning so much that I thought I would collapse under an avalanche of fat. I kept pushing, focusing on breathing properly as I barked out the count for the students—*ichi, ni, san, shi*—but I got to the end and made sure I held the last stance for a full two seconds to show them how important it was to finish their katas properly with Zanshin (remaining spirit). Then I marched over to where I'd picked my Arab up and put him back there, not saying a word as I resumed my position at the head of the class.

I don't think I'll be seeing him again.

Tuesday September 4

It's raining. The kid who got stabbed in the yard died today.

Wednesday September 5

Today I'm all alone. Jim moved out this morning; since we didn't know when he'd be back, or if I'd still be here then, I gave him my address in Canada. We joked that the next time we saw each other it might be on Canadian soil, but of course neither of us knows what the future holds.

It's night now, and I'm writing this lying on my new bed—one of the few perks of the move. The shrieks of my neighbours are louder tonight than usual, or maybe I just have more attention to give to them. It is beyond my power of words to describe the sound of that anger and agony night after night. I couldn't tell anyone about it now anyways, as I ran out of letter paper three days ago, so there is very little to do except be with my thoughts. This is good, as it's made me become more realistic about my situation, forced me to think things through more. I've resolved to give up all thoughts of escape—that fantasy would only compound my problems.

The lights are about to be shut off, so I'll end here.

Friday September 7

A busy day today with lots of news. I've been "hired" to work at the factory here, which should bring in a little money. My first day will be Monday. There is also some news from Tricaud. It was confusing, as always, his meaning lost in a sea of metaphor and flowery words, but I think the news is good—he sent a letter that said he will be applying for bail on my behalf once he has a couple more things. Finally! With it was a copy of a letter he wrote to Suzanne asking for another reference letter and a copy of some of my awards. I can only assume that this means that he has received a package from Canada and that once he receives this additional information we will be ready to go to the judge. My fingers (and toes and everything else) are crossed.

My order for new writing paper came in today, so I will write to him and Suzanne. It would be so good to have access to a telephone! To be able to get a response from someone instantly, rather than wait two weeks for an answer every time I have a question, would almost make this place bearable. I think it's even harder on the non-Westerners, who mostly have a much stronger sense of family than us, not to be able to make phone calls or have visitors. I must learn more patience, never my best quality, if I'm going to survive in here.

I also got another letter from Mia today. She is still upset with me—I told her that what I am here for is "not that serious," but I can't bring myself to tell her what I did—and she's not happy that I've decided to let Suzanne move into my apartment. She is pure fire, my Mia, and it is hard for her to understand that she can't help me the way Suzanne can while I'm here. It sounds as if the story has got out at the modelling agency too; I hope this doesn't mean I've lost that job now, I'll need the money when I return.

The weather has taken a nasty turn these last few days, with a biting cold that feels like November blowing through the exercise yard, and even seeming to rise up through the concrete floors. The sky is low and oppressive and grey, and as the temperature drops the tempers of the inmates are rising. I am noticing more and more talk of injustice in the yard, a bubbling frustration about the conditions in which we're kept, and it's now a given there will be a fight every time we are let out. It just makes this place worse, not even being able to take pleasure in the few hours you're allowed to escape this little room, never being comfortable enough to leave your back exposed. The anger is directed at our keepers, but the only outlet is each other, so the aggression flows to the only place it can. We become our own tormentors, punishing each other beyond what even those who punish us demand, opening a vicious circle of retribution. It is awful and feels unstoppable.

Saturday September 8

It is night again, and I am alone until morning comes many hours from now. It's a terrible feeling when you come in from afternoon exercise period and that door shuts behind you—there aren't many distractions after that, just you and your thoughts and the demons of doubt. The guys in the yard have warned me about this, how it's thinking that will do you in here, but I don't see how to avoid it. I've already asked myself all the obvious questions—Why did I agree to this? Why did I pick that line at the airport? How did I let myself get in this position?—but there are always new questions, an almost daily crop of fears and worries to contend with.

Last night those thoughts got the better of me and I spent the whole night tossing and turning, all the fears that are afraid of the light of day coming out to haunt me until I was scared enough that sleep became impossible. *What happens if Tricaud can't get bail for me? How long will I be here? Months? Years?* The mind rushes out to embrace the most devastating scenarios and you're forced to wrestle with what they would mean for your life. What would I do if I lost my dojo? If I've already competed in my last tournament? While you tell yourself these things will not come to pass, that there are people who are helping you and a way out of here will be found, doubt can never be extinguished completely. It draws its energy from weakness, so I have to search my own mind for reasons for hope, just to keep doubt at bay.

I've tried to push these fears aside, but I've noticed them coming out in other ways. I was trying to write a letter to Jon at the dojo this afternoon, reassuring him that I didn't expect to be here for long, but my hands began to shake so violently that I had to lay down my pen. And this morning someone bumped against me in line on the way out to the yard, an innocent navigational accident that I wouldn't even have noticed last week, but today I had to restrain myself from drilling him with a punch that would have sent him through the wall. Why? I don't know. But I know I must fight it. If I give in to these feelings, it will be almost impossible to pull myself out of the troubles I have brought on myself.

Detour on The Path

Sunday September 9

I decided to skip afternoon exercise period today; not to hide myself, but to give me time to explore.

I've begun to discover some amazing things about my own mind. With all of this time alone, I've started to let it wander wherever it wants to go, and it's taken me into the past, to places I'd assumed were lost. It began last night when I resolved to think about the good things in my life, and before long my thoughts had slid back deep into my childhood. The first things I remembered were the times spent in the woods near our home on the edge of Newmarket. Back then the area between Yonge Street and Bathurst was one large, uninterrupted forest, alive with life and adventure. My friend Brian and I spent every possible waking moment there, summer and winter, imagining ourselves as wild Indians. We taught ourselves to trap rabbits and skin them, to follow each other's trails through the trees, and to pursue whatever whim our imaginations threw at our feet. We were nine or ten years old, and as free as the animals with whom we shared the land.

By this morning, I could remember the feeling of the moist soil I used to crawl through in the fields outside my grandparents' house, darting secretly among the slender stalks of the asparagus plants whose tall, bushy heads shielded me from sight; the smell of baking apples wafting through the house when I came in; the starched stiffness of my father's collar on Sunday. I could remember all the way back to when I was six years old, every memory as vivid as if I were running to tell the stories to my mother after I walked through the door, and remembering brought a sense of calm.

I lingered longest on the memories of my first trip to Japan. Like this trip, I was expecting something larger than life and got it.

I had dreamed of the trip since I'd started karate, and spent several years working hard to save for it. I had originally planned to stay for two years and train, but then, six months before I was to leave, I met Suzanne and fell in love and the idea wasn't quite as appealing.

I was only twenty-three, a new second dan (degree) black belt, and I'd never been anywhere so unfamiliar. I was to travel to the city of Kumamoto on the southern island of Kyushu, about 100 kilometres west of Nagaski. There were very few foreigners in this part of Japan at the time, and almost no one spoke English.

Tsuruoka Sensei had arranged for me to spend two months living in the home of Chitose Sensei, a tenth dan grandmaster who lived on the outskirts of Kumamoto, who had been his own teacher. He was one of the most respected senseis in all of Japan, the head of the Chito Ryu style, and upon achieving the rank of tenth dan the Okinawan government gave him a belt sewn with real gold silk. He taught his classes in his backyard, on a square patch of bare ground, overlooking fields of rice paddies.

Leaving the life I knew in North America to life in rural Japan was quite a shock. I spoke almost no Japanese, so most of my communication was done by pointing and hand gestures. Chitose had five daughters and a son, and fortunately one of his son-in-laws spoke fairly good English, having spent time studying in the U.S., so when he was around he could translate for me. Otherwise I lived like a regular Japanese person—I ate my meals with the family and shared a room with Chitose's son, Yasuhiro. Eating was particularly hard, since the only utensils used were chopsticks—which I wasn't very experienced with then—which became difficult when trying to down something like a fried egg.

That was easy, however, compared to the training. The first of my three daily training sessions was in the morning as the sun came up over the rice fields. Chitose Sensei, who was in his eighties by then, used very traditional Okinawan training methods, such as wearing heavy iron *geta* (heavy shoes you had to grip with your feet) for practising kicks and regular use of the *makiwara*—a slender wooden post driven into the ground, roughly one centimetre thick at the top, wrapped in a pad of rice straw bound with rope—which I would punch over a hundred times with each fist for hand conditioning. There were also weights and tools for grip strength, and regular weapons training.

I suffered a great deal in those first few weeks. Training on the rough soil made my feet so tender I could hardly walk after two weeks. Chitose's training methods were also different from what I was used to, using higher stances with more inside tension than what I'd done before, leading to the discovery of a few new muscles that made walking all that much more difficult. After every class we would brush the ground with straw brooms to level the soil again.

I trained hard, usually more than four hours a day over the three sessions, focusing on repetition, kata and practising with the *makiwara*. There was very little sparring, but when they had competitions you had to put on armour—a hard shell, chest guard and cage over your face similar to kendo—because they would compete full contact and no one pulled their punches. To score a point you had to hit them hard, and if your hands were weak you'd hurt yourself—training in the countryside and fresh air I felt a much closer connection to how karate evolved in Okinawa.

In the afternoons I would sometimes go out with Yasuhiro, who now ran his father's organization along with his brother-in-law, to teach in the small adjacent communities. Foreigners were so unusual in that part of Japan that often children would follow me around, having never seen a white person before. Often Chitose Sensei would run the classes, and I was always struck by how happy and fit he was at his age. It was very inspiring.

These retreats into my mind are an escape, but also give me strength to know there is a place I belong. Here is temporary, but sooner or later, I *will* return home.

Monday September 10

I started work at the factory today. It's hard work—after half an hour of instruction, I was on the job grinding engine parts. There are twelve of us working in our 1,500-square-foot section of the plant, and with all the heavy machinery pounding against the pieces of steel it's hard to talk to anyone. There are several armed guards patrolling the factory, watching us from above as they pace a fenced-in catwalk, but with all the work to do there is very little opportunity for trouble. My job is to pick up part of the engine, the exhaust manifold, which weighs about twenty pounds, and then run it through a belt sander. The manifold is about three feet long and eight inches wide, and comes to me with jagged metallic edges that needed to be ground off with the sander. Lifting that bulk over and over all day long is exhausting—the pieces are brought in by the skid-load, about 150 parts a day—so I think they were happy to find someone with my strength. The only safety equipment is a mask to put over my mouth and nose and a pair of work gloves. The sander generates a huge amount of dust and I was covered in it by the end of the day, little particles buried in my clothes and hair. And there is so much lifting involved that I've already worn through the gloves they gave me. The good part is that because of the dust we're allowed one extra shower a week. It's enough to make me think they may recognize that we're human.

Thursday September 13

Already I hate the job in the factory. I've been so exhausted after work the last couple of days I haven't even had the energy to write to anyone—last night I went to sleep at 8 p.m. My arms are sore and my hands are already developing calluses despite the gloves. All this for a few francs so that I have something to eat to supplement the garbage they feed us. What a racket.

I came home tonight to find that I have a new roommate. No warning, I just walked in and there he was sitting on the floor. He doesn't speak any English, but I gathered from our brief conversation in French that he is from Guadalupe. His name is

Henri. It should be good to help me practise my French, but I was getting used to the privacy. I'm so tired I didn't even bother to ask him what he was in here for. I'll ask him tomorrow; now I need to sleep.

Friday September 14

End of the work week! I'm sitting here having a beer to celebrate. It's also a bittersweet day, as today is Suzanne's birthday. I've spent most of the day thinking of her while I worked, remembering in great detail each of the past seven or eight birthdays that we'd spent together. I just finished writing her a short letter, along with a birthday card that took me several hours to create—it is written entirely in French, so that she can translate and read each word slowly, and took many consultations with my French-English dictionary. In it I tell her about the big party I am dreaming of for the day I am freed, with great food and champagne. I can only hope it comes soon.

Sabaki
Step aside, to deal with

Chapter 8

Monday September 17

I'm having trouble writing this, as my hands are still shaking and I can't stop them. Less than an hour ago, all the anger, frustration and aggression in this place ignited, blossoming into a full-scale prison riot. Prisoners were smashing windows within their cells and many guards who tried to stop them were injured, but even more terrifying was how suddenly the violence welled up—one minute it was a boring, dreary fall day, and the next this place was ablaze.

The spark was a news item on the radio that two men had committed suicide in another French prison. Tensions here have been rising for weeks over our lack of rights—the authorities maintain that inmates who are under investigation but have not yet been formally charged (like me!) do not have visiting rights, for one. Since these investigations can take months or even years, men have had family and friends turned away when they came to visit. And of course, everybody knows this place is overcrowded and the government is pinching every penny it can short of making us sleep in tents.

So when the announcement came over the radio, everyone here understood the despair of those men. And they fought back. There is not very much in our little rooms to smash, but once a few people began the spirit of anarchy took over. Windows and porcelain toilets were smashed and the rage that is in most of us found an outlet. Lunch had just finished, so food trays became weapons. For whatever reason, some of the guards tried to enter the cells to subdue people, becoming targets themselves. Guards would pour in to rescue the injured and they would be attacked. I don't know how many were hurt, but they won't be doing that again. Visiting rights for all inmates have now been suspended, as have our exercise privileges.

I was in my cell when it happened, on lunch from my shift at the factory, but even though I was safe the riot has left me shaken. What happens the next time tensions blow up? I might not be lucky enough to be locked in my cell.

The strange thing is that some of us just got good news that makes it look like we'll be here for less time than we thought. A social worker here told me yesterday that, because of the overcrowding, the French parliament just passed a law that says all foreigners who are not charged with violent crimes are to be given conditional sentences. That means my sentence would be cut in half. Plus, I'm told that they usually give you one week off per month if you behave ok. So if I'm given one year like those cops said, and I get twelve weeks off for good behaviour, then I might only have to serve four or five months, and I've already served nearly two! It still feels like a long time, but at least it's not years and years—being here that long could break me.

Even if it's only another few months, I know I won't be the same man I was when I arrived.

Wednesday September 19

I feel terrible. I've been off work since yesterday, and I'm getting sicker and sicker by the hour. It started with a throat infection and a cold, and yesterday I felt like something had sucked all the clean air out of my head. Today I woke up with an infection on my legs; my skin is peeling away and I have dark, ugly red marks all over my thighs. Then after lunch I became nauseous and began to throw up. There's no escape from it in this little room, even when you flush it down the toilet the smell hangs in the air. I don't know how I could feel any worse.

I got a letter today from my friend Malcolm in Japan, telling me all about his plans to become an art dealer and use the funds to build his own dojo. Crazy Malcolm. He also sent me a topless photo of the latest woman he is dating which, considering my circumstances, does not make me feel any better.

Friday September 21

I still haven't gone to work since Tuesday, but I am recovering. My skin is still red and blotchy but isn't peeling anymore, and I haven't thrown up for twenty-four hours, so I guess I'm getting healthy. Healthy enough to enjoy a beer—today is Henri's birthday, so we are having a little party here in our humble room. My French is good enough now that the two of us can have a simple conversation, and he's told me a little about Guadalupe, and how he expects to be in much better circumstances by this time next year. I couldn't agree more!

I'm feeling good today because Tricaud finally came around this morning. He was his usual pompous, intellectual self, but this time he brought along the package Suzanne put together. She did a fantastic job. There are reference letters from friends, family and work colleagues, newspaper clippings, my tax forms and all the other business information we need to show what a good, responsible person I usually am. Tricaud has already replied to Suzanne to ask for one or two more things, and then he says he will apply for bail for me within the next two weeks. Two weeks! I could be a free man soon.

Freedom isn't cheap, though. Tricaud said that after I receive my sentence I'll have to pay a customs fine. The fine is set at the value of the dope I was caught with, which is $17,000. If I can't pay it (and there's no way I can), they'll send me back to jail for some more time. Usually, however, Tricaud assures me that they will settle for ten percent of the amount. Even that will be a stretch, but I'll have to ask my mother for even more money. So much debt!

Sunday September 23

The prison yard is not a relaxing place. Even on a Sunday morning, trouble can appear in the time it takes you to bend down and tie your shoe.

That's what I was doing when I heard the yelling. I'd been talking with John Blair, and was bent over to fix my laces before we started to walk again, when the angry voice began to rise about thirty feet away off to my right. Lumo, a large West African man I know from the factory and whose cell is right next door to mine, had backed a little Arab guy into a corner. The Arab, whose name I did not know, had a job serving the food that we ate for lunch and dinner, and I'd seen Lumo yelling at him before that he never got enough to eat.

Lumo is a big, powerful man—he looked like he could chew rocks, with his thick, prominent jaw, and his coal-coloured biceps are monstrous. I'd seen him in the factory lift an entire engine block with one hand, while using his other to sand it with a hand grinder. He did this several times a day. The little Arab was the opposite, perhaps 5' 5" with limbs that looked like they were built from matchsticks. Lumo was angry; the Arab looked scared.

Lumo was yelling about the food again, while the lunch server was trying to tell him that he couldn't help how much food he gave him, since there was always a guard standing right next to him to punish him if he gave anyone special treatment. The big man wasn't listening, and he had the little guy backed into a corner so that there was no way past.

I was watching this when I saw Lumo reach into his pocket and pull out a four-inch blade. It was a dining utensil that had been sharpened to a keen edge by rubbing it repeatedly against concrete and now it was a smooth and viable weapon. Lumo held it about three inches from the Arab's face and yelled a little louder.

Something inside me gave way. It wasn't the Arab's fault that he couldn't give him any more food, he was just a guy like the rest of us putting in his time. And Lumo didn't need a knife to hurt this guy, he could have destroyed him with his bare hands. The little guy was shaking violently, pleading for Lumo to put the knife down, but Lumo was just yelling.

I got up and strode over. Lumo saw me coming and took a step back, surprised. I took two more steps and pushed the knife away, putting myself between the two of them. No words were said. Lumo and I locked eyes; he was confused and angry, while I was barely holding in a wave of rage that had the adrenalin coursing through me like a bull set free from his pen. I wasn't thinking, just following some ancient instinct that had taken over. One more step and this was going to get very, very serious.

We stared at each other like this, bodies tense and poised, for several seconds without either of us moving. Even though we do not share a language, our souls spoke in that moment, communicating on a level beyond words. The animal that lives within all of us had risen up in me, and Lumo could see it. It was chafing against the few remaining restraints left in my mind, the last vestiges of civilized behaviour, and one aggressive move from Lumo would let it break free. We were perched on the brink—beyond it lay a struggle of life and death.

Slowly, Lumo let his gaze fall and turned his head, muttering, until the knife was hidden again and he was taking steps back into the yard. I watched him go, shaking. Part of me was glad he had chosen the wiser path, but part of me wanted to chase him down and have it out. I wanted a fight. Truth be told, I wanted to kill. There was so much anger in me, I just wanted to have somewhere to send it.

After several seconds had passed, I walked back to John, not even turning to look at the Arab I'd saved. What had become of me? I knew some sacred barrier had been breached. When I reached John we started walking again. No words were said.

— ★ ★ ★ —

Later that afternoon, I lay in my cell and thought about what had happened. When had I changed so much? There was a sick feeling in the pit of my stomach that hadn't left since the confrontation—now I knew something about myself that I had never wanted to. I could kill. I had known for years that I had the skill to take a life, but I'd never had an answer before to that question which everyone asks of themselves eventually: could I really do it? Now I knew, and I felt like something inside of me, something vital, had died.

Part of the reason for how I acted was being in this hellhole—normally in that situation my aim would have just been to stop Lumo, to defend. Now I felt even lower than an animal; an animal, at least, will usually only kill to survive, but I had been ready to go one step further. It was a horrible, numbing realization.

My mind wandered as I lay there, playing the conflict from the morning over in my head. It was mostly a blur, since so little thinking had been involved, just reaction. Then it clicked. Japan. The closest I had ever felt to today.

It was my second time in the country. I was training at the Japan Karate Association headquarters in Tokyo, living and working out in what was essentially the Mecca of Shotokan karate. I was to stay for five months, training six days a week, two or three classes a day, except Saturdays when there was only one class. We were training at a very high level, and every morning at 7:30 I went to a class taught by the chief instructor of the JKA, Master Nakayama, at his private dojo, the Hoitsugan. By then, Nakayama was a nineth dan, the highest-ranked living figure in Shotokan karate.

Because I'd needed to work a great deal to save up money for the trip, I had not trained as much as usual in the previous few months and I'd shown up in Tokyo a few pounds overweight and not in peak aerobic condition. Very quickly I learned this was a bad mistake. I couldn't get out of the way of people who were attacking me fast enough and they were giving me a terrible beating. I was in what they called a "foreigner class" every morning at 10:30 at the JKA, where half were Japanese and half non-Asians like me. The Japanese students were relentless. They were naturally very quick, and when I tried to block or dodge I was often only able to complete half the movement before they hit me. Because we were considered very skilled, we used what I called "controlled contact"—this meant it was considered normal for a punch or a kick to hit you above the eye hard enough to cut you and swell up, but not hard enough to crack the bone. All of us had enough control that we could throw a punch that would cut your lip, but not knock your teeth out. Of course, occasionally someone's teeth would punch *through* their lip—mouthguards were not used.

This kind of punishment went on week after week and my conditioning was not catching up. I became frustrated and despondent, thinking that maybe I didn't belong at this level. I started to think about leaving early and flying home, but the ticket I'd booked was not easy to change.

One night, after I'd been there for about six weeks, I went to the public bathhouse, a *centa*. Every part of my body hurt, as it had for weeks, but I hadn't paid much attention because I was getting used to pain as a normal part of intensive training. At the time, I had a broken toe, cut lip and swollen eye, all fairly painful. At the bathhouse, one had to sit on a little stool under a showerhead, with a mirror in front of you, as part of the process of washing yourself down before going into the hot tub. I rubbed some shampoo in my hands and raised my arms to my head; when I glanced at the mirror I noticed that my forearms were completely covered in a web of black and blue bruises. I was surprised, since I hadn't bothered to look at my arms before. I began to touch the bruises, and then hit them fairly hard, but the feeling was almost the same—a sign of nerve damage.

At that very moment I decided *Fuck this!* Enough was enough. I realized that the bastards who'd been beating me couldn't hurt me any more without killing me. It was like a light switch had gone on in my heart. *Tomorrow it will be different.* From the moment I stood up I was a different man.

That next day I changed my strategy. No longer did I try to dodge, retreat or to be as quick as my opponents. My biggest advantage was my size and reach and I started to use it. When an attacker came in I stood my ground and threw my arm straight out with a jab—it didn't always work, but once in a while they'd impale themselves on my fist. I was using the tactic of *sen no sen*, or attacking the attack. I hurt a few guys that way, but I didn't care. The way they treated me started to change. They could see I had gotten mean and they were afraid. They started to treat me with respect—they still came at me hard, but no longer were they taking advantage of me.

I wasn't going to let people take advantage of me here either, or take advantage of anyone just because they could. I'd run out of patience with that.

Wednesday September 26

Things have been mercifully quiet the last few days, and I have been thinking a lot about home. The last couple of days I've received letters from my father, Mia and Suzanne; again I'm reminded of why I need to get out of this place and how much I owe the people I love.

I hadn't told my father what I had done, only where I was and that I hadn't done anything serious. But Suzanne has gotten to him—he knows why I'm here, and while I know it must bother him, he doesn't condemn me for it and talks only of me getting home safely and quickly. It is good to feel his concern, I'd never felt it like this before.

Mia also seems to have forgiven me for all I've done to her. I still feel strongly for her and her feelings for me have not flickered like I feared they might with us being apart for so long. It is almost painful to read what she writes:

> *I've been thinking very seriously for more than a month now. No one has ever made me so happy. I've never felt so comfortable with anyone else. I really want you, Brad. I love you and I really need you. All my heart is yours and no one else's. I must know whether or not you feel the same way about me. Do you feel at all for Suzanne anymore? I feel I can wait for you if I know that you really want me.*

I have no idea how to answer her question. My feelings for Suzanne are so complicated, so tied up in our troubled but deeply shared past and our uncertain future, that I don't know how to separate my feelings for the two of them. Mia deserves an honest reply, but what is honest? The future is so hard to imagine now that I don't know what to think.

Suzanne is a rock. She has put my affairs in order, is monitoring how things are running at the dojo and is even taking care of slowly paying down my debts with any available funds from the school. There are many to pay—$400 for my accountant, another $400 for Cliff (Sue's stepfather, who did some work for me), more for the plumber and the furniture store. I will be broke whenever I get out of this place. And all the while her letters are full of nothing but love and hope. It is a mystery how I deserve it.

My last order for stamps was refused because I did not have enough money in my canteen account, so I am using my last two stamps to reply to Mia and Suzanne. After that, no more letters for a week until my next order goes through, assuming my money has arrived. It will be hard not to be able to "talk" to anyone from outside, since that's what I feel like I'm doing when I write, but I am so exhausted after working in the factory these days that I'm sure the time will fly by. The four or five dollars a day I earn hardly seem worth it for this grueling work, but it passes the time.

It is cold now, which only makes things harder, especially since the heat hasn't been turned on yet. Since I don't have any warm-weather clothing, I've had to borrow a couple of sweaters and pairs of heavy socks from a friend, and John has given me a coat so that I don't freeze at night. I can feel the cold of the sheet-metal bed frame through the thin foam rubber mattress, and we're lucky if they change the sheets once a month. It's amazing I'm not sick all the time.

I've been here for two months now.

Sunday September 30

There's a new face in the prison who's been entertaining me during exercise period the last few days. At first I thought he was just some joker, but now that I've spent some time with him I think he's one of the most amazing people I've ever met.

His name is Ivan. He's an older gentleman, probably in his mid-sixties, bent over and shuffling through the yard with the help of a cane, which is probably why I didn't take him seriously at first. He is originally from Transylvania, and has the strong jawline and thick, gray beard of a Slav. A very well-spoken man. When we first met, we did the usual round of questions—How long are you in for? What did you do?—and he answered that he'd been apprehended for pulling off one of the largest bank heists in the history of France. I looked at him and inwardly rolled my eyes, but as the stories began to flow over the next hours and days, I not only believed him but started to think that wasn't even the most impressive thing he'd ever done.

In his prime, he sounded like a modern-day Indiana Jones.

He actually carried a bull whip around with him. Never a gun, because he didn't want to really hurt people, he just needed to incapacitate them for a little while sometimes. He had been a criminal for most of his life, specializing in jewel smuggling. He would hide jewels in the most outlandish places to get across borders, embedded in food or tucked neatly inside pieces of equipment, and get away with it, since this was mostly in the '50s and '60s and before computerized security checks. And he did it all over the world—diamonds from South Africa, rubies from god-knows-where in Africa, the jungles of Asia, you name it.

Not only that, but he spent so much time in these places that he learned the languages. He speaks near-perfect English with me, then I'll see him wander off and strike up a conversation in Arabic with a North African, then prattle on with one of the guards in French. Apparently he speaks Vietnamese as well. He'd been a member of the Foreign Legion when he was young, and picked up a couple of languages there while fighting with distinction in Vietnam and a few other places. Claims to have been raised by an uncle in Kenya too. Africa was a favourite place of his, both to work and relax, and he'd pulled off many of his heists there where security was more lax. He told one story yesterday about the time he'd tried to hike across the border from South Africa to Mozambique, hacking his way through the bush with a machete to get around the border checkpoint and the guards, when one of the guards had seen or heard him and started shooting. Instead of running, he snuck back through the bush, disarmed the guard with his bull whip, and then left! It seems like too much to believe; his stories are fantastic, but he is not trying to impress you when he tells them. It's more like he's reliving the good times.

He actually got away with that bank robbery in France—he hasn't told me yet how he did it or how much money he got—and afterwards he decided to retire from his life of crime and bought a little restaurant in Portugal and ran that for a while, raking in $1 million in profits. But he got bored and sold it and went back to smuggling. This was when he was almost sixty! He was still being quite successful at it, but got scooped up by the cops when his ex-partner in the bank heist got drunk in a bar and started bragging to the wrong person. They scooped him up, and he squealed on Ivan to save his own skin.

Everyone knows Ivan will die in this place. Once the cops discovered who he was they charged him with more than enough to make sure of that. He knows it, but it doesn't seem to bother him—he seems comfortable here, telling his stories, having a laugh when he can with whoever happens to be there. He doesn't have any family, so there's no one to miss him and no one to miss. Even more than that, I think he knows he's lived the life of ten men and there's a price to be paid for that. But it's a price quite a few people would pay.

Tuesday October 2

Since meeting Ivan, I've started to wonder about some of the other people in here. I've been so focused on keeping my head down and staying out of trouble that I hadn't thought to investigate who were the more dangerous people I'm being held with, but during exercise period this morning I asked John what he knew. Smelling an opportunity to tell some good stories, he pointed across the yard to a group of men playing handball against the wall.

"You see that guy, the older one, who keeps winning?" John began, motioning towards a short, very muscular Italian-looking guy in his early fifties. "The reason he beats fellows half his age is that he's one of the most fearless men you'll ever meet. He's part of the Corsican mafia and they had him assassinate a man who was already in prison. The poor bloke must have known something they wanted to make sure no one heard. Our fearless friend disguises himself as a police officer and strolls into the jail by saying he needs to interview this prisoner. The guards bring him into the interview room, shut the door and leave the two of them there. The man you see there pulls out a gun, shoots the other bloke between the eyes, calmly puts the gun down on the table and waits for the guards to arrive. They appear and he's just sitting there like he's waiting for a bus. I suppose he had an agreement with the mafia that they'd care for his family and such for as long as it takes for him to get out."

I gave a low whistle. He was a handsome guy, with a stern face and dark eyes, thick wavy hair and built like a fire hydrant, but more than that he gave off the unmistakable air of someone you know you should not screw around with. It was impossible to miss his strength and confidence, but I'd never equated those qualities with a killer before.

John was clearly enjoying his role of opening my eyes. "You see that other bloke about twenty metres ahead of us on the track? Young guy? You want to know what he did?" He didn't wait for me to answer. "He had a torture chamber in his basement. He'd kidnap a woman, chain her to the wall and then torture her for a while before butchering her. Did it to a few women. Apparently the sicko went so far as to carve the vagina out of one of them."

I was flabbergasted. That guy? He was a skinny little bugger you wouldn't look twice at, round face, dark hair, no real defining features. I was sure he wasn't even thirty. More than anything I couldn't believe he was just walking around—I'm sure that in North America a mental case like that couldn't just wander around openly, even in prison; people would sort him out.

The whole thing made me feel ill. "Ok, enough of story time. Let's talk about something else." I was sorry I'd asked.

I'm still disgusted that I'm here with this kind of lowlife scum. It's made me want to get out even more, if that's possible. I'm tired today and the weather is getting very cold, and I still wonder how I could have been so stupid as to get myself into trouble like this. The whole day has left me depressed and angry. To make things worse, there's some Arab in the cell above me who's been chattering like a hyena the last three nights, yelling at his friends and shouting curses at god-knows-who until well after midnight. It's 8 p.m. now and I hear him starting up again for the night, and I know I won't be able to rest until he shuts up. Shit, I really hate this place!

Thursday October 4

I'm off work today because of a nasty accident in the factory this morning. I injured the index finger of my right hand—I damn near lost part of it—so I'm writing this with my pen pinched between my thumb and middle finger.

It was a simple thing, but so typical of all the ways they try to screw us in here. I'd picked up a new engine manifold piece, jagged and fresh out of the mould, and I was running the panel through the sander when my hand slipped—and landed on the moving belt. The sander—which usually grinds down metal edges with ease—ripped right through my glove and into the flesh of my finger, tearing off a swath of skin from the tip down to the second knuckle almost right to the bone. It's an ugly wound and it hurt like hell, and for a little while I was afraid I was going to lose part of my finger. They bandaged me up with a first-aid kit and sent me back to my cell, but they also made it clear that if I can't come back and work soon they'll give my job to somebody else—then I'll be stuck back here every day, broke and staring at the walls. It's all business! Not only are these assholes doing everything they can to make our punishment miserable, they're trying to make a buck off us! Which is pretty easy when you don't have to worry about pesky labour laws.

At least I'm not the only one angry. The rage here is approaching a boiling point again and today there was nearly another riot for the third day in a row. It all started a couple of days ago. There is a woman's wing at the opposite end of the prison (we are kept completely separate; I've never seen any of them) and on Tuesday the riot police went in there for some reason and kicked the shit out of them. That was just more kindling to the fire. Some prisoners started trashing their cells again, destroying whatever they can with their bare hands and screaming for hours on end, and several have been thrown into solitary. More than 500 people are on a hunger strike to get something done about the overcrowding and to get themselves the most basic rights. For one, the French do not allow conjugal visits, even after the trial, unlike many other European countries. The accumulation of abuses means this place is just ready to explode. I'm doing my best to keep my head down and not get involved, but sooner or later the flames will engulf me too.

Friday October 5

In the afternoon, the roller coaster careened off in another direction. Just before supper Tricaud arrived. His news was that he had gone to see the judge last week, only to find out that she was on vacation. Shit! How did he not know that? He did not seem worried and promised that he would go to see her immediately once she returns, so I suppose he knows what he's doing. His argument will be that it is much more damaging for me to be sitting here in prison than to be free. It's hard to disagree with that! He can say honestly that if I'm here much longer I could lose everything I have back home.

It's all too much for me to handle today. I just want to curl up and sleep until the day I'm released. Somewhere that is warmer, quieter and far more comfortable than here. The hardest part is that I still, after more than two months, have no idea when the day will come where I can take my fate in my own hands again. Until then I have to sit here, alone, and wait to find out what the next card is that fate will deal me. It could be anything.

Detour on The Path

Saturday October 6

The fire is coming closer. It came very close to burning me today.

The anger inside here has been bubbling for days and days, but now it has begun to take shape and get organized. Exercise period this afternoon began like any other, a warm, sunny fall day that broke the grip of the cold greyness that held us the past week. I was walking around talking to John and Rolf as usual when the regular announcement came over the loudspeakers that there were ten minutes left for us to return to our cells. Men usually begin to slowly file back inside when this happens, but today a dozen or so prisoners appeared at the entrance and refused to let anyone go in. There was a lot of milling around and confusion, and word spread that we were to stay outside as part of our protest. I don't know who decided this, but the prisoners blocking the entrance intended to make sure everyone participated.

As I was watching this, I saw my friend Paul, the young English kid, streak for the doors. In moments he was on top of the group, running at them at full tilt, screaming a war cry as he ran, arms swinging like two windmills. The men all turned towards him, ready to fight, when one tripped him and he went down. I could see three of the men starting to kick with big, swinging blows at his head and back. I thought he was a goner, and I was about to run over, but he popped back up like he'd landed on a diving board and started swinging at heads with his elbows, and in another second he was through the crowd and past the guards to safety.

Not a moment too soon. Seconds later twenty other men ran up and put themselves between the door and the crowd. There would be no more kamikaze breakthroughs.

The announcement came over the loudspeaker that exercise period was now over and we were to return to our cells immediately. A group of fifty or so was jostling near the entrance now, wanting to get in; two men pushed their way towards the door, shouting that they didn't want any trouble. They were promptly swarmed by a group of ten who began to punch and kick them mercilessly until the pair ran back to the crowd, one of them with blood running down his cheek from a gash under his eye. The crowd pushed forward towards the door, some of them being shoved unwillingly by those behind them, but every time they met the group of thirty they were pushed back with a flurry of fists.

I stood back about fifty feet with John and Rolf, not wanting to find myself stuck in a crowd if things really got ugly.

After a couple of minutes of this, the loudspeakers crackled to life again and people began to point at a figure in a window twenty feet above us.

"Uh oh," John said, shaking his head. "That's the prison director."

"What's he saying?"

"He's saying we bloody well better get inside or they are going to bring in the CRS."

"Who's the CRS?"

"Riot police. Not very cheerful."

Oh great. A number of people were turning and looking behind us at the opposite end of the yard. There were two great steel doors built into the far wall. They extended to the full height of the enclosure and if opened were wide enough to drive a good-sized truck through. People were pointing at the doors and looking panicked, and I suddenly realized that the police were already there, standing just on the other side, waiting to be released.

The loudspeakers crackled again. "Well, things are going to get interesting now," said Rolf, looking grim. "That was our last warning."

I was stuck. I could take a beating from the men blocking the door or I could get my head used as a baseball by the truncheons of the riot police; I was in trouble either way. I edged backwards, making sure I was in an open area, and looked for some way I could squeak through to the door.

Fortunately, I didn't have to. Panic had spread rapidly through the men being kept outside, and the growing crowd began to push forward en masse. The rebels stood their ground and punched anyone who got within range of a fist, and there were many screams as blows connected, but the sheer weight of numbers finally overcame them. Two broke through to the door, then two more, then a flood. I jogged up to the back of the crowd, but by that time the fight had left the rebels and they gave up. I went back to my cell and collapsed on the bed, thankful that I'd escaped a battle I wanted no part of.

I thought that was the end of it, but an hour later I heard the director's voice crackle over the loudspeakers. The group after us was doing the same thing! Because the prison was so large, the exercise periods were done in shifts, and it was a group of about 150 inmates who lived above us out there now. A few minutes later the director's voice came on again. Then a third time. Then I heard a completely new sound.

Henri was with me. "They are opening the gates for the CRS!" We could not see the exercise yard from our cell, but the men across the hall had a clear view and everyone on that side of the prison was shouting and telling us what they saw.

We hardly needed them to. I have never been on a battlefield, but now I know what one sounds like. It is mostly screaming, terrible gut-wrenching screams of pain, punctuated with the thuds of bodies being struck with police sticks or falling hard on concrete. We could tell from the sounds and the shouts of our neighbours that the police were not holding anything back—besides being armed with truncheons, shields and full body armour, we could hear the frantic barks of police dogs and the pop and hiss of tear gas canisters. It was clear the police were hitting anything that moved, that no one was spared; the men out there were completely unarmed and didn't stand a chance.

Well, almost unarmed.

"Holy shit!" Henri said. "They have pulled out the posts from the soccer field and are ramming the police with them!"

"The goal posts?" I said incredulously. It didn't seem possible—those posts were six inches thick and eight feet high, embedded into the ground with concrete. How could anyone do that?

"Yes! They are hitting the police with them, ramming their shields."

It was a war out there. I don't know what made the men fight back so hard, but they did not give up easily. It took more than an hour for the police to finally subdue them. And the screaming did not let up. Horrible, horrible screams. There was no way that the resistance had held up that long, so the guards must have locked the prisoners inside the yard until every last one of them was beaten. It was terrifying to listen to even from the safety of our cell—there was no way to block out the relentless cries of pain. It was obvious that some of the men were being beaten quite badly, bones breaking, being shown no mercy.

How, how, how did I get into this place? And how do I get out?

Jisei
Self-control

Chapter 9

Monday October 8

After the chaos on Saturday we were locked down in our cells for the rest of the day. No one knew how long it would take for things to get back to normal, but at 10:30 Sunday morning the electronic latch on the doors clicked open and we were free to see the carnage for ourselves. It was grim. Most of the debris was gone, but the gaping holes where the goal posts had been were still there, and in several places the walls were splattered with blood.

It was a subdued group that morning, most of us speaking quietly in groups of threes and fours; no one joked or played the usual games to kill time. Most of us thought the CRS had been called in too soon and had come down too hard. I didn't say much when others complained—I knew that some men had gotten the shit kicked out of them for no good reason, but I was more worried that the injustice would make people hungry for revenge, and the CRS would be called in again, and a whole new cycle of violence would begin.

The whole situation irritated me, mostly because I was afraid and didn't want to fight the CRS. I was still angry this morning, especially since it was time to go back to the factory. When I returned to my cell at lunch, there was a letter waiting for me from Suzanne.

I tore it open, and right away began to feel sick—the bad sick that lives deep down in your gut. After being my rock of support the last months, my lifeline to the world, Suzanne was losing heart. Her fears were slowly overtaking her optimism. She'd replied after reading my last letter and almost every paragraph I'd written had struck her like an accusation. A joke I'd made about her slipping information to my father had come off like a claim that I didn't trust her; a passing comment about some trouble the guards had given me over a cute musical card she'd sent had caused her to panic and think that she'd gotten me into serious trouble.

I finally see that I've put her under more stress than I'd realized and it's starting to take its toll. I'd told her in the letter that I needed more money for the canteen, meaning that she should take money out of the dojo's business account and send it to me, but she is trying to come up with it from her own pocket. (A bad sign that probably means the account is dry.) Also, she's just started a new job, on top of everything she's putting into helping me, and it sounds like it's wearing her down too.

Far worse was a passing comment she made about all the messages on my answering machine from women she didn't know. This made me so guilty that my stomach churned like a mid-summer storm—I don't know what to say.

After thinking about it all afternoon, I've decided to apologize. For everything. For all the womanizing, all the rumours she's heard about me. I don't really know what the right words are, but I want to put them down on paper so she can hold them and have some reason to think I'm not a terrible person. I don't know if it will help either of us, but at least it's doing something. Doing anything that improves my situation feels like a small victory.

Tuesday October 9

French classes started up again today so I was able to get a few hours off work, but I'm still in a lousy mood. The food is getting even shittier and there's no doubt now that I'm getting fat—what should I expect after being locked up all day and fed this crap that has all the nutrition boiled out of it? I can't imagine what I'd look like if I was in here for a few years. Probably like a pig being fattened for slaughter.

The shower today felt like they'd pumped the water in from the Arctic. I hate this place!

Thursday October 11

I'm so exhausted today that I almost can't write. During the last couple of days there seem to be more pieces to grind than ever and I'm barely sleeping at night with this bloody Arab above me chattering almost 'til dawn. Just the sound of his voice when he first starts up makes me wince. I barely have the energy to fall into bed when I get back from work, and the shouting and insults begin almost the moment I lay down. If this was someplace sane I would have called the cops on the guy weeks ago.

Even worse, there is something wrong with my eyes. My vision is getting blurry and I can hardly read. I don't know what's causing it—the dust at work that seeps into everything or the stress—but it's making it hard to work. But I don't want to stop because I need the money.

They can't keep me in here forever, can they? The time keeps slipping by. I have to believe that with each passing day I am closer to freedom. Any other thoughts would break my spirit now.

Saturday October 13

I really don't know if I'm going to make it through this. I've never been so close to the edge in my life—this ignorant, mother-fucking Arab, when he's not screaming across the way to his buddies the next building over, he keeps playing his ugly bloody racket he calls music all through the goddamn night. I scream at him to shut up but it doesn't do any good. I'm going to hunt him down in the yard tomorrow, and if I can figure out who he is I'll shut him up for good.

My eyes are worse too. It's making it very hard to work. I'm going to try and get them checked out tomorrow.

It seems that everyone is out to get me. Yesterday, at the end of the day in the factory, we all lined up to leave the work room, and I went back to my cell to pick up my towel and soap for the shower. I was about to step back out when the guard put his hand out and stopped me.

"No shower for you, Jones."

"Why?!"

"You were talking in line. Stay in your cell."

What I hate is how they treat us like children. I was a filthy, stinking mess—my hair had so much dirt in it I couldn't get a comb through it, my arms were practically black from all the crap I'd cleaned and I smelled like a bag of shit. I had to try and wash myself in the tiny sink in our cell—where we only get cold water, and you have to push in a button with one hand to keep the water flowing while you try to clean yourself with the other. I wasn't able to really get clean until our regular weekly shower this morning. And then I couldn't sleep last night because of that ignorant fucking Arab.

I'm a wreck! My hands won't stop shaking as I write this. If I don't let off some steam soon, someone is going to get killed!

The only thing that would help would be to get some news about my case. Anything. By next week I'll have been here three months and I still have no idea what's going to happen to me. Of course, Tricaud didn't show again yesterday. He *has* to come next Friday. I hope by then he'll have gotten in touch with my *juge d'instruction*. I need some news. Now!

John Blair told me yesterday about a guy who tried to get back to his cell during the riot last weekend. Apparently he was rude and pushy about it, so the guys who started the riot cornered him in the yard the other day. When it was all over they'd stabbed his bloody eyes out! With those butter knives they buy for their lunch and then sharpen, little three-inch jack knives. Unbelievable! I'm making a special effort to stick close to Paul for the next while in case they have it in for him too.

Today is one of those days when it's impossible not to think of home. All I really want is to get back to my dojo. Dammit, I wish I knew when I could!

Monday October 15

There was a good knife fight today in the yard between some Arabs; I have to admit those pricks really know how to use a blade if someone's pissed them off. One of them got cut up pretty bad before his friends pulled the other guy off. The guards, of course, just stood around and watched—if the Arabs want to take each other out, it's less work for them.

I heard from John that the troublemakers who started the last riot got moved out over the weekend; I think they've spread them around some of the other buildings here.

No mail today.

Wednesday October 17

I'm feeling a little better because I finally got to see a doctor yesterday. I'd been off work for two days because I couldn't see properly (felt like a blind old dog who wasn't good for anything), but the doctor gave me some drops for my eyes and today they are getting back to normal. Funny how not being able to make money for them gets their attention. I must have really complained to the right person, because they finally let me see a barber too, after weeks of asking. Got it shaved right down to the scalp, so it's much easier to look after.

I've received four letters in the last two days, so I'm feeling less cut off from the world. Still, each letter keeps asking questions I don't have answers to—what's the news on my case, have I heard anything from the judge, have I found out when I'll be released? No, no and no! It's bad enough that I don't know anything, but it doesn't seem like anyone else does either. Just the same old shit.

Friday October 19

I can't fucking believe it. They screwed me again. Now I know the guards here really are just assholes.

Once again, I went back to my cell to pick up my towel and soap after work. I *really* wanted a shower, it had been days. I was turned towards the door to leave when one of the guards put his hand out to stop me.

"Jones, not today."

"*Why?*"

"For talking last week."

The door closed and I lost control. Punished twice for the same "crime"! I started kicking the door, as hard as I could, convinced I could break it down. Then I tried to do the same with our little cupboard on the wall. *It was so unfair!* I was yelling the whole time, and Lumo next door pounded on the little opening between our two cells that we can speak to each other through.

"What's the matter?"

I told him.

"Oh, those pricks!"

On top of everything else, with the French legal system against me and my incompetent lawyer, I now have to fight the idiot guards. Why? I'm not looking for a fight, I just want to keep my head down and get out of here as fast as I can. Instead, I'm left in this pit to stew in my own filth.

To make matters worse, Tricaud went AWOL again today. The bastard! It's been two weeks since he told me the judge was away on vacation and I haven't heard a word from him—how long can she be gone? Now it'll be at least another week until I get any news; the thought of it leaves me cold. Another week of questions with no answers. And nothing I can do about it. My hands are shaking again as I write, it makes me so angry. And that bloody Arab upstairs is chattering again.

My roommate Henri doesn't have any more waiting to do. He left this morning to get his judgment. It's evening now, the temperature is dropping with the light, and he hasn't come back. Maybe they let him go! I hope so—if he gets out, maybe I'll be next.

But I doubt it.

Saturday October 20

It's morning now, the earliest I've woken in weeks. Last night's anger is gone, replaced by a dull ache, like a steady drizzle following a hurricane. It's quiet, the kind of sleepy Saturday when back home I'd be enjoying a cup of coffee before heading off to the dojo for morning classes. Breakfast won't arrive for an hour or so and most people here are still sleeping; Henri is back from court and slumbering a few feet away. They heard his case late in the day yesterday, but now have to decide what to do with him. He got back in after dark last night, and expects to be told his fate very soon.

I'm sitting at our tiny desk waiting for the day to come. Outside, a dull, heavy sky looks as if it has given up fending off winter. The sun has only been able to just light the backs of the clouds with a warmthless glow, surrounded by the leaden grey sheath of the sky. It's raining lightly in that way that you know you'll be listening to for the rest of the day. Looking out beyond the concrete walls and steel bars, a nuclear winter couldn't look much worse.

I've got my daytimer open in front of me, the one they allowed me to keep when I arrived. All week I've been staring at today's entry, written months ago, and each time I do my spirit gets a little heavier. It was written with such optimism, long before any of these troubles:

October 20: World Karate Games begin in Holland.

A year ago I was at the World Karate championships, in Cairo, and the memory is one of the proudest of my career, probably of my life. When I wrote this year's reminder, I fully expected to be there again. Today I cannot imagine being any further away, being any less proud, or feeling any worse. If a year ago was the peak then this is the valley, and I can't believe the distance I've travelled in twelve months.

We were a fun-loving, wide-eyed group that landed in Egypt. There were ten of us representing Canada, from British Columbia to Newfoundland, and we knew that we were small fish in a very large ocean of talent. We'd be fighting the cream of Europe and the best of Japan and we were looking forward to seeing what that meant. Each of us was confident, having trained since childhood to be able to compete at this level, and we knew we had nothing to lose. As our coach spelled out for us on the flight over, "We're not going to win, so let's have a good time."

The event I'd won at the nationals with my partners, Kim Dunn and David Tsuruoka, was team kata, the first win for me after five years representing Ontario. We were good friends as well as teammates, having spent hundreds of hours training together and honing our bodies over the previous eighteen months (not to mention that my teacher was David's dad, Masami Tsuruoka, the father of Canadian karate), and each of us was excited, awestruck and nervous as hell, but the one thing we were sure of was that we knew our routine and nothing was going to throw us off. Team kata is easily dismissed by aggressive *karate-ka* in the fighting events, but it is a technically excruciating event—perfecting one's own technique so that every movement exudes crisp, graceful motion is only half of what's needed; this technical perfection must also be done in perfect synchronicity with your two partners. Done well, the movements acquire a beauty and flow far greater than the sum of the individual efforts, and demonstrate what a well-trained fighting trio can execute.

The championships were taking place inside a police and military training centre—most of the audiences were Egyptian soldiers. During the opening ceremonies, the soldiers who trained at the base put on a display that left our jaws hanging. The ceremony was outside in brilliant sunshine, and as we sat looking around with mild curiosity at the strange surroundings, hundreds of men dressed in bright orange belts and snow-white karate *gis* marched out in formation until they filled an entire soccer field. On cue, they began to perform a kata—probably five hundred Egyptian men in total, all straining to prove themselves to us in unison. It was a beginner's kata, and if you looked closely you could see that their timing wasn't perfect and the odd small mistake slipped into their technique, but looked at as a whole, as an army of karate warriors, the sight was awe-inspiring. The Egyptian military used karate as part of its basic training (part of why they'd lobbied so hard to host the championships) and they'd been working for months to prepare for this day. They went through three katas in total, and at the end all the competitors stood and gave them a raucous ovation—their effort had been sincere and they had honoured us with their work.

A few days later, finally, the morning of our event came. We loosened up together and rehearsed the little things we had to watch for in our performance, the angle of a hand at the end of a movement, the timing of a turn. I'd done this so many times with Kim and Dave that it was more ritual than practice—a way to stay fresh and relaxed. We joked about the fragrant stench of where we were warming up, a little service tunnel in the bowels of the stadium, comparing it with the manly smell of the fire-hall bay where we often trained (and Kim worked). The trick, we knew, was how to harness the adrenalin from all the excitement in the air and transform it into focused energy—not only to find the right level, but to make sure we all hit it the same way, at the same time.

Once warm, we went out to watch the competition. In our event, there were teams from twelve countries, mostly from Europe and a couple of others from the Americas. The Japanese team was the favourite; they were so composed, had beaten such a high level of competition to get here, that I couldn't help being in awe. We watched a few of the teams ahead of us and, while the calibre of competition was excellent, we could detect little flaws in their technique that gave us heart. We could beat these guys.

Soon it was our turn to step onto the hardwood. No one expected much from a team from Canada, so there was barely a ripple from the spectators when our name was called. We came out and bowed to the five judges—one at each of the four corners of the floor, and one in the middle ahead of us—called out the name of our kata and moved into position. Our formation was something unique. Most teams performed in a pyramid, one man at the front and two behind, but we inverted the structure so that Dave and Kim, who were both much shorter than I, were in front and I watched from behind. As I moved behind them and emptied myself, I thought, *This is it, our one shot.*

Our kata was *nijushiho*, "twenty-four steps." It's a challenging kata. The movements build up like a wave, slowly rising and then crashing hard. It is furious and powerful and all over in forty seconds.

There was no signal, so we had to time our start from the moment we bowed to the judges so that we began in unison. My mind had become a blank canvas, its only function to take inventory of the body's movements and make the necessary adjustments—relax the shoulders, release tension—putting the left brain to sleep and letting the right brain take over. *Slide forward. Elbow* strike. *Pivot 180 degrees. Double punch.* I had to tune into the internal rhythm we'd developed during our thousands of repetitions, not looking at my partners but *feeling* their timing, trusting my body to know what was right. *Back stance. Sweeping backhand block. Horse stance. Elbow smash.* Even though the movements had been written into my body it was different every time, the interplay with my partners and the crowd changed with each performance.

And then it was done. We held the final movement with full intensity, capturing *zanshin*, not letting the energy disappear. Then we bowed to the judges and I gave in to the rush of elation—we'd nailed it. I knew from being there, from the flow between us, that our performance had been perfect. Kim and Dave knew it too, and we didn't need to exchange a word to tell each other. We waited patiently on the floor for each judge to give us our score.

"7.6"

"7.4"

"7.5"

"7.7"

"7.6"

Huh? We were deeply disappointed. We knew our scores would be just in the middle of the pack, but our performance had been much stronger than that. We bowed to the judges without displaying any emotion, but I knew the result was based more on Canada's lack of standing as a karate power than anything that had happened on the floor.

In the end, the medals went to the Japanese, the Italians and Belgians, but we knew we'd been as good as anyone. Our teammates had seen it too, and they congratulated us and told us what we were already thinking, that'd we'd been robbed. In the end we were ranked ninth, only one place out of the second round. It was sad, but it was a pinprick of bad feeling compared to the overwhelming pride we felt at having represented our country, and ourselves, as well as we ever had.

And now I'm here, only a few hundred miles from where the scene is being played out again, but as far away as I can imagine in every other way. *How?* How can I have lost everything in so short a time? How can I have thrown away everything important to me? How can I go from being so high, so proud, so invincible, to *this*? I can barely keep myself from sobbing, trying to understand how, when someone offered me a shovel, I dug myself a hole this deep. And how will I ever climb out?

I'm afraid, very afraid, that for the first time in my life I may have lost what I never thought I'd lose: hope. The way back to a normal life seems so long, so uncertain, that I just don't know if I'll ever be able to find it again. I don't know if I have the strength. I don't know if the best part of my life is gone forever. And I don't know how bad it can get—I think it could get much, much worse.

And I don't think I'm ready for that.

Sunday October 21

News from the outside world:

Suzanne wrote to say that DeHavilland called, letting me know they might call me back to work soon. What a pisser! If that call had come a few months ago I wouldn't be here. Now I'll probably be stuck in this cell when the call comes, and there goes my chance to work for them again. Shit!

And there was a message for me when I got back from exercise period that Malcolm, of all people, had tried to visit yesterday! I don't know why he's in France; he hadn't told me that he was leaving Japan. Maybe he was planning to surprise me—with any luck, he brought some clothes with him, my rags are really starting to fall apart. It probably doesn't matter, since he was turned away, not having arranged permission from my judge for his visit. Maybe he'll try again if he's here for a few days.

I've been sitting around thinking about Suzanne's letter for much of the day. We've become so close again that all the troubles we've had in the past now seem so unimportant. And I can tell she feels the same way. We just can't shake each other off. I can't imagine us apart, even if we end up marrying other people.

I miss her so much! All I want is the simple uncomplicated life we knew. Every night I roll over and I can almost feel her curled up next to me. Her warmth. The down of her soft skin. The fragrant smell of her hair. All I want is to fall asleep with that feeling.

That's what hardens my soul, the worst part of being here. This place is putting wrinkles on my face, but it's ageing my spirit too. I am already a different man than when I walked in here. I now have the heart of an angry tiger. It knows that I've been very close to killing a man and the thought of it didn't bother me. It sees people being beaten up or cut with a knife and sees something natural. It's entered a wilderness where only the strong survive. And it wants to live.

Wednesday October 24

The grey skies that cloud our lives

Are sure to clear

As dawn breaks the endless night.

I wrote this poem last night as I was sitting around feeling sorry for myself. I decided to call it "Endless Night." It reminds me of a universal truth I'd almost forgotten—that nothing lasts forever. The bad times will eventually give way to the good. What is down will bounce back up. This too shall pass. As easy as these things are to say, it's just as easy to stop believing them. Sitting here, imagining all the things that can happen to me, I had stopped believing in this truth, but I know in my heart that it's true. I just have to believe. And turn that belief into action. As difficult as it feels, nothing is impossible. I have friends, I have something to return to, I have time on my side. Sooner or later, time will fix this. I will walk out of here. I know that.

I'm thinking a lot about John today, he's in court for an appeal of his original sentence (Five years! But he was smuggling cocaine, more serious). It makes me feel better to at least see that the system hasn't ground to a halt—even something as small as that feels like progress. It's one case closer to mine being heard!

Thursday October 25

No work today, there's some kind of national strike so there are only enough guards for "essential services," which doesn't include watching prisoners manufacture car parts for fifty cents an hour. It's a good thing; I feel myself getting sick again, being in the factory would have been miserable.

The usual morons tried to take advantage of the skeleton staff today, and there was a huge fight in the yard between the Arabs and the Chinese. Man, those guys don't screw around. You can only fight that way if you feel hate, for each other or this place or your own life. The knives came out, of course, and a lot of guys got cut up, but what was worse was that nothing seemed off-limits—full-strength kicks below the belt, eye-gouging, hair pulling, three guys on one. It was ugly. Two of the Chinese were cut up pretty bad, one of them was slashed in a long, smooth line from the corner of his mouth to the back of his ear. The guards weren't about to throw themselves in the middle of that, so they just sat back and watched until the Chinese realized they were outnumbered and things were about to get really bad, so they ran off to the other side of the yard. I just leaned against a wall near the exit with Rolf and Jim and watched, hoping that one of the Arabs who got cut was the prick who lives above me.

With all this time today, I wrote a long letter to Mia. I don't want to expose her to most of the stuff that happens in here, so it's hard to come up with a lot to say other than I miss her. I'm distracted today too; I can't stop thinking about what news Tricaud will bring tomorrow. I'm sure the judge is back by now and he's gone to talk to her. In the very least, he should be able to tell me when he'll have something to tell me. Even that would make me feel better!

Oh, and I'm out of money again. Shit!

Friday October 26

Back at work today. No Tricaud. Fuck! Fuck! Fuck!

Sunday October 28

Feeling shaky today. Spent half the night vomiting with some sort of flu. Not surprisingly, it isn't helping my mood at all. It's probably depression that's making me sick. I'm just tired of waiting. I'm going to write Suzanne, my mother, my father and anyone else I can think of and tell them to telegram Tricaud and ask what is happening with my case. Maybe he'll start to feel some pressure to do something. I don't know what else I can do.

I got a really nice letter from my dad yesterday. He told me some things he'd never told me before, including that "he missed me very much and he loved me very much and he doesn't care what I've been up to as long as I make it home safe and sound." Let me tell you, it really made me tear up. I know saying something like that must have been really hard for him. I only wish I knew how to tell him how much it meant to me.

Tuesday October 30

Tricaud finally arrived today. I almost wish he hadn't bothered. He came by at 3 p.m., dressed in his three-piece suit and French cufflinks, and nonchalantly told me that there was nothing new to report. According to him, I just have to wait. What the hell is that?

I also found out from another guy waiting for Tricaud that I am only one of fifty-four clients he is representing. That doesn't leave much time for me. And I've already paid him in advance, so there's not much reason for him to worry.

Shit! Sometimes I could just scream! How could I have been such a bloody fool! The French system isn't justice, it's business. Everywhere you turn it's money, money, money. I feel like I did when I first came here, hopeless and helpless.

The one piece of good news Tricaud had for me is that French law says if a prisoner does not receive a meeting with his *juge d'instruction* within four months he must be set free. For me that's November 25, so at least I should know something before then. He told me to write him if I hadn't heard anything by the 23rd so he can prepare to apply for my release. That still feels a long way away.

Henri moved out today, sent off to another cell without receiving any news on his sentence, so I'm alone tonight, which I think makes everything feel worse. The bastard took the French-English dictionary too. I've been told I'll be moving up to the third floor soon to live with John Blair—that would be an improvement, although it won't help my French. When that happens I'll also be allowed to change jobs and become the new cinema operator. There's no pay, but it's a hundred times better than working in that bloody factory and you get a shower every day. That's worth a lot.

I'm worried about Suzanne, her letters are more and more lonely. She says she sits around at night and reads my letters, but I wish she would go out and not wait for me. I keep telling her this, that I might be here for a long time, but I worry that she's holding out. I don't want to be responsible for bringing her life down any more than I already have.

Keiko
Consider the past

Chapter 10

Friday November 2

It's early morning, and the dawn has not yet broken. The horizon is a misty red and it looks like the birth of a beautiful day. For some reason I've been waking very early these last few mornings—probably a lack of activity catching up with me.

There has been no work yesterday or today because of a national holiday, so I've decided to spend the time writing a letter to my judge. I want her to understand how desperate my situation is, how my business and even more is at risk. I want her to feel I've already been given a just punishment. I was talking yesterday with a new Englishman who is in here, Guy, who said he finally got action on his case when his brother came down from England and screamed at their embassy staff and kicked his lawyer in the ass. I wish I had someone over here who could do a little ass-kicking.

John Blair told me yesterday that Indira Ghandi has been assassinated in India. Thank god I wasn't in the country when that happened! I can't imagine trying to go through customs with a case full of dope in those conditions. Thinking back now, I still can't believe I made it out of there—and I thank God I did. While this place is no picnic, I'm sure prison in India is a hundred times worse.

I do wish the conditions in here were a little easier, though. It may sound ridiculous, but I'd kill for a pair of running shoes so I could do some exercise. You can't do much with prison shoes—I get blisters from just walking around the yard in them. I bought a pair of running shoes about a month ago from a guy in exchange for a carton of Marlboros; they were too small. So I gave them to a Frenchman for eighty francs' worth of stamps. But he hasn't given me the stamps yet! That's almost a week's factory wages wasted. We get paid 700 francs a month (about $100 Canadian), but half of that is put aside for when we get out. It's ridiculous—I'm spending more on stamps and paper than I'm making in the factory. For what? Every night when I blow my nose the Kleenex is black from all the dust I've been breathing in.

I've been alone in the cell for three days now and, while it has its good points, it's pretty lonely. All you can do all day is sit around and think. I heard that "Desert Moon" song again and the first part still makes me cry. I can't help thinking of Suzanne every time I hear it. And wondering how long it will be until I see her again.

Sunday November 4

Time to turn up the heat.

I wrote a letter to Suzanne today asking her to write to my judge—on behalf of my five instructors and herself, my secretary (at this point, I don't think a little embellishment can hurt)—to ask for information on my case and how long I might be away. It is important, of course, because the business is going badly in my absence and she and the others are wondering if they should be looking for other jobs.

It is a desperate, shameless ploy, but I'm prepared to try anything to speed things up and get more information. I don't know what else I can do. I also suggested she get in touch with Karate Ontario and have them write a letter on my behalf. It can't hurt. At this point I am short on ideas, but desperate to find a way to get out of here. I've spent four days sitting alone in this cell, and I'm about ready to drive myself out of my mind.

Today has been hard because it is Mia's birthday. I still get long, emotional letters from her (I got one three days ago) telling me how much she loves me and how she is waiting for me to return. On one hand, I feel incredibly lucky to know I have people thinking of me and waiting for me, but on the other hand, I feel like a bastard for putting them all through this. I've been lying here thinking of her dark, elegant face and imagining her thinking of me lying here in this dank cell, and I can't picture any expression on that face that I'm proud of. I'm sorry, Mia.

Monday November 5

Back to the grind today (ha!). Life at the factory was as miserable as I remembered it, and there was an unending stream of car parts to grind down. By now it's dark when I wake up, dark when I go into the factory, and dark when I get out, so I feel like I never see the sun.

I wish it was dark enough that people couldn't see me—I've never been so fat and out of shape in my life. I hate being unfit more than almost anything, it's making me feel like shit. Hell, I only shave once a week, I must look like shit too. I know the whole thing, this place and how I live here, is killing me slowly. It feels like I've been plucked off the face of the earth, thrown in a box and forgotten.

Shit! I can't let myself get down like this. I have to find the energy to fight, even when I'm not in fighting form, or God knows how long I'll be here. I just need to get my judgment, so I know how long I have to fight for. I just hope to god I don't get some crazy long sentence. But even if I do, at least I'll know. I'll be able to sleep properly at night. I'm surprised I don't have an ulcer by now with all the lying awake at night, wondering how things will turn out, playing out all the scenarios in my head.

I hope they move me soon. It's getting pretty lonely here by myself, it's already been a week since Henri moved out. I only get to talk to someone for an hour a day—you're not supposed to talk when you're working. Writing letters helps, but it's just not the same as having someone to talk to.

Judgment. If I can get that, I can get through this.

Wednesday November 7

My spirits rose a bit with the mail today—four letters! Carol, Sheila, Elias and Trish in B.C. Carol even sent me a harmonica—now I can get my revenge on that damn Arab upstairs. When I read these letters, even the most basic things about my friends' lives, it gets me out of this place for a while, at least in spirit.

Still, the story of where I am and what I've done seems to have spread further than I'd hoped. I never wanted people to know this about me, never wanted them to think "Brad Jones, dope smuggler" when they thought of me. Now it's too late, and there's nothing I can do about it.

Friday November 9

Three more letters today—I've got lots of writing to do this weekend. Fortunately, I'll have lots of time, as they sent me home from the factory today at lunch because I don't have any proper work clothes. All of my clothes are starting to look like rags, ripped and embedded with enough dust to choke myself on, and they didn't have anything for me to wear. Now I'm not even dressed well enough to work in a prison!

I also got a new roommate yesterday. A sweet little guy from Cambodia. He looks half-starved and like he had a rough ride before he landed in here. He speaks a little French, so we talked a bit when he arrived, but he's mostly been sleeping. I think he's a refugee with some immigration problems. Typical of the French to throw him in with killers and rapists while they figure things out.

Detour on The Path

Saturday November 10

I'm thinking about firing my lawyer. I was talking to Jorge, a Venezuelan in here for smuggling cocaine, in the yard today about how Tricaud didn't seem to be able to make anything happen.

"You should try my lawyer," Jorge said with a shrug. "He's good, no bullshit you know, he just tells you what's gonna happen."

"Mine always sounds like he's giving a philosophy lecture."

"Not Kunitz, man, he doesn't waste time. He's done this for years, he knows how everything works."

Doesn't waste time. That's what I need, not these half-answers I get from Tricaud. And Jorge is not the kind of guy who takes any bullshit, and he's in much more serious trouble than I am, so if he's not complaining his guy must be alright. As we walked around, he told me how his father had gone out to find the best lawyer he could in Paris (he comes from a well-off family) and this was the guy he came up with. Seemed like a much better idea than picking someone's name off a list.

Jorge gave me Kunitz's address, so I'm going to send him a letter and see if he'll meet with me.

Monday November 12

Dull and grey today. No mail came, but new prison work clothes arrived. I hope they move me up to live with John soon. Not a lot else to write about.

Tuesday November 13

Well, I'm alone again. I got back from work at the factory and the little Cambodian was gone. God knows where. I'm so tired from work that I don't even care. I must have lifted 200 engine manifolds today. I know I should write some letters, but I just don't have the energy. What is happening to me? I never used to get tired like this. I need to get some better food from the canteen, but I'm almost out of money—it's either fresh food or stamps and paper, I can't afford both. How am I supposed to make a choice like that? I guess it'll be stamps and letters; the food is terrible, but I think I would really start to lose my mind if I couldn't communicate with the outside world. That's the only hope I have of getting out of here.

I'm so tired of this place. More and more I find it hard to be around people. Instead, I sit in here and dream about my old life. Today I was thinking back to training with Nakayama sensei in Japan. I bet if I told most people in here that I trained with the top student of the man who is called the father of modern karate (Funakoshi Sensei) they wouldn't believe me! I hardly believed it the first time.

That first trip to Japan, I eventually made my way to Tokyo after three months with Chitose Sensei. I knew I wanted to go to the JKA—the headquarters of the Japanese Karate Association—but Tokyo was so strange to me that I got lost right away. A stranger took pity on me and asked if I needed help, then walked me all the way to the door of the JKA, considerably out of his way.

I walked in, in awe to be standing at the gate of the temple of Shotokan karate. Tsuruoka sensei had given me a letter of introduction, and I gave it to the instructor who was at the desk. After reading it, I was told how much the fees were and to show up for training the next day. They asked where I was staying and I didn't know—I'd come straight to the JKA before even making plans for where to spend the night. Someone walked me outside and led me down the street to a place a couple of blocks away that had a small sign over the door which had a little JKA logo and read simply "Hoitsugan"—Nakayama's private dojo.

It was a plain building, with the dojo sunken a few feet below ground and some rooms on the floor above. I was shown one of the rooms, which were extremely basic—a mattress on the floor and some dividers between rooms. There were only three other people staying there at that time. The only rules were no girls and be ready for training at 7 a.m.

The next weeks, and again when I came back to the Hoitsugan during my second time in Japan, would be some of the most intense training of my life. Nakayama sensei taught the early morning class. The dojo was only about fifteen feet by twenty, and there were normally only six to eight people in the class, mostly foreigners. We were expected to warm ourselves up and be ready when he arrived. He usually came in wearing a cardigan over his *gi*—he was in his seventies—and when he entered we all lined up behind him as he kneeled on the floor. The classes were more technical than physically challenging, but Nakayama revealed his subtle and complete knowledge of every movement, nudging our form into line whenever it was lax.

After an hour with Nakayama we would usually grab some breakfast and then go to the 10:30 a.m. class at the headquarters, and then a third class in the evenings. Tanaka would teach a class one day, Asai another, Osaka—a world kata champion—another. These were the people who were in all the karate books I'd read, the best teachers of the day—and they were still young, most of them in their forties. There were some tough guys in those classes, from as far away as Britain, Egypt and South America, and our teachers pushed us to be sharp and hard. I never knew what to expect from one day to the next, and I would get nervous every day walking up the stairs of the JKA to class.

Nakayama always impressed me the most. He was still fit and mentally very sharp for a man of his age, but what struck me was his calm and gentle way. He was humble and never seemed to rise to anger. One day a reporter from *Fighting Arts* magazine from England had come to class to interview him (in English, which Nakayama spoke fairly well), and started telling him about a famous British martial artist, listing the several different disciplines in which this man had attained a black belt rank. Nakayama nodded as the man spoke and didn't say a word.

"Do you know this man?" the reporter finally asked.

"No," replied Nakayama. "But he must be very good. I have studied only one martial art style my whole life, and I am still not very good."

That, I thought to myself, is the mark of a true master. This from the man who founded and designed the sport of karate!

I felt better after remembering these old stories. It's so easy to forget who you are in here, and to let your better self wither away.

Wednesday November 14

Some good news! Jim got back here from his stay in the prison hospital today and they've put him back in the cell with me. How good it is to have a slice of home! He'd been gone for more than two months, but the second he opened his mouth, a little bit of the weight I'd been carrying fell away. To have something familiar given back to you—someone who talks like you, who understands where you've come from—just makes the time pass a little easier. It was all I could do not to jump up and give him a big bear hug.

It's incredible why he was away so long. The operation (for hemorrhoids, the poor bastard) happened not long after he left, and the recovery was only supposed to take a few weeks. But they lost him! Not literally, of course, but administratively they officially had no record of where he was supposed to go. So he ended up being stuck there for ten weeks, sitting in a hospital bed, when he was perfectly fine for half that time. Didn't matter what he said, or how well he was, they couldn't do anything for him until some official somewhere got the right piece of paper. Unbelievable.

I had two beers left (warm), so we drank them to celebrate while I caught him up on all the stuff that's been happening here (mostly who left, who got their sentence, any new guys to watch out for). He sat there and smiled, nodding in his serene, composed way. He looked like being in this prison cell was a lucky break he'd caught, which I suppose it was, looked at in the right way. After we'd talked for a couple of hours he said he was going to turn in—it had been three months since he'd had a drop of alcohol, so I guess it hit him harder than you would think. It's probably my imagination, but he looks like he's aged while he's been away. I wonder if he was thinking the same thing about me. I gave him back the bed, it seemed only fair, so now I'm writing for as long as I can before laying myself down on my piece of thin foam rubber on cold concrete. Just like old times.

Thursday November 15

Sometimes it amazes me how many different ways they can come up with to screw you in here.

Today I found out that it was no accident that I got Jim back. Or at least they were trying to give me something good so that I'd shut up when they screwed me over. Because they've screwed me over big time.

I asked for this damn cinema operator's job more than six weeks ago and they told me I could have it. Not only would I get a shower every day, but I wouldn't have to work in that factory every day and be so exhausted.

But they told me today that I can't have the cinema operator job because the factory won't release me. I'm too good a worker! Apparently I do the work of three men and have made myself indispensable. I can't believe that shit! It's only because I've been doing it for a while and I've gotten good at it. And they told me I can't quit because they won't give me the cinema job then either. So it looks like I'll be stuck working in this bloody factory as long as I'm in here.

I'm also starting to get bad reports about Tricaud from people in the yard. Once I started asking around, I'm finding out that everyone says the same thing about him as I do. I hope this Kunitz guy writes back soon. One of the guys I hang out with occasionally, a French guy who speaks some English, named Anois, got set free today. And one of Paul's buddies, Mick, was getting his judgment today. So things are happening. At least for some people!

I got a letter today from Mia. She has apparently been in touch with my father—he called her—and they talked for about fifteen minutes. She says he even invited her up to meet him sometime. He sounds like he's very worried about me; it's not like him to reach out to people or to get emotional.

Saturday November 17

I finally got some good news about lawyers. I can't believe how long it took.

First, I met with Tricaud yesterday. He seemed confident that something would happen soon—he reminded me that the law says that I have to have a hearing with a judge within four months of being arrested, and my four-month anniversary is only eight days away. So within eight days I'll either find out where I stand or I'll be a free man. Still, I don't really know how Tricaud is going to argue that I should be given bail. I asked him if he thought I would be released and he gave me one of his stupid non-answers that didn't tell me anything.

Then today I met with the new lawyer that Jorge recommended, Kunitz. What a breath of fresh air! When I first walked into the room where he was waiting to see me, I was immediately impressed by his appearance—he was tall and lean, probably in his mid-forties, well-dressed in a good suit, with a full head of dark hair, and a chiselled face. His dark eyes locked on me and there was a scar that ran alongside his nose to his upper lip. He looked like he'd been through some things and had come out the better for it. I couldn't help thinking of a shark.

He wasted no time with pleasantries. "So, what happened?"

I'd put the basics of my arrest and what I'd been caught with in the original letter that I'd sent, so I spent the next few minutes filling in some of the details on where I'd been, how the hashish oil had been transported and what the story of my life had been before I had made this incredibly stupid mistake. He nodded along, scribbling notes in a small steno pad, and not saying anything until it was clear that I'd said my piece. Then he looked up.

"One year, maximum."

I was flabbergasted. Finally the direct answer I'd been waiting four months to hear! I didn't have time to let the feeling set in, as Kunitz was starting to rattle off a list of forms and letters I'd need to get, so I scribbled them all down while still feeling slightly in awe. His English was near-flawless, with only a mild accent, so we whipped through the list quite quickly. This guy was on the ball, in full command of his situation. He waited patiently for me to finish copying down my to-do list, then said his fee was 7,000 francs if he wanted me to proceed.

"You're hired."

He told me where to send the paperwork he needed, then indicated that the meeting was over. The whole thing lasted less than ten minutes. I left feeling like I'd made more progress in that time than I had in the previous four months. Finally, something was happening! The first thing I did was sit down and write a letter to Tricaud telling him he was fired. The next one was a little harder, a letter to my mother asking to borrow yet another thousand dollars for Kunitz's fee. If it means I'll get to see her sooner it will have been worth every penny.

Once I started telling guys in the yard about Kunitz, several of them asked for his address so they could write to him. Seems like I'm not the only one around with lawyer problems. I also heard that Mick got his judgment yesterday and was released. Maybe I'll be next!

Brad Jones

Monday November 19

I nearly developed writer's cramp from all the letters I had to send out this weekend—six in total. They certainly had a much lighter tone than some of the ones I've sent out lately. I know nothing has really happened yet, but it *feels* like things are about to happen, and that's a big improvement over the last months. It took me so long to write them all that I stayed in yesterday and missed the weekly cinema, but I didn't care. My canteen money ran out today so I feel like I have no time to waste—the only thing worse than being in here is being in here and being broke.

I think I must be driving Jim nuts talking about all the things I'll do when I get out. I must remember that he's already had his trial and he's going to be here for a few years; he's been very patient and seems happy enough for me, but if I were him I'd probably be sick of hearing about how soon I'll be out of here. I hope I'm right.

Wednesday November 21

Every time you start getting a bit of hope here, this place knocks you back down again. Everything is just so hard. I ache all over from sleeping on the floor and I still can't get a proper night's rest anyway with all the screaming that goes on for hours.

Paul got two pieces of news today. He found out his trial date is a few weeks from now, but I guess he found out a bit too late, because he was also diagnosed with an ulcer. Poor guy. I just hope they don't send him to the hospital and lose him like they did with Jim—he could miss his trial for something like that.

Sent a letter off to Kunitz today. It's four days from my four-month anniversary, so supposedly I should either have my hearing or be set free by Sunday. *If* Tricaud knew what he was talking about. I bloody well hope so. I can't handle any more of this indefinite waiting.

Detour on The Path

Thursday November 22

Surprise! Guess who showed up today? Tricaud, of all people. He very humbly glossed over the fact that I fired him, saying, "I don't mind working with other people"—I guess he doesn't want me to ask for my fee back. It didn't matter, because I would have been ready to forgive him burning down my dojo after the next thing he said:

"You have a meeting with the judge tomorrow."

I could have kissed him. He didn't tell me much more than that, just when I'll be picked up to go to court tomorrow morning and to dress as well as I could, but I'd heard everything I needed. Finally! After 120 days of rotting in this cell, some progress. The relief was overwhelming. *Now, at least, I'll know.* That was all I'd ever wanted.

A few hours later I received a telegram from Kunitz telling me mostly the same thing that Tricaud had. I'm starting to get nervous now, thinking about what could happen. What if they decide I shouldn't be released? How long would I have to stay here until my trial? I couldn't imagine another four months, especially knowing that was just until the trial, then I could be in here for God knows how much longer. What if it's more serious than people have been telling me? What if I'm here for two or three years? Would I survive that?

I have to remain calm. Go within myself. My fate is in my hands now, at least a little bit. I can fight now.

Friday November 22

My cell door rattled open at 7 a.m.

"On y va."

I was led down the hall by a pair of guards, down some stairs and then down another hallway, until I was back where I'd first arrived in the prison. I hadn't seen this area since that first night, and now, in the light, it didn't look as menacing as it had then, just a drab, grey institutional room. Several other guards were waiting and one of them told me to put out my hands, then slapped on a pair of cuffs, hard. I was marched into the back of a waiting van with half a dozen other prisoners. None were friends of mine, though I recognized a couple of them, so I just nodded and said nothing. One of my cuffs was removed and attached to part of the van. We waited for two more inmates to arrive and then the doors were shut and the van pulled away.

There was nothing to look at except for the drawn faces of the other passengers, so I shut my eyes and focused on staying calm. There was still a voice in me saying, *What are you doing here? You don't belong with these guys.* I blocked it out—the time for denial and defensiveness was long past. I had to admit to what I'd done, it would gain me nothing to play it down or be dishonest about it, but at the same time I had to convince the judge that it was an aberration, a horrible mistake. If I could convince her that I was just a regular guy, a good guy, then I'd be Ok, but her job was to look for criminals and make sure they were locked away. I had to make her see that I was different. I had dressed as well as I could, in jeans and a T-shirt (washed thoroughly the day before in the garbage can that was my only laundry facility) and a pair of prison shoes. I'd managed to talk my way into having a shower the day before too, since I would be away all day today, so my hair was clean and combed and I'd risen early to shave. It was all I could do.

We bounced along the road for twenty minutes or more. The rough ride caused the one handcuff to chafe against my wrist, which was starting to hurt, and leave a big red welt. Finally the van stopped and the doors opened to the basement of the Palais de Justice, where I'd been taken after my first night in the police station. More guards were waiting for us, the handcuffs were re-applied, and we were escorted to another large holding cell that could keep about twenty of us. The door was shut and we all sat down to wait.

Detour on The Path

I had no idea what time my hearing was scheduled for. We'd left the prison before breakfast so my stomach was rumbling, but I did my best to ignore it. The one thing that was better than last time was that my French had improved and I could now understand much of what was being said over the PA system, so I was less worried about missing my name. It didn't seem like there was much I could do, so I just tried to relax.

It was several hours before I was finally called. My back was stiff because there was nowhere to lie down or walk around. The two guards waited for me at the door, looking bored, then led me through the catacomb of hallways and up a flight of stairs. I walked through a door and suddenly I'd left the prison system and was walking among civilians again—real people! It was a strange feeling. I couldn't help gaping at everyone who strode briskly past, the women especially, but no one paid any attention to me. They all looked so clean and formal, so purposeful, striding confidently to their destination. I almost felt like I'd stepped onto a movie set it was so strange, but so good at the same time, like I'd found my way back through the looking glass.

And then they were gone, as I was whisked through the lobby and into a hallway lined with offices. We stopped and my handcuffs were removed, and I stepped into an office with all the familiar trappings—the plush leather chairs, the wall of books, the mahogany desk, the French flag. The woman from the Canadian embassy was there and so was Kunitz, sitting back in one of the leather chairs and chatting amiably with my *juge d'instruction*, the same cool, middle-aged woman who I'd been interviewed by four months before.

Suddenly I had to fight down a wave of panic. The next several months, maybe years, of my life lay in the intentions of this woman.

No one else seemed very tense. From what I could tell, they were making small talk in French and when I entered the room the judge motioned for me to sit down in the chair in front of her, next to Kunitz.

"How are you, Mr. Jones?"

"Good, thank you."

"I'm glad to hear it." Kunitz stood up and shook my hand, saying how "glad to see me" he was. Everyone smiled and I sat down, and then the judge turned to me.

"Are we ready to begin?"

"Ok."

Then the questions began. Who was Rico? Where was he? How had I gotten involved? Who else did I know? They were all the same questions I had been asked before, and I answered them as truthfully as I was able and hoped there were no contradictions in my story. Kunitz said very little, nodding occasionally and jotting down the odd note, tapping his knee with his pen, clearly listening closely but not indicating what he thought. The tone of the interview was very polite, almost like a job interview, and the main point seemed to be to check if I'd changed my story at all, or suddenly "remembered" any new information that might help me get released. I couldn't tell what the judge thought of my answers; most of the time she was writing things down in her book, and it was impossible to tell if she was pleased or not.

This went on for several minutes, no more than ten, when she stopped writing, looked up and smiled politely.

"I think I have all I need here. Thank you for your time, Mr. Jones."

I stood up and the guard was at my elbow. I shook hands with the judge and Kunitz then walked out of the room. The guards re-applied the handcuffs and took me back the way we'd come, and in a couple of minutes I was back in the holding cell with the others.

I had no idea how it had gone. Was it good or bad that it had gone so quickly? I replayed as much as I could in my head, looking for any indication of approval or disapproval in her placid demeanor, but I couldn't find any clues. Why had Kunitz said so little? He had stayed after I'd left—what for? Why didn't anyone tell me anything?

I took a deep breath and let it out. There was nothing to do but wait. I knew that it wouldn't take long—no one else I knew who'd had their hearing had waited more than a day or two—so I just had to be patient. I was desperately tired of waiting, but what else could I do?

I sat in the holding cell for another two hours before they put us back in the van. I was back in my cell in half an hour, Jim contentedly reading a book on philosophy, a cold tray of food on the writing table. Home sweet home. I filled Jim in on the details while I ate, and he assured me it sounded like all had gone well.

I wish I knew. I wish I could be sure.

Saturday November 24

I was up at six, unable to sleep. I knew Kunitz usually did his rounds on Saturday morning, so I was hoping I wouldn't have to wait long for news.

At about 10:30 a.m. the intercom buzzed and the door to my cell swung open. I walked down the hall to the central control room to find out what they wanted.

"Ton avocat."

My lawyer wanted to see me. Thank god!

I had to stop myself from running to the meeting room. When I got there, Kunitz was waiting with a smile on his face. He offered me a seat.

"So, what happened?"

"Sometimes, Mr. Jones, miracles happen, and I think one just happened to you."

I smiled. That sounded good. "So am I being released?"

Kunitz wasn't quite ready to give away the ending when he had a good story to tell.

"Let me tell you what happened. It turns out that yesterday was the last day of work for the good judge, before she moves on to another position. You were her last case.

"After you left I started to lay out all your documentation. The tax records, the business license, the letters of support, the awards. But before I did that I opened up your comp card from the modelling agency—the one with you standing bare-chested—and put it in front of her: 'Does this guy look like a criminal?' You are lucky you are so attractive to women! After that I started to hit her with all the documents that showed what a good citizen you are but, to be honest, I think it was—" He paused, searching for the right word, clearly enjoying the moment. "My appeal to her femininity that made her decision easier." Then he laughed, the first time I'd seen him do so.

As embarrassing as it was, the photo was a smart move—it was taken when I was in peak condition, just after the world championships, and I'd never looked better.

"So it worked?" Excitement was bubbling up inside me like a volcano about to go off.

"She is going to recommend that you be released."

I found it impossible to speak. *I was going to be released.* I slid back in my chair and smiled the stupidest, happiest grin that had ever crossed my face. *Released.* A deep, contented sigh slipped out, saying how I felt better than I could with words.

"Now you'll have to make some arrangements first. You'll have to get some money sent over to pay your fines. Have it sent to me. And then there will be some paperwork. But it shouldn't take long. When they release you they'll give you a trial date which will probably be in a few months. Make sure you're here for that."

"No problem."

"I should emphasize, Mr. Jones, how lucky you are. You were her last case. If you had been passed on to her successor, that person would have wanted to interview you all over again, and the process would have started from the beginning. You are a very lucky man."

For the first time in many, many months, I felt it. Maybe my luck was finally changing. I was going back to the real world.

I went back to my cell and told Jim, who slapped me on the back and congratulated me. By mid-afternoon word had spread, and I spent most of the exercise period accepting congratulations from people. Finally, it was my turn. I wrote a short letter to my mother, explaining everything that had happened, and asked for her to send one last loan right away. *I'm coming home, Mom. I'm coming home.*

Sen no sen
Seizing the inititive earlier

Chapter 11

Sunday November 25

My dear sweet Suzanne,

By now you have spoken to my new lawyer and he has explained the deal he has arranged with the juge d'instruction for my release.

With any luck I will have already spoken to you by phone by the time you receive this letter. If I am released I have you to thank for most of it. It is my past that is saving me. I couldn't have proven any of it without all those things you put together and sent over for me.

I'm being very optimistic and saying this could be the last letter you receive from me from prison.

My four-month anniversary at Fleury Merogis has brought a fresh wind of hope that has me feeling the best I have since stepping on the plane in Toronto. Suddenly the little hardships of prison life don't bother me. The quality of the food has improved. The late-night chattering of the Arabs now sounds like the songs of birds. Every time footsteps ring out on the concrete floor outside my cell I think that this could be the man who will come to release me. I know it will take a few days, but I can hardly wait. I've even put my few possessions in order and decided who I will give them to.

I'm feeling very proud of myself for hiring Kunitz to take

over my case. Who knows how long I would be here if I were still in the hands of Tricaud! I know Kunitz will get this done.

Lost in the excitement of my meeting with the *juge d'instruction* was a letter from Suzanne in which she finally acknowledged she is seeing other people. I added a post-script to my last letter to let her know how relieved I am that she's not waiting for me. Even now, knowing it's unlikely that she'd be waiting years for a man locked behind bars, I know it is the right thing. Still, she will be the first person I call when I am released. There are so many things that I would tell only to her.

Thursday November 29

I am still here. The last several days I've been distracted and tense, waiting for someone to tap me on the shoulder and tell me I am free to go. At work it's been difficult to concentrate and I've had to be extra careful to avoid injuring myself again. The evenings, like this one, are the worst, since prisoners are always released at night, and I'm sitting here listening to footsteps in the hall wondering if they're coming to my door. I am writing fewer letters, since all I want to write is that I am no longer in prison.

I've spent a lot of time thinking about the last time I was free to walk around Paris. I was twenty-one and naïve and all I can remember of those two short days in May was how fun and carefree the time seemed. Some of the guys in here have told me where I can go for a good meal, where is a good place to stay, or where to go if I want to find a woman for the night. What a way to spend my first night in Paris! I really just keep hoping that I will be able to go home for Christmas. No one has told me anything about how long I'll have to stay in France or when my trial might be.

I got two letters from my brother Brian today. Apparently Mom called him in tears after the last letter she received (before the good news). Shit! I have so many people to make things up to when I get back. Brian will be home with the rest of the family for Christmas. What a Christmas it would be if I could join them.

Saturday December 1

Kunitz finally came to see me today. As always, I feel much better now that I've talked to him. Apparently he's just waiting for the bail money to be sent over from home—once that clears he'll ask for me to be let go immediately. He spoke with Suzanne a couple of days ago and the money will arrive shortly. Seven thousand francs. I will be digging myself out of this financial hole for a long time. At this point I don't care how much it costs, I just want to get the hell out of here. It should happen this week.

Yesterday, a woman from the Canadian embassy came to visit. She had come to tell me about a prisoner exchange that is being organized between Canada and France.

According to her, there are nine Canadians currently in prison in France—seven of us here at Fleury Merogis—and nine Frenchman in prison in Canada.

I listened politely to what she had to say, but I had a hard time paying attention. She was in her early thirties and dressed well in a fairly conservative long skirt, with heavy glasses and long, black hair, and while she wasn't really my type, she was also the first woman I had spoken to at length in more than four months. I asked her every question I could think of. I could hear other prisoners yelling crude remarks at her as she left, but it didn't seem to bother her. I did learn that the prison conditions in Canada were, not surprisingly, far better. At home I could have studied some university courses and the food is more humane. Sentences for dope are also about half of what they are in France. I'll have to remember to be more careful about where I'm caught! I don't think anything will happen in time to help me, but Jim really wants to get transferred. He's only seven months into his four-year sentence, so going home could make a big difference to him and could even lead to him serving less time.

She also mentioned that the prison director had told her that Fleury Merogis was designed for 4,000 prisoners and it now has 5,300. And they wonder why people riot.

Wednesday December 5

I've done little but work and think the last several days. I'm trying very hard to keep my spirits up, but it's difficult because my mind is outside these walls. Today, the engine parts felt like I was lifting an entire car and all week I've only been able to work at half my normal rate. I'm sure it's my lack of training—I can't wait to start getting myself back in shape.

The mood in here has taken on an edge in recent days and it was very tense in the yard this morning. The North Africans were chattering like frozen hyenas; most of the poor bastards have never felt cold like this and it's only going to get worse for them. There was a lot of taunting back and forth and a bit of shoving, but nothing really serious. I just keep my head down and stay out of their way, and keep hoping that by tomorrow I'll be gone. Tomorrow. Tomorrow. Tomorrow.

Paul and his accomplice Steve were supposed to have their trial yesterday, but Steve's lawyer didn't show up. His lawyer is Tricaud. This is also making me nervous. Their trial has been rescheduled for next week.

The last few nights I've found myself reciting "Endless Night" in my head to lull myself to sleep. I say it over and over, like a monk saying the rosary before bed. I don't know why I've started saying it now, but I feel peaceful when I do. One of the first things I will do when I get home is have it engraved on a plaque and put it up in my dojo. Perhaps at least my students will learn something from my mistake.

No news of my release.

Brad Jones

Thursday December 6

Jim moved out today, they transferred him to another cell for some reason. It is very quiet tonight, there are no stars, and even my neighbours seem tired. I sent a letter to Mia, who I hadn't told of my release yet, although I'm sure she must have heard. No mail. No news.

Friday December 7

Fuck! Tricaud came again today even though I had fired him and said that the money is still not here. What is taking so long?! I don't know whether to believe him or wonder if the prick is keeping it for himself. How would I know? I feel sorry for the poor bastards who only have him to represent them and have to listen to his bloody French metaphors. I'm sure this would all happen so much faster if I could just make a few telephone calls.

Tricaud also said that I had a ninety percent chance of release. It was only after he left that I started to wonder about what that meant. What is the ten percent chance of me not being released about? I thought this was guaranteed? If he was here right now I don't think I would be able to stop myself from throttling him. Kunitz is supposed to come tomorrow and I hope he can tell me straight what's going on.

Saturday December 8

Kunitz didn't show up today. Maybe Monday (the day after tomorrow). No explanation as to why.

I got a long letter from Sue's sister Sheila this afternoon. She must have sent it just before my good news got to her. In it she included a copy of the character reference letter she sent to the judge—it is always very strange seeing what other people write about you. Reading it has made me feel better, because it reminded me of *who I am*. Not just a nameless prisoner, but a normal person. It's so easy to forget that in here. It was a very good letter and it made me sound like quite an upstanding person, talking about how much I worked to support the dojo, my attitude towards karate and even how good I am with kids! I'd release me! I don't know what effect it had on the judge, but it couldn't have hurt. Sheila said in her letter that she was trying to make it sound more like "from one woman to another" rather than from the friend of a defendant to a judge. What a great kid.

Monday December 10

Paul and Steve got back from their trial today. They each got two-and-a-half years. That shocked me when I heard it, though I tried to put on a brave face for Paul. I guess his crime was more serious than mine, but we've spent so much time talking about how he'd be out of here in no time that I'd started to believe it. This has made me start to sweat because I realized I might have to go *back* to prison after my trial. That can't happen. There is no way I'm ever coming back here once I get out.

Paul and I went off on our own during the afternoon exercise period and talked about how to stay strong while he's in here so that he can get his life back on track once he gets out. He's so young and bloody hot-headed that I'm afraid he'll do something stupid and get himself stuck here for a really long time. It doesn't help that his tough-guy south London accent seems to set something off in the Arabs, so that the second he opens his mouth they're on him. I told him to just keep his head down and find something else that's important to him to keep him going. He sounds like he wants to keep training and this should help teach him some discipline and discourage others from going after him. I promised to send him some instruction books when I get out and to try to help him as much as I can.

It looks like Kunitz is not coming today. I have been given no indication of when I will see him. All this lawyer stress is probably why I haven't slept properly for almost a week now. With all my tossing and turning, I can't be getting more than two or three hours of proper sleep a night. There is nothing worse than not being the master of your own fate.

Wednesday December 12

This morning, finally, some news. A telegram came from Kunitz that said he has received the money sent by my mother and will try to secure my release for the day after tomorrow. God, I hope it works! I will do anything to get out of this place. The last few days I have felt more like a prisoner than ever before; the feeling that *I shouldn't be here* has become overwhelming. The few things I hope to take with me are sitting in a neat pile on my desk and I've decided not to write any more letters until I am a free man.

Thursday December 13

An unexpected change—I have a new roommate. He's a Tamil from Sri Lanka and doesn't speak much English (or French). I think the poor bastard must be very scared and confused about why he's here—from what I can gather, he fled his country to escape a civil war and applied for refugee status when he got to France. I'd sure hate to be a refugee in France. He's tried to tell me his name twice today, and I still can't figure out what it is. He's lying on the floor now, on the foam mattress, trying to sleep. The poor guy has nothing—no food, no money—so I gave him half of my canteen order for this week. I figure I probably won't be needing it—I'm getting out tomorrow!

Detour on The Path

Friday December 14

I knew things must have gone wrong when it was Tricaud who showed up today.

Apparently my application for release was refused because I need to give the judge an address for where I'll be staying in France. Could someone not have pointed this out to me earlier! It's like this is the first time anyone here has tried to make bail. Once I get an address, they say I should be released early next week. Honestly, I have never seen a country that was more disorganized administratively. If someone wrote down the meaning of life and handed it to these people, they would lose it.

Sunday December 16

Kunitz showed up yesterday and gave me some more details. He will take care of getting me an address, and once that's done I'm free to go. I will need to stay in France for one month and then they will return my passport. I would then have to return for my trial. Guess I won't be home for Christmas! I don't bother to question how it works anymore, I just accept it. This will all end soon.

There is no electricity today and it's absolutely freezing in here. Outside it has been grey and bleak for days and today feels like winter is very close.

My new Tamil friend has been making exercise period more difficult for me. He doesn't know another soul in this place, so he follows me around everywhere, probably because he is terrified of most of the other prisoners. This wouldn't be so bad, except that he insists on clinging to my arm the entire time, so that it looks as if we are two star-crossed lovers waltzing around the yard. I know he doesn't mean anything by it—I gather this is a normal thing for men to do back in Sri Lanka—but we sure get some funny looks. I don't have the heart to tell him off about it, so I guess I'll just have to deal with my new reputation.

Brad Jones

Tuesday December 18

My god, if the world depended on the competency of lawyers, we would still be living in the fucking Stone Age. It's been four days since Tricaud and Kunitz found out I just need an address to be released and I'm still here. Why does this take so long? I decided to take matters into my own hands and spoke to one of the social workers here. He said I could use his address (even though I won't be staying with him) and he promised to contact Kunitz today to let him know. I hope this works. Only seven days 'til Christmas.

One of the guys from the factory was told by his lawyer this morning that he would be released. He told us when he got to work. He sure looked happy.

No mail today. I haven't heard from Suzanne in a while.

Thursday December 20

Tricaud came by today (where is Kunitz?) to tell me that they got the address and they will have a hearing with the judge tomorrow. I don't know how many times I have said this already, but I really think this could be my last night in prison. My god, I hope it is! It's now been almost two weeks since I've slept through the night. I get up every morning wondering if it will be the day. I am so tired of waiting, and I am afraid to hope anymore.

An English friend of mine, Charles, was released two nights ago. He and his wife have a little house in the countryside, about one hundred miles north of Paris, and he's invited me to go there for Christmas if I'm let out in time. It sounds wonderful.

My Tamil roommate was taken to court today for the hearing on his refugee claim. He has been there all day. It seems like the pace of trials and judgments is picking up, like they are trying to clear out as many people as they can before Christmas. I don't know what this means, but I hope it works in my favour.

I have been lying in bed, alone in my cell, for the last couple of hours. It is fairly quiet and I can only hear a few other voices around me. The last few days I have been thinking about Suzanne more and more. Even if I am released before Christmas, I will not be home for the holidays. I've been reliving the last few Christmases in my mind and they seem so clear, so vivid. The huge stocking Suzanne made for me and all the kids running around when we visited her family. Feeling her warm little body next to mine when we woke up on a frosty Christmas morning, always early. She feels so close that I could reach out and touch her face right now. She was always so happy at this time. This is the first time I will be away from home for Christmas, and the first time we will be apart in many years. I will miss being home, but really I miss her.

Friday December 21

Again, it was Tricaud who came to see me today. He and Kunitz submitted all the information for my bail application yesterday and now the judge has five working days to make her decision. Unbelievable! That could mean a couple of weeks with all the holidays. Tricaud seems very confident that I will be out within the week, but I don't know who to trust anymore.

My Tamil friend apparently had his application rejected and will be deported. The poor bugger must be terrified. I'm not sure what he did or how bad the situation is in Sri Lanka, but he is convinced that he will be killed if he has to go back. In any case, he has moved out and won't be spending Christmas in this hellhole. I am on my own again.

Saturday December 22

Shower and yet another French film today. I am resigned to the fact that I'll be spending Christmas in prison. Shit! Shit! Shit!

Monday December 24

This Christmas Eve is a day I'll remember for the rest of my life.

I woke up alone and thinking about how I hadn't seen a single familiar face since I'd got here. It had been a rough, sleepless night, like most of them have been over the last few weeks. I kept thinking *I'm not supposed to be here, I'm not supposed to be here,* and the words had been rolling around my head for hours while I struggled to drift off.

Because it was Christmas Eve we had the day off work, so when I stepped out of bed I had nothing to do but draw out the few pieces of baguette and lukewarm coffee that was breakfast. I didn't bother writing, or practising my French or anything, I just lay in bed and waited for the morning exercise period. The weather outside matched my mood, grey, sulky and lethargic.

When the cell door opened and I went out, I made no effort to walk around or take any form of exercise. I sidled up to the fence and struck up a conversation with Rolf, hoping his thunderous laugh would be the perfect antidote to my foul mood. He cackled as I cursed the prison, the Arabs, and whatever else came into my line of sight.

After we had been talking for about ten minutes, a fight broke out across the yard, about 100 feet away from us. I turned to see a group of about twelve men beating on two others, all of them Arabs. I didn't know why they were fighting—there are so many brawls, it's impossible to know what sets them off—but seeing such an unfair fight made me furious. There is a strict honour code to combat that has been instilled in me, and seeing this kind of mismatch was a clear breach. I watched as the two men broke free of the group and ran to the exit door, about thirty feet to my right, which was always locked while we were out in the yard. They were pounding madly on the heavy steel door and screaming for one of the guards to let them in, but the guards were either not there or had no interest in helping an Arab of any kind, no matter what the circumstances. After a few seconds, about ten of their opponents descended on them and started to really beat them, trapping each in the corner and kicking them with abandon. The poor guys didn't have a chance and would probably have been killed if left for more than a minute. One was screaming with what air he had left in his lungs, and it sounded like someone being skinned alive.

I started to run towards the men, not thinking, just knowing that this had crossed a line. I bulled through the group at top speed, and started pushing a few of them out of the way. I knew that in this kind of situation I had to keep moving so that I could confuse them and not give them an easy target—when I grabbed the first guy I threw him hard against the wall and used my momentum to spin in the other direction, charging at the next attacker. After doing this a couple of times I managed to get myself between the gang and the beaten bodies of their victims. I think they were quite taken aback by all this—they'd never seen anyone, never mind a large Westerner, get involved in their wars before. They began to throw a few punches and kick at me, but I was able to block all of this fairly easily, knocking away their awkward lunges, as these were just thugs who weren't trained in fighting techniques. I did not have to attack, as they backed off fairly quickly, probably now remembering that I taught karate. Instead, they screeched curses at me in Arabic and many of them spit from a safe distance.

It was then that I saw Paul being held up against the fence by another group of Arabs. Apparently, when he had seen me dive into the group he had rushed to help me, but several of the gang had grabbed him and pinned him against the wire fence, two of them holding him while several others whaled away. Paul was stronger than he looked, but he had not been training with me for long and was no match for several opponents at once. Once again, I ran and threw myself amidst the group, challenging them and getting myself between Paul and his attackers by shoving aside two of the cowards who were throwing punches. Faced with a formidable opponent, the group lost its nerve and, after a few more half-hearted flurries, which I was able to block without having to counterattack, they started to back off. The joy was lost for them once they were faced with a real fight.

Paul, who had already been in a few brawls in his short nineteen years, was cut in several places and would have a few bruises but was not seriously hurt. What had been aggravated most was his temper, and he cut loose with a stream of curses at the backs of his attackers that they probably would have admired if they'd understood it. He was most upset with one guy in particular who had cut open his lip, and he was screaming at the man, swearing he would get even. By now, the adrenalin was pulsing through me and I was riding the wave of release that comes with combat. Finally, it seemed that there was something I could do to change my situation, rather than sit and rot until someone let me go free. The blood-lust rose up in me.

I told Paul to go after the guy who'd attacked him and I would hold the rest of the gang off while he got his piece of vengeance. Paul didn't think twice and took off at a run after his target, leaving me to catch up. He came up behind him, shouting curses and making it clear across the language barrier that he would gladly take the stocky coward in a fair fight. They yelled back and forth at each other, puffing up like roosters at a cockfight, and one of them pointed to the sheltered area under the prison block.

The shelter, where I had been teaching my karate lessons, was where most of the outdoor fights took place. It was at the far end of the enclosure, as far as you could get from the entrance to the prison's exercise yard, protected from the weather and the eyes of the guards by an overhang from the adjacent building. The whole area measured about thirty feet by forty feet. When the other inmates saw that a fight was going to happen they streamed into the area to watch. There were about 300 men in the yard that day, about eighty percent of them Arab.

Detour on The Path

Because Paul had run ahead of me, many people were already in the shelter when I got there; I was still about twenty feet away from Paul when the fight started. The two managed to exchange a couple of punches, the crowd circling them and egging them on, each landing some heavy blows. After only a few seconds, someone from the crowd jumped on Paul from the side, then another, and then another, until men were descending on him like rats.

I was already pushing my way through the mob and I managed to get to Paul before the entire yard piled on top of him. I grabbed the first guy I saw and threw him headlong into the man beside him, then reached for a third guy and threw him against the nearby concrete wall as hard as I could. I was able to shove away enough men so that Paul could get to his feet, but now the attacks were starting to rain down on me. I was in a bad spot, with Arabs around me on all sides, so I lunged towards the wall and turned my back to it to cut off that line of attack. Suddenly attackers seemed to be coming from out of the ground and I had to deal with them coming from several directions. Up to that moment I hadn't needed to do more than block and throw, but now I started to strike back. I took a fighting stance and lashed out at a large guy coming at me from my right, hitting him with a sidekick to the solar plexus that made him crumple as the air left his lungs. I then spun to my left and shot towards a wiry man who was being pushed at me by the crowd, hitting him with a kick between his hip bones that caused him to double over. My training had taken over now and it was no longer about finesse, it was about survival. Every time I turned in a direction, I could see men cringe as the mob shoved them into the circle. With my peripheral vision I could see bodies flying back into the crowd as I attacked. I knew I had to keep moving as much as possible and create space for myself so that the sea of prisoners couldn't converge on me. I moved straight ahead and delivered an open hand strike to another man's face, then moved left for another sidekick to a fat man's gut, then ahead again with a backfist strike to another's jawline.

While I was attacking, I could see through the crowd that several prisoners in the yard were yelling at their friends still inside the building to throw down anything that could be used as a weapon. One of the things we were allowed to have was a small penknife, rounded at the top, to cut and butter the baguettes we got most mornings. Many prisoners—always thinking of their next fight—sharpened these knives against any concrete surface they could find, grinding the blade until it had a sharp point. I knew that many of the Arabs often ran their blades through garlic, so that any wound delivered would become infected and leave a scar. Several of these blades were now raining down on the yard from the cell windows and people picked them up and rushed into the fray.

As I sunk the edge of my *shuto* (knife hand) into the temple of the man in front of me, I could see a smaller man on my right with one of these blades. He was standing with the knife held in front of him and his right leg extended straight ahead, looking for an opening to rush me. I turned to deliver a sidekick to the extended leg, but I hesitated, knowing that a sharp kick to the knee would cause his leg to bend backwards at an impossible angle and rip the knee's ligaments apart, crippling him. Just at that moment, I saw that someone else was attacking me from the left, so I turned and blocked the lunge, dispatching him with an open-handed thrust to his cheekbone. Out of the corner of my eye, I saw the man behind me raise the knife up above his head and jump at my back. There was no time to turn and block, so I threw myself forward to evade the stab, and as I did my right foot caught my left heel and I stumbled. As I was falling, I felt the blade rip through my jacket and steel graze against my shoulder. I landed awkwardly on my right arm and heard something "crunch," but I popped back up as quickly as I could, terrified that the man would take a second swipe while I was down on the ground. I knew I couldn't hold off the group indefinitely, so I started to run, bulling my way through the men straight ahead of me, and I managed to get out into open space. Two or three from the crowd followed me, but now that I was out in the open again I had no trouble fighting them off.

Miraculously, Paul, whom I had assumed would be ripped to shreds by the mob once we were separated, had also managed to push his way out of the enclosure and was now running towards me. He was in rough shape, with blood streaming down his face from several cuts. I started to notice a horrible shooting pain in my right shoulder and I had to hunch over and hold it to stop it from becoming unbearable. Something was very wrong. We ran to the exit door at the end of the yard.

Several of the guards were hanging out the windows watching and somehow picking out people they thought had been responsible for starting the trouble. These people were later taken away, and would probably be thrown in solitary. Paul and I pounded on the door and, surprisingly, were let in along with the original two victims. The guards, who bore no love for some of the more difficult Arabs, had seen us fighting and had decided that the enemy of their enemy must be their friend. When we got through the door, they took one look at us and led us directly upstairs to the prison infirmary.

Now that the rush of battle was over, the pain in my shoulder had become horrendous. As I sat on an unforgiving steel bench waiting for an X-ray, my whole right side was on fire and I found it impossible to do anything but hunch forward to minimize the pain. The results of the X-ray came back quickly—a dislocated shoulder. My arm had popped out of its socket so that it was more than four inches below where it was supposed to be. The old bearded doctor shook his head and made it clear that they couldn't fix the arm there. I would have to be taken outside the prison to a civilian hospital. They gave me two Aspirin and sent me back to my cell to wait, telling me not to eat anything.

On the way back to my cell, under the watchful eyes of a very unnecessary guard, I realized that I had never been hit by anyone in the entire fight. And somehow I had come away with the worst injury!

It was still only 11:30 in the morning. I was alone in my cell with nothing to do but think about how much pain I was in. While I was out, the guards had brought my lunch and left it on the small table nearby. Because it was Christmas Eve, this was one of the best meals of the year, with fish cakes, rice and a large helping of ice cream. I watched what would have normally been the highlight of my week melt into a gelatinous pool that I was both forbidden, and also incapable of enjoying. Time moved as slowly as my heart rate was fast. I tried sitting perfectly still, hunching over, lying down, standing up and would have balanced on my head if it would have made the excruciating pain in my shoulder any more tolerable. I tried to concentrate and focus my mind, but I was too upset, too angry. Before long I started to feel nauseous and light-headed and my muscles started to seize up and shake, strong indications that my body was going into a state of shock. I could hear Paul, whose cell was only a few doors down from mine, calling for me. The doctors had stitched him up and told him that he had no serious damage, but he didn't know what kind of injury I had. I managed to stagger over and lever open the window in the cell and yell that I'd "talk to him later," before collapsing back on the bed.

Close to two hours passed before the PA system crackled to life.

"Jones!" was the only word broadcast, but the door of my cell gave an electronic click and swung open. I walked through and slowly made my way to the glassed-in control room, thankful that I was finally being taken to the hospital where I might get some relief. The officer in the room looked up and silently pointed towards the adjacent office of *le chef,* the prison director.

I knocked on the door with my good arm before entering. The director's office was a denial of the surroundings, as clean and orderly and stately as our surroundings were dank, cramped and filthy, a room designed to assure the few bureaucrats who visited the grounds that this was a place of civility and progress. The director, a lifelong civil servant, sat behind a large desk with a stack of papers on either side of him, methodically working through each sheet while moving it from one pile to the other. He looked up from the one in front of him, folded it in half, and motioned that I was to take it. As he handed it to me he grunted, "Allez a ta cellule," and took the next sheet off the pile, my brief audience clearly over.

Confused, I walked out and started back to my cell unescorted. As I was walking down the hallway, I unfolded the sheet. There was a large stamp across the middle of it that made its meaning impossible to misinterpret—*REFUSÉ*. My release had been refused. Refused! At that point, my eyes blurred and my mind stopped processing the rest of the words. *They weren't going to let me out!* I got back in my cell in a daze and sat heavily on the bed. This was a different kind of shock. The pain in my shoulder was still urgent and constant, but now it was matched with a numbness of hopelessness. I sat, dejected and confused, and thought that I must be the unluckiest man alive. I looked over to my writing desk at the picture of Suzanne and thought of my family, at home and together, probably sharing a coffee around the kitchen table and blissfully unaware of what kind of hell I had been dropped into. I felt small, forgotten and used up. Not knowing what else to do, I lay down on my good arm, faced the wall and closed my eyes.

I'm not even supposed to be here.

Shin, kokoro
Spirit, heart, mind

Chapter 12

I LAY LIKE THAT FOR WELL OVER AN HOUR, trying to stay absolutely still. It was the only way to lessen the pain, but it was impossible—the muscles on my right side were spasoming violently, tentacles of pain shooting through me as the head of my humerus bone pressed against my rib cage. That was followed by waves of nausea, and I bit my lip to stop myself from crying out. *Can't somebody help me?*

I lay like this, on the brink of throwing up and utterly hopeless, until I heard the voice on the PA system call my name again and the cell door popped open and a guard was waiting for me grunting that I should follow. We walked down a couple of flights of stairs, me stepping gingerly so that my arm didn't bounce, until he opened the door of a tiny holding cell and indicated I should wait inside. There was nowhere to lie down so I sat, my eyes closed. After a few minutes the guard came back to put a pair of handcuffs on me—it was such a ridiculous idea that I just stared at him, with a look that said "You've got to be kidding," so he left and came back a few minutes later with a pair of leg irons. He clamped them on my ankles and left me to sit. The pain was as bad as it had ever been, the spasms still shooting through my side sporadically, but I did my best to stay calm.

I sat for close to half an hour, staring at the walls and shaking, before the guards came back. There were a couple of them this time and they led me to the back of a waiting van. The chain of the leg irons was too short, so I could only shuffle about twelve inches at a time, and when we got to the van, I couldn't lift my foot high enough to step in. The guards had to grab me and heave me inside while I bent over so that I wouldn't smash my head, trying desperately to keep my balance so that I didn't keel over and land on my shoulder. I was the only passenger, so they slammed the doors shut and we pulled out.

We drove for about thirty minutes, me cradling my arm the whole way to protect against the frequent bumps in the road. Two cops were waiting when the doors opened at the end of the trip, looking very serious as they stood outside the doors to the ER of the civilian hospital. The fresh air felt good, but it was brisk and cold and I was only wearing a short-sleeved golf shirt and a old jacket, while the people walking into the hospital were in winter coats and hats. I had to hop out of the van, because of the short chain around my ankles, grimacing at the landing.

The officers stood on either side of me as I shuffled through the doors into the waiting room. Doctors and nurses walked around in their crisp whites, and a couple dozen people sat waiting for treatment. Tiny plastic Christmas trees with blinking lights were scattered around the room and it was cleaner than anything I'd seen in months. Seeing all these regular people I had the same feeling as I did entering the court house, like I'd returned from a long journey to a strange dimension. Except this time almost every head in the room turned to stare at me. I looked like hell—my hair was dishevelled and dirty, and I hadn't shaved in several days. The knees in my pants were ripped and bloody from when I'd fallen during the riot and I was wearing the same old jacket that was too small for me, trudging in wearing leg irons with cops at each elbow. I was so, so ashamed. *I am not a criminal!* I could tell from how people were looking at me, staring and whispering, that they must have thought I was a depraved murderer or rapist (or both), and I wanted desperately to tell them that I wasn't that kind of person, that I was not so different from them, just a regular guy who'd made a big mistake.

Instead I just kept my head down and stared at the floor. *Oh god, they are all staring.* I felt so small I wished I could have shrunk to a size where I could crawl right through one of the cracks in the tiled floor, anything to get all those eyes off of me. I'd never felt so ashamed, so worthless, so unlike who I thought I was.

I sat like this for about twenty minutes before they led me into a room. There were two more guards, a doctor and a nurse alongside a long metal table.

"Let's see if we can get that shirt off you," the doctor said, in very good English. He helped me wrestle out of it, gingerly, which took several tender minutes, then he got me to lie down on the table. "Ok, just relax, I'm going to try and set this."

I asked for a moment to compose myself and took a couple of deep breaths, trying to relax. He grabbed my arm and held it so that it was at a ninety degree angle to the joint, then slowly started to twist. He was trying to torque it, so it would roll back into the socket. It started to slip back in, about halfway, then suddenly popped back out from the pressure. *Fuck!* The pain was incredible, and I kind of screamed through clenched teeth as my arm dropped back down. He tried it again, with no better result, then a third, and then a fourth time, the bone jumping back out of the joint and hitting my rib cage after nearly resetting on each attempt. They'd given me nothing for the pain, no drugs or sedatives, and after the fourth try my body started shaking violently and I couldn't control it; the chains from the leg irons were rattling against the table and making a terrible noise.

The doctor looked at me sympathetically. "Ok, I'll be back in a minute." He had the nurse come over and hold my arm out and away from my body, gripping it by the wrist and elbow, which was actually the most comfortable position for it to be in.

I looked up from the table. This was the first woman I'd seen this close since I'd been in prison. She was beautiful, with green eyes and sandy blonde hair, with the perfect composure of a French woman.

"So," I said, in my bad French, "what are you doing tonight?"

"Rien."

"Me either. Why don't you pick me up down the road at eight o'clock?"

The guards got a good chuckle out of that, and she gave me a really nice smile, one that stayed with me long after I left the room. It made the whole thing almost worth it.

The doctor came back in with my X-ray from the prison hospital. In it, you could clearly see that my arm was a good four inches below the socket.

"We can't fix this properly here," he said. "We're going to have to send you to the prison hospital and they will have to operate."

Great! This was the hospital that used to be a dungeon, the same hospital where they'd sent Jim for his hemorrhoid operation and lost him. *Now they'll probably lose me too! I'll never get out of here!* I sat up and tried to wrestle my shirt back on, but couldn't do it, so I just draped my coat over my shoulders and was escorted back through the reception area and into the van. The ride back to Fleury Merogis was cold and bitter.

When we arrived my leg irons were removed and I was brought back to the same holding cell to wait for the prison doctor. I felt miserable. It was Christmas Eve, I was in tremendous pain, and after all the hope of the past weeks I again had no idea when I was going to be released. I couldn't understand why I'd been dealt such a cruel hand by fate—I deserved to be punished, but not like this, it was too much. I was still cold so I tried getting my shirt back on, wiggling and shimmying until I was finally able to slip it over my head and guide my arm through the hole. The pain was crippling, and all I could do was sit there, hunched over, wondering how long it would take for someone to figure out how to fix it.

Finally, after many minutes of trying to sit as still as possible, something in me snapped. *Fuck this.* I stood up and walked over to the bars of the cell. I grabbed my right arm by the wrist with my left and lifted it up so that I could clench the bars with my right hand at chest height, then turned myself sideways. I took a couple of deep breaths and then pulled as hard as I could.

There was a crunch and a snap, an ugly sound, like the bones of a chicken leg being torn away from the flesh, and I felt the arm moving. I pulled downwards and straight back, using my legs for power, and after I'd yanked as hard as I could I stood up to catch my breath. Suddenly I was able to stand up straight. The pain still radiated out from the joint, but I was able to move the arm around and it didn't make the pain worse. *It must be in!*

Just then the guard, one of the same ones who'd taken me to the hospital, came over to check on me. I pointed at my shoulder and started moving it around. "Hey look!" His eyes grew large and he hustled over to the office nearby. I could hear him saying that I'd fixed the arm myself, and one of the other guards, who'd also come with me to the hospital, came over to see. I showed him how I could move my arm around and he nodded, clearly impressed.

After a while the prison doctor showed up and checked things out.

"Seems ok," he said in French. "I'll have the guards bring you some pain killers to get you through the next day or so."

He then unrolled a long piece of gauze and wrapped it underneath my right wrist, tying a knot behind my neck to make a very rudimentary (and flimsy) sling. That was it—he left and the guards took me out of the holding cell. Amazingly, despite all that had happened, it was still only late afternoon and the day's second exercise period wasn't over yet, so I was sent back out into the yard.

Before they let me out, a couple of the guards who stood watch over the yard stopped me. They'd seen the fight that morning.

"You practise karate or something?" one of them said, miming a chopping motion.

"Yeah."

"Oh, you are good. There were Arabs flying all over the place when you were fighting."

I couldn't remember the details of that and had no idea how

many people he was talking about, but I could see they had a new respect. They had no love for the low-life Arabs either, so I guess they felt like we were now on the same team.

When I stepped outside Paul and Rolf saw me immediately and came rushing over. Paul was pretty banged up, some cuts and bruises and the beginnings of a black eye, but could have been a lot worse. They asked how I was and what had happened to me, so I retold the whole story. No one else in the yard paid much attention to me—these fights happened all the time, so as long as I was alive there wasn't much unusual about it.

After that it was back to my cell for a long night. When dinner arrived there were no painkillers, so I was left to lie there, alone, and suffer. The more I lay there the more unfair things seemed to be. The throbbing in my shoulder was still relentless, always there, making it hard to think about anything else. *Why were things so bad?* It just didn't seem right that I had to go through all this for the mistake I'd made. It didn't make a difference if you'd mugged someone or raped and murdered an entire family, you were treated like a piece of shit either way.

The lights went out and I lay in the dark, unable to sleep. I started to think about my family and friends, gathered at home with their loved ones on this special night, sitting around the tree and laughing over an eggnog or some Christmas cake. Were they thinking of me? I started to remember all of my past Christmases, every one of them, reliving the joy from when I was a small child. Would I ever be happy like that again? Or would my next Christmas be like this one, desperate and miserable? I thought of the looks from the people in the waiting room today, what kind of person they'd seen me as. How will I ever reclaim my old life? It was hard to imagine a future when the present was so riddled with pain.

I lay there, alone and afraid, and waited for the morning to come.

Brad Jones

Tuesday December 25

I woke up this morning full of rage. That prick who attacked me is going to die.

I figure I have nothing to lose anymore. With my release refused the light at the end of the tunnel is gone, and I have no idea how long I'll be here. I can't imagine staring at this guy day after day, knowing he tried to kill me, and doing nothing. The penalty for killing a prisoner in here is six years—for all I know I may be in here that long anyway, I think I may as well get my satisfaction.

I saw him in the yard this morning and we stared at each other. I got a better look at him—short, stocky, tightly curled hair, an ugly son of a bitch. I could see he was nervous when I looked at him. I thought of rushing him right then, but until my shoulder heals I'm vulnerable, and I don't want there to be any mistakes. So I kept to my side of the yard, Rolf and Paul and John all staying close to me, while he stayed on the opposite side, surrounded by his cronies. He can see my intention, I'm sure of it. I hope it terrifies him.

The authorities were at least able to treat us with a little human decency today. When I got back from the yard there was a piece of cake waiting, not half bad, and they showed us a movie in the afternoon. Still, it is impossible to forget what day it is. Despite all the distractions, my mind keeps going back to home and family, and the beautiful scene unfolding there without me. It's a bit like imagining what the world would be like if you were dead.

For all their Christmas generosity, the guards here are still stupid. When the breakfast tray was brought in this morning, the pain killers were on it. The guard apologized and said they just forgot to bring them last night. I threw the pills back at him—they're no good to me now.

Detour on The Path

Thursday December 27

They pulled me out of my cell today and put me on trial. I couldn't believe it. It was a hearing for the fight I was in, to see if I needed to be punished. As if they haven't done enough!

I was taken to a little hearing room next to the director's office. The director and a couple of other men I didn't recognize were seated there behind a table, and a few of the guards were also in the room. Once I entered the meeting began, but no one actually spoke to me directly. There was no translation, so I could only pick up bits and pieces of what was being said—the director and his officials seemed to think I had started the fight and they wanted to know how to punish me for it! I knew the standard penalty for starting a fight was some time in solitary confinement—no exercise period, no bed to sleep in, just you sitting on the floor in a tiny room, alone with your thoughts. I'd seen guys who'd come out of that and they weren't in good shape.

They discussed "my case" for several minutes before one of the guards came to my defence. He said (as far as I could tell) that I'd only been trying to defend myself and I'd been trying to protect someone else who'd been attacked. After that came out the whole process ended quickly, and the "charges" were dismissed. I was extremely relieved, but didn't even have a chance to thank the guard who spoke up for me before I was whisked back to my cell.

That's where I am now. I've been sitting here for twenty-one hours a day the last few days, since I can't work in the factory because of my shoulder. I stare out the window or try to read. I haven't written a letter to anyone in more than two weeks, because I just can't bring myself to tell anyone about what has been happening. I need to have something good to tell them.

Brad Jones

Saturday December 29

Kunitz came around today for his regular whirlwind session with all his clients. He raised his eyebrows when he saw me and asked what happened, so I gave him a quick recap, but I didn't want to use up too much of my precious ten minutes. I asked him about my release being refused and he brushed it off.

"Ah, don't worry about it, some stupid administrative mistake, I'll get it fixed on Monday."

I feel a little better; I may get out of here soon after all. At this point I've stopped getting my hopes up, but we'll wait and see what happens.

Monday December 31

It's New Year's Eve and I'm still all alone here in my cell. I feel terrible—I spent all of yesterday in bed with a bad cold, and feel only slightly more human today. It is cold and my shoulder is giving me trouble—it's still in the same sling, but now it aches, a slowly building throbbing that worries me. I can take it out of the sling and move it around a little bit, but it's most comfortable resting and supported.

I've been lying awake at night listening for footsteps again. They usually come for you between 11 p.m. and midnight, with no warning, so I stay up until about 1 a.m. before letting myself drift off. I don't expect them to come, but there is a little bit of hope left that I can't extinguish.

It looks like I will start 1985 in here. I hope the new year brings better luck.

Tuesday January 1

No matter where you are, there is always a party for New Year's. At about 11:30 last night the noise began. Everyone started banging their metal cups and plates against the bars of the windows, and by midnight almost everyone was doing it; the noise was unbelievable. People lit up little scraps of paper and threw them out the window, so it looked like it was gently raining fire. I sat with the lights out and watched, mesmerized by the strange beauty of it. The yelling and banging just made everything more surreal. There was even a countdown at midnight, and shouts of "Happy New Year" in many languages. It was quite a little party.

Today has been quiet and dull. I am very lonely. I think tonight I will pray for my release.

Thursday January 3

It is true. Miracles do happen.

Last night I was lying in bed, trying to put myself to sleep by reading a book, when the footsteps came. I had heard them enough times by now that I did not get excited, just kept reading my book, but I could still hear them. They got closer, as they had before, but I kept reading. They stopped, very near, but I did not look up. I could hear a key turn in a lock, but I did not think it was mine. I was facing the window, but out of the corner of my eye I saw my door swing open, and a guard stepped in.

"Partage!"

Oh my god, he's come for me.

"Partage!"

I leapt out of bed and started gathering my belongings. *I'm leaving!* I could not believe it. I asked the guard if I could have one minute to say good-bye to Paul, who was just a few doors down, and he grunted that I could. I'd already assembled all my belongings that I didn't want to bring with me—writing paper, envelopes, magazines, my thesaurus, my little coffee pot and heating coil—and put them in a little box, so I grabbed that and ran down the hall. I'd even written up a little "will" in fancy script, to designate who got the privilege of receiving these meagre possessions ("To Rolf, I bequeath my magazines…"). I pounded on Paul's door while the guard sauntered down to open it.

"I'm free! They're letting me out!"

Paul had known I might be released, so he was all smiles and congratulations. I gave him the box to distribute to my heirs and we said our good-byes.

"You take care Paul, keep your head down and get out of here as fast as you can. Write me so I can find you when you get out."

"Will do mate. Go enjoy Paris."

I ran back to my cell and gathered the few things left in there—a change of clothes, comb, photos. The guard led me downstairs and took me to the large grey room I'd been processed in when I first arrived. My suitcases were brought out and laid on the counter, and I saw all the things I'd set out with from Toronto—my suit, my regular clothes, watch, wallet. I signed some forms and then they started counting out cash for me—the money I had left over from the last amount that Suzanne had sent, plus the half of my earnings from the factory that had been set aside. It all came to a couple of hundred dollars. I collected it, gathered my bags, and then the guard started walking me towards the door.

I had no idea if anyone was going to pick me up, where I would go, or even where I was exactly. The whole thing was surreal, and happening so fast that I didn't have time to think. We got to the door and the guard opened it, standing aside so that I could walk by.

Fresh air. Stars. Freedom.

Tricaud was waiting for me. He smiled and shook my hand, offering his congratulations, then escorted me to his car. His girlfriend was there, a pretty, intellectual-looking woman, so I got into the back seat. It was a beautiful car, a Jaguar. We pulled out of the parking lot and I stared, dumbstruck, as the distant lights of central Paris began moving closer.

"We are going to take you to a little hotel where you can stay," said Tricaud. "In a couple of days you should go see Monsieur Kunitz at his office."

I nodded, unable to find words.

"Congratulations, you are a free man!"

"Great!"

I was back in that stupor of disbelief I'd felt when I was arrested. I'd dreamed of this moment for so long it seemed impossible that it was happening. I continued to stare out the window, not really thinking anything, just aware of a quiet elation in my gut.

The lights from the holidays were still up in the streets, giving the city a ghostly beauty. After forty-five minutes or so we pulled up to a small hotel on a peaceful little street. Tricaud came inside and checked me in, then handed me the key to my room.

"Congratulations again, Mr. Jones," he said solemnly, shaking my hand. "Bonne chance."

I thanked him and walked up the flight of stairs to my room. I unlocked the door and dropped my bags on the floor. It was a small, simple beige room, with a bed and a wardrobe and a little side table. The washroom was down the hall. Not knowing what else to do, I sat down on the bed.

It was the strangest feeling. I knew I could go anywhere, do anything, but I was paralyzed. All I could do was sit on that bed and stare at the door. It was after midnight by this time, but I wasn't tired; I just sat there, staring. *I could walk through that door if I wanted.*

I spent the whole night that way. I must have lay down at some point, but I didn't really sleep, just dozed off for a few minutes here and there. Most of the time I was curled up, as if I was expecting to be hit; I was like a dog that had been beaten and was waiting for the next blow. I was still in the sling and the dull throbbing in my shoulder was still there. By the time the sun peeked through the window I was sitting up on the bed and awake.

I decided to have a shower and put on clean clothes. God, that felt wonderful. The water was warm and I could stay in as long as I wanted. I shaved, combed my hair and put on a shirt and pants that still had specks of dust from Pakistan.

I walked and walked and walked. Paris was grand and full of life, but most of all it felt good to be moving, to be able to go more than fifty metres in any direction without hitting a wall. I stopped in at a little patisserie and bought a coffee and a croissant, which melted on my tongue—it was indescribable to put something in my mouth that was fresh, just out of the oven. I walked for hours, all over, taking in the sights—it was hard not to stare at the women, or to get over the feeling that everyone was staring at me. There was a gradual feeling of euphoria building inside as I went, the slow granting of permission to let myself believe I was once again just a regular person. The same words kept rolling around in my head.

I am free. I am free. I am free.

Saturday January 5

Of course, life is still not without its problems.

I wanted to call home right away, but this was not as easy as I thought. There was no phone in my room, and I couldn't figure out how to call overseas from a payphone. Finally I asked the woman at the desk of the hotel (which took some effort, since I no longer had a French-English dictionary) and she told me I had to go to the big central post office and use their phones there.

It was a bustling brick building down near the Louvre, open twenty-four hours a day and every day, unusual for France. The bureaucracy of making the call was more like what I was used to—I had to fill out a form with the number I wanted to call, give it to an attendant and wait until a phone was available. I sat for close to twenty minutes before my name was called and I was directed to a little booth with a sliding door where I picked up the phone and waited for them to make the connection.

My first call was to Suzanne. It was so *good* to hear her voice again, and she was ecstatic to hear I was free and wanted to know right away when I was coming home. I explained how I was going to stay in Paris until my trial, so I could close the door on this chapter of my life. I had no idea how much the call was going to cost me (I was still broke) so I had to rush through the explanation and promise to send her an address in Paris where she could write me. I went through the whole process again to call my mother and let her know that I was ok, then went and paid for my calls.

I have little to do—I'm not supposed to go and see Kunitz until Monday—and I have to be very careful about stretching my few dollars, so I walk a lot. Last night, after spending most of the day roaming the streets, I stopped in at a cozy little neighbourhood restaurant for my dinner. There was a young woman there, in her early twenties, and a much older man—he must have been eighty—sitting two tables over from me and they were speaking English. The girl was quite beautiful, dark-haired and very slim, with full lips and perfect ivory skin, and she spoke with an east-coast American accent. I couldn't help but eavesdrop—she seemed to work for the older man, who was giving her his undivided attention, in some kind of fashion business. Before long I had struck up a conversation.

We made small talk for a while—where we were from, the beauty of Paris—while we ate; I danced around an explanation of why I was in the city. Her name was Jacqueline, and she was the in-house couture model at the fashion house owned by her companion. She had moved to Paris a couple of months before.

Finally, our meals were wrapping up.

"We're going down to the Champs Elysées, would you like to join us?" she asked me.

"OK."

We left the restaurant and stepped into a huge black Mercedes that was waiting for us, Jacqueline and I sitting in the back. As we chatted, the lights leading to the Arc de Triomphe approached, tall and majestic, mesmerizing in its beauty. The two of us got out and walked up and down the strip, browsing the windows of the impossibly expensive shops and sharing stories.

We got close very quickly.

Friday January 11

I had my first meeting with Kunitz a few days ago. It was all smiles and handshakes, just a chance to check in and see what the next months had in store. I am out on bail and must stay in France until my trial—some of my friends in prison had told me to skip the country and go home, just cross over into Belgium and get on a plane, but after I asked around I found out that Interpol would issue a warrant for my arrest, and I'd likely be picked up next time I tried to cross a border. It's best to finish things, to stay and take my medicine rather than have this hanging over my head for the rest of my life.

Kunitz told me that I should have a trial in the next couple of months—the sooner the better since I can't work and have no way to support myself. I am to check in with him every couple of weeks to find out when we are to go to court and to plan my defence.

In the meantime, I have been spending most of my time with Jacqueline. For some reason she has taken a liking to me—she has led a very sheltered life and my stories about competing and travelling in Japan seem to have a great effect on her.

It turns out that she is in Paris because she's run away from home. She left because her parents wanted her to marry some lawyer who she didn't like (she is also trained as a lawyer)—so she ran away to Paris. She's no poor orphan, though—she told me she was raised on an estate in the Hamptons, and her father owns a large national grocery chain. Now she is the house model at the couture house owned by the man I met on our first night, her job to model all his creations for clients who come in to shop. Apparently he is one of the original couturiers—and he has fallen in love with her and wants her to marry him. He's even offered her a deal—"I'll die soon, so marry me and when I'm gone the entire business is yours." I think she's crazy not to take it, but she has too much pride and refuses. Still, he can't complain that she doesn't deserve the house model job; she has the body of a mannequin, an hourglass figure with a twenty-one-inch waist.

After a few days together, knowing I was living in a hotel, she suggested I stay with her for a while. She has a room in the basement of a building near the Eiffel Tower, arranged by her couturier, in the Trocadero, an upscale neighbourhood. She's taken care of by two old ladies who bring her all her meals. They even bring us breakfast in bed! Fabulous breakfasts with coffee, croissants, toast, fruit and jam. Jacqueline seems to think this is normal, which makes the truth about her circumstances so much funnier.

We were walking into the building one afternoon when she saw a well-dressed couple walk past us on their way out.

"I don't understand," she said, shaking her head. "All of these nice people, they come in here, they stay for two hours and then they leave."

I laughed, having figured out what that meant days ago. "It's a love hotel."

"A love hotel? What is that?"

"You know, where men take their mistresses. A place you rent by the hour."

She was shocked—she didn't even know that was possible. She is incredibly naïve that way, since her life has been so sheltered. She actually told me that she and her friends used to ride the bus for kicks back home, just to see what it was like.

At the same time, she is also very talented and artistic. She can draw beautifully, has her Grade 8 in piano and is an excellent singer. Sometimes she'll burst into song in the middle of the Metro.

She's not always easy to take, though—I'm burning through the money I'm saving by staying with her because she told me that "a lady never pays for anything." Since I can't work, I'm getting Suzanne to wire me a couple of hundred dollars every two weeks from the dojo account. I hope it holds up.

I'm meeting with Kunitz again next week to get information on my trial. The sooner it comes the better. Paris is nice, but I want to get home.

Nintai
Patience, perseverance

Chapter 13

I SPENT THE NEXT MONTHS carving out a simple life, full of waiting.

Not being able to work, I found myself with more time to fill than I ever had before, but with almost no money to spend. With nothing else to do, I set out to explore Paris. I had to preserve every franc so I rarely even took public transit, instead choosing to walk for hours and hours every day. I'd set out in the morning, often with the sole intention of getting to a new place, letting my mood dictate the day. Sometimes I'd be a tourist, and would treat myself to a visit to one of the famous sights—I spent whole days wandering the halls of the Louvre, or strolling the banks of the Seine, popping in to take a quiet moment gawking at the stained glass of Notre Dame or climbing the white steps of Sacré-Coeur for a view of the city. I paid my respects at the grave of Jim Morrison, marvelled at the ornate detailing of the furniture at Versaille and was awestruck by the millions of human bones lying beneath the city in the catacombs.

More often I shied away from the tourist hordes and explored the grand boulevards and winding sidestreets of the *arrondissements*. Over time, I learned my way around the city quite well, and probably know it better today than I do Toronto. While I didn't appreciate it at the time, it was a gift to be stuck in Paris, of all the places in the world, with lots of time to roam and think. It was just too bad that I was so sick of waiting and thinking.

My first meetings with Kunitz didn't help my frustration. At first there was nothing to report, then after a few weeks things got worse. Since I'd been the last case heard by the judge who'd granted my bail, a new judge had been appointed to oversee my progress through the justice system—and she wasn't happy. Kunitz had found out—somehow—that this new judge did not agree with her predecessor's decision to have me released, and now was doing everything in her power to delay my trial. She knew that, since I was unable to work, I'd be struggling to make ends meet.

Kunitz just gave me a Gallic shrug and said there wasn't much we could do. There were limits to how long the judge could put things off, but it all depended on how difficult the judge felt like making things for me. I couldn't help thinking, *Why is my fate never in my own hands?* After my first month out of prison, I was back in the old, familiar waiting game.

Meanwhile, Jacqueline was becoming more and more of a problem. At first we had lots of fun, learning the city together and spending quiet nights cozying up when it was too cold to go out. But her naïveté and strange artistic temperament slowly started to drive me crazy. She was always looking for hidden, deeper meanings to ordinary things, and, having been raised as a spoiled only child, she was used to having even the most basic things done for her. I couldn't stand that. At the same time she was convinced we were meant for each other. She drew a detailed (and, to be honest, quite beautiful) plan of what our dream home would be like, and in her mind I would be working as an executive for her daddy's company. It was all too surreal, moving from being surrounded by rapists and murderers to being the supposed future husband of a wealthy heiress, all in a couple of weeks.

One day, after Jacqueline and I had been living together for a week or so, I was strolling through the Trocadero and saw a man with a karate *gi* slung over his shoulder walk into a fitness centre. I followed him inside, and found out from the staff that there was a lunchtime karate class there every day during the week. I was thrilled—my shoulder still wasn't fully healed, but I could move it around pretty well and didn't need the sling anymore. I decided to come back the next day and test it out.

I went and bought myself a *gi*—no small expense on my budget—and arrived eager the next day. It felt so good to go through the old movements after so long. I was rusty, and there were some things I couldn't do without feeling pain in my shoulder, but I felt the best I had in months. I started coming to the class every second day, then every weekday, gradually re-acquiring my conditioning.

I also decided to improve my French—if I was going to be here for a little while, I could at least finally learn the language properly. I signed up for a month's worth of classes at the Alliance Française—as I saw it, there was no point in signing up for any longer than that, because my trial would probably be soon and I didn't have the money for anything more anyways—and began showing up for lessons every morning. I quickly got into a nice routine: French classes in the morning, then over to the fitness centre for karate at lunchtime, then back to the school in the afternoon to study in their language lab. The language lab was free, and I could spend hours listening to tapes and working on my pronunciation. It filled up the day nicely and my French rapidly started to improve.

Not long after I started at the school I made friends with one of the instructors at the language lab, Lucy. She was a petite young Jewish woman from Morocco, very soft spoken, who had lived in Paris for most of her life. We hit it off immediately, going to cafés for conversation and spending most of the time laughing. She was a sweet soul and the first person I'd met since I'd left Canada that I could really talk to. Before long I had my first friend in Paris.

While things really seemed to be coming together in some ways, they were stressful as hell in others. With all the money I was spending on classes, and with Jacqueline, I really had to make every franc last. It was winter, and cold, but all the clothes I had with me were summer clothes—packed in July for the heat of

Southeast Asia. Very soon I was scouring the flea markets around the city, mixing and matching ratty old sweaters and a heavy coat with the few nicer clothes I had. I knew that the more I took from the small amount in the dojo account, the harder it would make things for my friends who were running the school.

I also got a message from Suzanne that DeHavilland had called and wanted me to come back to work. If I'd been at home this would have been great news, but I knew that if I didn't return to the job soon they'd fire me. Of course it was impossible to go back, but I remembered that my union's regulations stated that if I was unable to work because of an injury or illness I couldn't be fired. I still had a shoulder injury! I paid a visit to the Canadian embassy and explained my situation, and they had one of their doctors examine me and give me a note explaining that I was unable to work because of my shoulder. DeHavilland wasn't happy about it, but it worked.

Most frustrating was the waiting. Weeks passed and there was still no news on my case. I dropped in to see Kunitz at least every week, and each time he said, "Come back in a couple of days and I'll know something." I was happy to be free, but the feeling of helplessness was building again.

In some ways the waiting was harder this time because I had much less communication with my friends and family back home. It was difficult to write letters now because there was less time in the day, and I didn't know how long I'd be at the same mailing address. I didn't want to write about my life in Paris; all I had to say was how much I was looking forward to being home, and how soon I hoped I would see them. Overseas phone calls were expensive and could only be made from the central post office in the 1e arrondissement. I called home when I could to speak to Suzanne or my mother, but the conversations were always brief and more of a chance to reassure them that I was alright.

After living with Jacqueline in our little basement hotel room for a month or so I decided to leave. We just couldn't understand each other's different worlds and her eccentricities were making me crazy. I was so frustrated that I left her a note saying I was sorry and walked out. It wasn't how I would have liked to have handled it, but I knew she wouldn't just let me go.

I started moving around from little hotel to little hotel. I was living in the cheapest places I could find, usually just the most basic of rooms with a washroom down the hall somewhere that was shared by the entire floor. The places were rarely clean or anywhere that I wanted to spend any more time than I had to, but I had a place to sleep where no one would bother me. I kept moving because I knew that Jacqueline would be looking for me. She had showed up at Kunitz's office right after I left her, demanding to know where I was. Kunitz could honestly say that he didn't know, but she camped out in his office for days and days, waiting for me to show up. For two or three weeks afterwards I had to phone ahead to ask him if it was safe for me to visit.

On the positive side, my training was starting to go well. By chance, the man who taught the classes at the local fitness centre happened to be the brother of Serge Chouraqui, one of France's national team coaches. After a couple of weeks he suggested I go train with Sensei Chouraqui at his dojo, the Sporting International Karate Club (or Club Daguerre, as everyone called it, after its street address). It was a very simple building, unremarkable from the street, with just one main training room and a second smaller room with mats, but it's one of the best schools in Europe. When I arrived there were three former world champions training there.

The midday class was excellent, since the traditional French two-hour lunch gave everyone the chance to come in and train. It was a very intense class for brown and black belts, and my cardio conditioning had deteriorated so much that I had a hard time keeping up at first. Slowly I was able to work my way back to a competitive level, and after a couple of months I felt more like my old self.

By early March I didn't know any more about my court date than I had on the day I'd been released. I stopped going to classes at Alliance Française, thinking that the trial *had* to be soon, but also because the fees were stretching my budget too far. I did still spend time with Lucy. Her mother ran a movie house that showed old films from the '40s and '50s, so we'd spend the evening there, or chat in a café. Sometimes we took day trips together—my favourite was out to the Champagne district northeast of Paris, where we hunted around and found the simple grave of Dom Perignon, simply marked inside a tiny country church.

As spring came to Paris, Suzanne came over for a visit. I wanted to thank her for all the help she'd given me, so I told her to take some money from the dojo account and fly over for a week. It's hard to describe how good it was to see her—she was the first tangible piece of my old life that I'd seen in more than nine months, the first bit of my history I could hold in my arms. It was a happy reunion, and afterwards we had the best time we'd had in years; now that we were comfortable just being friends we could let ourselves simply enjoy each other's company, without the pressure of a relationship.

I had a special treat for her. A friend I'd made at the dojo worked for the French government and he made arrangements for us to stay in the countryside at a former hunting chateau of King Francois I, an elegant mini-castle in the woods from the sixteenth century, with traditional furnishings and a full moat. He told me that Kissinger had even stayed there once. We spent a couple of days there walking and relaxing and enjoying the exquisite French cuisine.

A strange thing happened when we first arrived. We'd only been in our room a few minutes when I noticed an oddly shaped coin on the bed. I was sure it hadn't been there when we'd walked in. It was oval-shaped and copper-coloured, only about a centimetre-and-a-half in length. When I picked it up I could see that it had an image of the Virgin Mary, her arms open in a welcoming gesture as she stood on top of the globe. We couldn't figure out where it came from, and we guessed it must have fallen out of the pocket of Suzanne's jacket, which she'd borrowed from her boyfriend. I kept the medal, not really knowing what it was, but thinking it was not the kind of thing you just throw away.

Suzanne told me some more about how things were going at my dojo. Finances were still tight, but George and Jon and the others who'd agreed to run things had found a way to let it exist. The debts were still there, but all of them together were keeping the wolves at bay while still running the classes. I wished I could have flown them all to Paris to thank them.

After Suzanne left I went back to the struggle of trying to fill my days. After more than three months Kunitz still had no more than a shrug to answer my questions on when this whole thing would be over. A guy I met at Club Daguerre had been letting me sleep on his couch for a number of weeks, which took some pressure off my finances, but I couldn't do that forever. I was really starting to get frustrated again—I couldn't help feeling useless and anxious after months of just waiting around and spending the little money I could scrounge up. As much as I hated to say it, at least in prison you didn't have to pay for food and a place to live.

One other strange thing happened to me. Not long after Suzanne left I was preparing to go on another short trip, this one to the Alsace with my Australian friend Bill from the Alliance Française, when a Japanese woman that Lucy knew gave me another of the medals I'd found on the bed at the chateau. This one was actually just a photo of the medal in card form, but she explained to me how the coins were known as the "miraculous medals" and whoever possessed them would receive graces from Mary. I had never followed a religious practice, but it struck me as strange that this famous medal I'd never heard of would suddenly show up twice in such a short time.

Finally, in the first week of June, I got the word. The trial would take place in three weeks, a full year after I'd agreed to Rico's proposal.

There wasn't much to do to get ready, since the case had been prepared for months. By this time I was staying in a small apartment that a friend of Lucy's had lent me while he was away, not much more than a room with a mattress on the floor. The one thing I did was borrow some money from Lucy and buy myself a one-way ticket home, leaving two days after my court date. I knew the odds were that I'd be let off with a fine; at the same time, there was still a chance I'd be sent back to prison to serve more time, and sometimes that fear would creep in and keep me awake long into the night.

Most of all, I was looking forward to certainty. One way or another, I would know how much longer my actions would haunt me.

Not surprisingly, I didn't sleep much the night before the trial. I got up early and put on my best clothes, the same suit I'd worn all through Pakistan and India. I didn't need to be at Kunitz's office until later in the morning, so I decided to walk to the Metro station, which was about half an hour away from my apartment.

It was a beautiful day on the cusp of summer, and I took my time. Partway through my walk there was a small church that I'd passed every day in the last few weeks. I had never paid much attention to it, but as I went by, my thoughts occupied with all the different possible outcomes of my hearing, I decided that today might not be a bad day to go in and pray.

The door was open and I stepped in and took a moment for my eyes to adjust to the low light. It was a very simple church, plain and quite old, with a few paintings and statues of Catholic saints. I sat down in a pew at the front and closed my eyes to think. The medallion I'd found on the bed at the chateau was in my pocket, and I did my best to calm the turmoil in my mind and ask for…protection of some kind.

After I'd been sitting for a little while, the strangest feeling came over me. The best way I can describe it is as if my body was full of fluid, and then someone pulled a plug I didn't know about in the bottom of my feet. Slowly, slowly, all the fear and tension drained out of me—I could actually feel the line of tension descending downwards from my head to my torso and dropping all the way to my ankles until it was gone. All that remained was a feeling of peace and tranquility. When I opened my eyes I looked up to see that I'd been sitting in front of a statue of the Virgin Mary. I got up and went outside feeling wonderful, and continued on to the Metro.

I got to Kunitz's office and we shared a quiet drive out to the Île de la Cité where the Palais de Justice was located. I was still feeling calm when we got to the courthouse, and waited patiently for our turn to come. It didn't take long before we were called.

I walked in and was escorted by a court official to a little box in the middle of the room where I was to stand, Kunitz on my right and the prosecutor on my left. There was also a woman from the Canadian embassy standing just a little behind me on my left to translate the proceedings. In front of me were the desks for the three judges—the French use a system derived from the Napoleonic code, with a main judge (known as the court president) sitting in the middle and a little above two other judges on either side of him.

The three of them entered and everyone stood up. It was time to begin.

The prosecutor made his case first. The crux of his message seemed to be that I was a terrible person who should be locked up. He spoke quite quickly and the translation was poor so I missed some of the details of what he was saying, but he took great pains to point out every legal and ethical problem he had with my actions. By the end of his five minute speech I felt horrible.

Then it was Kunitz's turn. He was much more deliberate, going through all the material we had provided, showing that I had a clean record and that I was someone who had earned many accreditations and awards.

"Here's a person who has made a mistake," he said, addressing the judges. "Perhaps the price has been paid already, and maybe we should see about ending this now."

He sat down and the head judge continued to leaf through my folder, examining each item. I had been holding the miraculous medal in my palm all through the proceedings so far, and I clasped it extra tightly right now.

Finally, he spoke.

"How could someone who teaches children, who competes and represents his country—how could you do such a thing?"

My brain was racing. "I've been asking myself the same question for the last eleven months." I wanted to say more, to have an insightful answer, but that was all that came out.

He nodded and closed the file, and the three of them stood up and left the room.

Now I really started to panic. Had I said the right thing? What did his nod mean? Kunitz made a motion that I should relax, but every fear that I'd been holding at bay during my long nights of thinking came back to me at once. What if they sent me back? What if the fine was so large that I couldn't pay it? What if this isn't over? I clenched the medal even tighter, so that it was digging into my palm.

The wait went on for about ten minutes, but felt like hours. The thought that I couldn't shut out was *I can't go back to that place.*

The three of them walked back into the room and sat down. The time of reckoning had come.

They wasted little time with legal niceties and the court president got right to the verdict.

"We have reviewed your case and your sentence is three years."

No.

I'd understood him in French, and didn't even hear the voice of the translator. *Three years!* I tumbled into a fog and was gone from the courtroom, not hearing another word that was said. *Three years!* I could not believe it. My whole insides caved in at that moment and I fell into a place of pure fear, completely beyond the markers of rationality. All that existed was the hell I was about to re-enter. *I won't last three years in that place.* The only answer that made sense was to end my life right there, there was no way the person that I knew was going to survive.

From somewhere far away I could hear the noise of the courtroom. I wasn't sure what it was at first, then I realized the translator was speaking to me.

"Oh my god, you are so lucky!"

Lucky?

Kunitz was beside me and smiling, shaking my hand. I couldn't understand what kind of twilight zone I'd just stepped into.

"What do you mean lucky?"

"Your sentence is very unusual," the translator exclaimed, still very excited.

Then Kunitz explained what had happened: while my penalty was three years, the time I'd spent in jail up to now was sufficient and the rest of the sentence was suspended. However, I was also banned from the country for the next five years and the judge had made a point of saying that I'd be dealt with harshly if I was ever caught committing a crime in France again—I would pay the penalty for that crime, plus the rest of this sentence would then have to be served. In addition to all this, I had to pay a fine equivalent to about $20,000.

"We'll talk about this fine," Kunitz said as he guided me out of the court room.

He drove me back to his office and explained what my options were. The best one was for me to leave the country now, and I would forfeit the bail I'd paid for my release (about $5,000) in lieu of paying the fine. After some time, the fine would be expunged from my record.

Kunitz dropped me off and shook my hand. "That's it, we're done. Bonne chance."

I walked back towards the Metro relieved and still in a daze. It was finally over. On my way back to my apartment I looked at the church where I'd stopped during the morning and realized it was a church specially dedicated to the Virgin Mary. *Of course.* I shook my head at the strange memory of it all.

When I got home I realized I still had one more problem: the authorities had not returned my passport. I was to leave in two days, but I couldn't see how it was possible without that. And I only had a few dollars left to get me through. I was about to call Kunitz when another plan came to me.

The next morning I showed up at the Canadian Embassy and got a meeting with a woman who seemed to be a senior official. I put my case to her:

"Ok, here's my situation: I don't have any money, and I don't have anyone I can call who can provide the kind of money I need to pay my fine and get them to give my passport back. So I don't have a passport but I do have a ticket home—for that reason, either the embassy helps me to get a passport or I'll have no choice but to camp out here on the front steps until the situation changes."

I think the woman understood the desperation of my circumstances, and she did not get angry with me. After a moment to think about it, she replied that, "I can't really make a decision like that, I'll have to go and call Ottawa." She paused to think for another moment. "Ok, I'll go call Ottawa."

She left the room and I took a look at the clock on the wall: 10:15 a.m. Which meant it was 4:15 a.m. in Ottawa.

She returned after about a minute. "Well, I tried calling Ottawa but no one answered. Considering that your flight is tomorrow, I'll have to make a decision…We'll have to issue you a temporary passport. You go get a photo and I'll get the paperwork started so we can have this done today."

I thanked her profusely and bolted out of the office onto the street, looking for somewhere I could get a passport photo. It had

Detour on The Path

worked! The embassy was only a block from the Champs Elysées, so I ran in that direction, eventually finding a little booth in the closest Metro station. I returned to the embassy as quickly as I could, and in a few hours I had a sheet of paper marked "temporary passport." It had my photo and flight information on it and was only valid for the one day, and I was told to return it to the immigration officials when I landed in Toronto.

I spent that last night enjoying a beautiful dinner with Lucy, eating outdoors overlooking the Seine. I was still a little nervous that something would go wrong, but this was probably going to be my last night in France for quite a while so I tried to enjoy it.

When I got to the airport the next morning the customs officials looked at my piece of paper a little oddly but waved me through.

I was on the plane, which was sitting on the tarmac waiting to taxi to our runway, when an announcement came over the PA system: There was going to be a delay. The police had to board the plane.

Oh god.

A murmur went through the plane and I started to squeeze my arm rests. *What could it be?* The door opened and the police got on.

They walked right by me.

I couldn't believe it, but they were there to talk to somebody else. Some other man was escorted off the plane, the doors closed and we taxied for take-off. I don't think I took a breath until we were in the air.

When we finally left the ground an overwhelming wave of relief came over me. *I am free. Really free.*

When I went through customs in Toronto, I showed them my temporary passport and they told me to go over to the immigration desk to give it to them. The man there took a cursory glance at it and shrugged, then walked away.

Thank god. It was over. The last obstacle to my return was gone.

I walked through the doors to the arrivals lounge, where Suzanne was waiting for me—I hadn't told anyone else I was coming back. We drove back to my old apartment, which was now hers, and I sat down and looked around.

I'm home.

Mukin shûri
The way to success has no short cuts

Epilogue

A FEW DAYS AFTER I GOT HOME, I went to pay a visit to Tsuruoka Sensei. I had told him nothing of my adventures and, as far as I knew, he knew nothing of them.

My apartment was just a few minutes away from his dojo, so I walked over about an hour before class. I knew he was usually there at that time, as I used to often come over before class to speak with him. The dojo had not changed, and he sat in the same place as he always had—the same close-cropped beard and glasses, the same *gi* simply worn, looking fit for a man in his mid-fifties. It felt like only days had passed, rather than a full year.

When he saw me, his expression did not change and he did not get up. He offered me my usual seat and we looked at each other for a moment.

"So, where have you been?"

I told him the whole story, holding nothing back, from my decision to my reasons to what I had seen in Asia to the long, hard days in Fleury Merogis. I tried my best to give as true an account as I could, without justifying things or looking for sympathy, so that he would know the whole truth. He was, in many ways, like a father to me, and I wanted him to know everything.

He listened impassively, not saying a single word or doing so much as raise an eyebrow throughout the entire retelling. When he could see that I was done, we sat quietly together for a moment before he spoke.

"You are very lucky."

"What do you mean by lucky, sensei?"

"Most people do not learn what you have until their last days. You have learned these things early in life, and now you can take that and do something with it."

I nodded, not really understanding what he'd said right away. We moved on to more mundane things and I started training with him again that day. Life returned to normal.

I thought about what Tsuruoka Sensei told me for a long time, grateful for that and the many other pieces of wisdom he shared during the thousands of hours I spent training under his guidance. It is because of his lesson and the others I've learned while reflecting on those terrible twelve months that you hold this book in your hands. I have hidden my story from most people for many years, but now my hope is that, by showing how my karate training helped me to overcome these extreme challenges, and sharing the lessons I have learned from them, my story will help you to face the challenges of your own life with greater resolve.

This is, of course, a cautionary tale. What I did was wrong and I was justifiably punished, however harsh that punishment seemed at the time. I now know that there are no shortcuts in life and, however well-intentioned my actions were, if nothing else my account demonstrates the importance of taking responsibility for what you've done. That year was the darkest time of my life, and it took monumental amounts of work afterwards to put myself back on my right path. It is a lesson I have learned very well over the last twenty-plus years, and I believe that taking it to heart has been one of the keys to my success since that time.

I also want to show—especially to martial arts students—how karate can be applied in real-life situations. Too often its usefulness can seem distant in the controlled circumstances of the dojo, and this beautiful, practical art is often recognized only as a path to fitness. It is much, much more, and in my time of crisis it safeguarded not only my physical well-being, but my mental and spiritual health as well. I sincerely hope that my students can draw confidence from this for their own lives, without having to go through what I did.

And finally, what I have learned since this episode is how important it is to forgive—both others and yourself. When I returned to Canada, for a long time I was very angry, at those I thought responsible (like Rico) and mostly at myself. It was only after I "let go" that I was able to put my trials behind me and get on with my life—until then, I was still a prisoner. Writing this book and sharing my story is my final act of letting go; by casting light on my dark secret, and trusting the people in my life to understand what and why I did what I did, I am lighter and freer.

So what path have I taken since I returned? With a great deal of hard work and help I was able to build the life I had dreamed of during those long, lonely nights of incarceration. It certainly was not easy at first—I was in worse financial shape than when I'd left and the dojo was still struggling to survive. But I worked hard and caught some breaks. Eventually I got my job back at DeHavilland, and enrollment at my school began to grow. I continued on with my competitive career for another five years before retiring, but never achieved quite the same heights; competition seemed less important to me after that year, and some of the fire that motivated me had gone out. I began coaching Canada's national karate team in 1994, and in 1996 was inducted into the World Martial Arts Hall of Fame.

More importantly, I was able to live a normal life again. I returned to Newmarket and built up my school, watching it grow slowly from occupying a modest second-floor room to needing a larger space and then a larger space yet again. Today I'm proud to own a world-class facility that serves more than 250 students, and to have been lucky enough to have taught many thousands more and instill in them a little of the strength that karate has given me. All in all, I do feel very lucky—there have been times of trouble, of course, but I've always felt there was someone looking out for me, never more than when a "miraculous medal" showed up again in the most unexpected of places, as it did when the dojo was again passing through a difficult period some years later and forced to move after sixteen years because of the sale of the building.

Many of the people in this story are still in my life. All of those who helped keep the dojo alive in my absence are still with me, either at our dojo or running their own schools, and we are in regular contact. My steadfast friends who wrote and supported me while I was in prison are still there for me today, for which I will always be grateful. My romance with Mia did not survive the ordeal, but my friendship with Suzanne remains strong and her help in digging up copies of the letters I sent her while I was in France was invaluable in helping put this book together.

As for Rico, I never saw him again once I returned. None of the help I was promised if I was caught ever materialized. Several years later, a friend directed me to a newspaper article in the *Toronto Sun*, telling how Rico had been convicted as the leader of a hashish-oil importing ring, smuggling narcotics into Canada in typewriter cases. The prosecutor in the case estimated that Rico had made a profit of more than $2.2 million during the four years he ran the scheme. He was sentenced to eleven years in prison.

As I say in the story, when I wrote the poem "Endless Night" it reminded me that my trials would eventually pass, and it gave me the strength to hold on until the good times returned. A copy of the poem now hangs on the wall in my dojo, and as the years have passed I've come to realize that the words have another interpretation—that just as the bad times give way to the good, so too do the good sometimes vanish behind a cloud. Too often we rush along fretting about life's little problems, ignoring the bigger picture of how good our life is just then, and missing the chance to savour our good fortune. When I look up and remember how bad things were when I penned those words, I remember to appreciate all the things that have passed since then.

Today I am back on my path, living the life I always wanted, more driven and focused than I have ever been. My ordeal exacted a heavy price, robbing me of my innocence and taking from my eyes a playful light that has never returned, but I am stronger for it. I know now just how precious life is, that time wasted is never regained. It has made every moment since that much sweeter.

To Etienne,

Ryu su fu sen kyo.

"Running water in a stream faces no barriers."

From your fellow Karateka,

Rolf

May 23, 2015